OUTSIDE/INSIDE
…JUST OUTSIDE THE ART WORLD'S INSIDE

— OTHER TITLES BY MARTHA KING —

POETRY

Women and Children First, 2+2 Press, 1975
Weather, New Rivers Press, 1978
Islamic Miniature, Lee/Lucas Press 1979
Monday Through Friday, Zelot Press, 1982
Seventeen Walking Sticks, (with art by Basil King)
    Stop Press, 1997
Imperfect Fit: Selected Poems, Marsh Hawk, 2004

PROSE FICTION

Little Tales of Family and War, Spuyten Duyvil, 1999
Separate Parts: Six Memory Pieces, Avec, 2002
Seven & More, (with art by Basil King) Spuyten Duyvil, 2006
North & South, Spuyten Duyvil, 2006

OUTSIDE/INSIDE

…JUST OUTSIDE THE ART WORLD'S INSIDE

Paul — Thank you for being here

MARTHA KING

[signature]

12/9/18

BLAZEVOX[BOOKS]

Buffalo, New York

publisher of weird little books

BlazeVOX [books]

blazevox.org

21 20 19 18 17 16 15 14 13 12 01 02 03 04 05 06 07 08 09 10

BlazeVOX

Acknowledgements

My grateful thanks to the editors and their magazines or websites
where earlier excerpts from *Outside/Inside* appeared: Sanjay
Agnihotri (*Local Knowledge*); Brigid Hughes (*A Public Space*);
Rob Cook and Stephanie Dickinson (*Skidrow Penthouse*);
Geoffrey Gatza (*Blaze VOX*), Trace Peterson *(EOAGH)*, David
Plick (*Construction*); Pam Brown and other editors (*Jacket*).

Thanks too, to these readers who offered me encouragement, fact-
checking, enthusiasm, and vital editorial suggestions during the
long gestation of this book: Christina Clifford, my dogged one-time
agent, Andrei Codrescu, Dianna Douglas, Laurie Duggan, my sister
Charlotte Furth and her daughter Bella, David Gitin, Mary Emma
Harris, Mitch Highfill, Vincent Katz, Kevin Killian, Burt
Kimmelman, Kimberly Lyons, John Mullane, Elinor Nauen,
Elizabeth Robinson, Lynn St. John (for editorial help as well as his
wonderful photographs), Alice Sebrell, Michael Seth Stewart,
Cathryn Davis Zommer and finally and always, Basil King.
Any and all errors are mine and persist here despite heroic attempts
by these friends to keep me on the straight and narrow.

My apologies to anyone whose name I've inexplicably left off. My
memory is very sharp until it isn't.

for

by

and with

BAZ

as ever

Contents

OUTSIDE/INSIDE

...JUST OUTSIDE THE ART WORLD'S INSIDE

Preface
An End Note to Begin with

There is supposed to be a sense of completion to memoirs. Three

parts. Life lived, the effects that lingered now X is over, and the it's-

never-over part. Maybe three parts more: Lessons learned. Burdens

still carried. Clarity sought. And the coda of forgiveness of self and

of others. That's a common form. But sometimes the coda is

revenge or denunciation, or a jeremiad warning all you stinkers out

there that you've got nothing to say for yourselves.

The problem with memoir conventions is that the jury is

still out on a fundamental assumption firmly believed by the main

character and narrator, Martha King, about the value of the art of

her partner Basil King.

Who is Basil King? How important is his art? What

happens to a memoir when the conclusion is still so open? How are

you to read it? And who is Martha, Martha Winston Davis King?

Why, in defiance of all the tropes of male-female relationships in

the late 20th early 21st centuries, has she lived her life in the context

of his?

Beyond that, it's quite possible that you don't know who

most of the people she writes about are. So you'll have little outside confirmation of her assertions, on which accepting her descriptions might depend.

Suppose you simply read this as fiction?

It seems to me today's readers often assume a tale's protagonist is the author and the author the protagonist regardless of what the work is called or how preposterous that idea might be. Regardless too of how many post-modern devices a writer lays out to snare or deter this.

The best I can suggest is don't worry. Don't worry if you recognize names and don't worry if they're from out of the blue. If this is just a tale to you, trust that in a tale real events occur and so do inventions. In a tale some events will match a common history you've witnessed or learned about and some will offer a window into a world you never suspected or never had an opportunity to know.

So here, whether you find recognition or novelty, with side stories and digressions as in any other long narrative, everything serves to embellish or leaven the experience of sharing it with me, Martha King, by reading on. I certainly hope!

PART ONE

My Black Mountain

If I had not been. If I had not been always in transition, moving from New York City winters to Virginia summers, always the new girl, the one no one knows, the one with the Southern accent, the one with the Yankee accent, the rich or the not-really-rich one, the one from the house with all those books, from East 86th Street on the Upper East Side, or the commuter suburbs of Chappaqua, Pleasantville, and Mt. Kisco, or the Hudson River town of Ossining where the men, mostly Italians or fled-from-the-farms old Anglos, didn't take the train but worked at the penitentiary or in factories that lined the riverfront....

If I had not been the faculty brat, in and out of university classes and campus buildings all over Chapel Hill from the time I was fourteen. If I had not had such comfort with poverty, which gave me a feeling of calm and normalcy. A childhood in the deeply depressed South from 1937 when I was born to the early fifties gave me this although my family was white and white collar.

If I had not been any of those things I would still have been just as desperate to leave home the summer I was eighteen. And I would have found a bohemia somewhere, a gang of people at odds. All runaway kids know this. But would I have met Black Mountain people, who with all their diversity have a certain ineffable stamp? It was accidental for me. I was passing through my days without deep attachments. I felt everything could be exchanged. Everything almost was.

I almost didn't spend the three summer months when I was eighteen at Black Mountain College. My time there was bracketed by a legal rule, *in loco parentis*. It accidentally steered me there just as powerfully as it was invoked by my father to keep me away after that one summer.

I meant to spend the summer of 1955 in Cherokee, in the Maggie Valley of North Carolina, in the mountains way west of Black Mountain. I had been hired as a dancer for *Unto These Hills* – a drama about the Cherokee expulsion and the survival of a remnant band. This shameful story of U.S. colonialism had been tarted up as a public entertainment by a playwright from the University of North Carolina at Chapel Hill; it was presented over the summer months in an outdoor theater near the Cherokee reservation, to the great improvement of the local economy. It still is a summertime staple after several rewrites to present a more balanced picture of Cherokee culture.

In 1955 not a single Cherokee performed in it. The all-white cast was mostly made up of drama students from Chapel Hill – by Playmakers, and I was one. At that time the Playmakers welcomed townies and I'd ingratiated myself by showing up for auditions and volunteering to paint sets, scour for props, and even serve as a prompter if I were not cast. The balance of the actor/dancers were from New York, professionals who competed for a summer of full employment, with communal benefits. The company became "Indians" with the use of full body makeup for the first act, transformed themselves into white settlers for a middle act, and daubed the body paint on again for the tearful finale. My sister Charlotte had preceded me in this job two years earlier, and my parents, brother, and I had visited her there, so I knew just what to expect, down to the twice a night detergent wash-down to accomplish these racial change-overs. I also knew what to expect: amenities provided by a Cherokee boarding school: a dining hall, dormitories, classrooms, and off-time dance and theater work, squeezed out of the six-shows-a-week, dark on Sunday, drill.

I had been hired. I had the job. I was in the drama department office to sign my contract when someone noticed my birth date. I'd been around the Playmakers for years, and people had forgotten I wasn't a college student. Or so they said.

Sudden awkward silence.

There had been a recent "problem." A father was suing the department for failing to protect his twenty-year-old daughter from a romance with an older actor. *In loco parentis* universities were to be, for white girls under the age of twenty-one in the 1950s South. The assistant director lied nervously. "Gee, Martha, we thought you were a lot older. We're really sorry." Which might have been true. Not his difficulty. Mine. It was March. My summer escape route was obliterated.

Was this before or after I bought a copy of the *Black Mountain Review* at the Bulls Head Bookshop in the basement of the university library? I'm not sure, though the magazine gave me a jolt. It was the issue with a portfolio of Franz Kline's black and white paintings, and a two-page essay by Robert Creeley in a language and tone I had never encountered in my life. What was this art? This pared down but intensely exploding abstraction? I knew abstract art as controlled and cerebral, hard edged and clean. And what was this crazily direct/indirect way to write about it? This terse hip-talk? What was this magazine anyway, typeset and published in Palma de Mallorca? I had looked it up to find out where it was. Balearic Islands. Spain. Spain meant Franco to me. A curtain had closed over the whole country after the Spanish Civil War.

But Black Mountain College was not in Spain. It was right here in North Carolina. I looked Black Mountain up too and realized that I knew the region well, but not as a place where a Robert Creeley wrote or a Franz Kline did paintings like these.

The summer Charlotte was performing at Cherokee, my parents had taken me and my brother for vacation in the western part of the state. We were to stop and see her (inspection?) and the play too (for our parents' liberal interests), but then we drove all the way to Fontana Dam, at the Tennessee border of the state. It was the largest dam and lake in the TVA system, which was then an icon of New Deal progress. My father was excited about this visit, where multidisciplinary regional planning had created essential flood control, inexpensive hydroelectric power, and a place of affordable public recreation. That was the description.

The reality was hideous. Floods were controlled, for sure, but the lake water levels had to be manipulated to serve the needs of the giant electric plant resulting in a wide scar of rank red mud ringing the steep sides of Fontana Lake. There were plank walkways across the mud flanks and floating docks to accommodate swimming and fishing. Swimming was spooky to say the least: once in the water, the bottom was hundreds of feet below. The "affordable vacation cottages" were the prefab village that had been erected for the dam construction workers in the thirties: dark, cramped, and mold-stained. We left after one day.

We roamed after that, stopping mostly in what were then called "tourist homes" – local houses with rooms of unpredictable cleanliness or privacy for rent to transients. There were no reliably predictable motel chains in those days. There was an actual motel in the town of Cherokee where we stayed. It had a huge fake Plains Indian-style teepee out in front, and the road through the reservation was chockablock with stands selling Cherokee souvenirs made in Japan and Taiwan. The real Cherokee had been agriculturists, weavers, and readers, who wore woven turbans not feather headdresses.

After leaving Fontanna we headed east, by-passing

Asheville, and went up the Blue Ridge Parkway, down at Spruce Pine, and over to a state campground called Carolina Hemlocks – all of us agog at the scary mountains, the mild mountains, the cool, crazy changes.

From the campground we drove through the Toe River valley on Route 80 right past Rhonda Westall's farm at Celo, where later my parents would spend every summer, and our daughters in the 1970s had idyllic vacations. From Celo it's less than fifteen miles if one could go right over the Blacks to the Black Mountain campus on the eastern side.

Everything in that Appalachian hemlock forest territory was the familiar sad beautiful bad roads and rickety bridges over rivers full of water-rounded boulders, was smoky blue mountains, was over-farmed flatlands, dotted with small churches and cabins with porches and many kids, kids with sores on their heads and calloused feet. Nothing therein had ever suggested the world I was discovering in books and films: Soutine, Morandi, Georgia O'Keeffe– Anais Nin, Bertolt Brecht, Raymond Radiguet. Nothing in the *Black Mountain Review* recalled them either, except that it did, and it danced on my senses, and drove me batty to get at it, to figure it out.

So after the collapse of my Playmakers job I wrote to the school for a catalog. I asked about summer school, scholarships, and work/study programs.

Arrived: no real catalog. A mimeographed description of a

summer program and two brochures for summer institutes from several years earlier. A printed application form. I filled it out. A formal typed letter arrived for me, signed Constance Wilcock, Registrar. Much later, I found out this was the woman I came to know as Connie Olson, Charles Olson's partner. ("When the fort is under attack, and there are only three people left, they run around a lot," Ralph Maud of the Charles Olson Society told me.)

The UNC library yielded a little more: Several full catalogs from the 1940s. Socialist kids building the campus. It radiated a kind of Putney School, Quaker wholesomeness. It was all about weaving, pottery, theater. It was only 300 miles to the west of Chapel Hill. I could get there on a bus!

I was supposed to work in the summers, not ask my parents for money for a school. I had worked since age twelve, first at babysitting, then selling popcorn at one of Chapel Hill's two movie theaters, saving up the money I wanted for books, records, art supplies. That summer I had about $70 banked. The round trip bus ticket would eat $20 of it.

I asked my parents if they'd ever heard of Black Mountain College.

"Ar-rumph," Lambert said. "Eric Bentley went there." Radical theater was his image.

"Black Mountain girls do post-graduate work at the abortionist," said Isabella. Sexual liberties was her image. That prissy housemother air was another of her change-ups, for she was the one who had taken thirteen-year-old me to foreign movies, to *La Ronde, Devil in the Flesh, Les Enfants du Paradis.*

More correspondence with Black Mountain followed. Was there a work/study program or could I get a part-time job in the town? More no's; too far, not feasible. Finally I got a postcard, a BMC letterhead postcard, with the by-now familiar black circle logo, on which was typed: "Come with what money you have in hand and what you are used to for cooking. – Charles Olson, Rector."

Too bad I kept none of those papers. The postcard was the best. I remember folding it up in tight little squares. What I was used to for cooking was my mother. I wrapped up an old hotplate, two saucepans, some picnic cutlery, some clothes and stuffed my duffle bag.

Thus, Black Mountain College in the summer of 1955. The squalor didn't shock me. I was used to southern intellectuals hunkered down in bottomed out chairs, living the country life with walls of dusty books and a pump in the kitchen. I liked the sweet quietude of a well-regulated outhouse where you tossed a small scoop of white lime or grey wood ash into the hole after use. Black Mountain College had flush toilets. But almost everything was battered. A gut busted ruin.

"They've left," said the buildings and grounds. And yet not.

"What do you mean?" "Do you mean it?" These two demands circled like twin lenses. Everyone was free to hold up everything said or done to them. Anything and anyone could be – was – fiercely scolded if the focus were sloppy or careless.

They hadn't gone. They were here, talking fiercely. There was no shared unspoken agreement to spare the feelings of the less competent. They meant you to prepare yourself to mean something and then to challenge or defend it. They meant you to think of art or poetry or even politics as more important than the indexes of your personal importance. They believed the outside world was real and could be affected by things *you* did, things *you* thought. As for the obvious poverty, it didn't automatically mean powerlessness. We were in a modern world where a moneyed class no longer had sole purchase on intellectual life. Independence could often mean poverty, especially for those who broke with the canons of received opinion. Examples were everywhere: the hand-to-mouth struggles of Merce Cunningham and his troupe of dancers, the poverty of Willem deKooning, Philip Guston, or earlier still, of James Joyce or D.H. Lawrence. Poverty did not mean meaning-lessness. It did not give a person a pass from obligations.

I walked through neck-high weeds to the library. A one-story wooden prefab from World War Two surplus. *Dissent, Origin.* Black Sun. Carl Jung. Jane Harrison. Books from Black Mountain's own print shop: *The Double-Backed Beast, The*

Dutiful Son. Pages in beautifully made books, shining in the sunlight.

"They've left."

True enough, no one staffed the library. The pot shop and the print shop were closed and padlocked. I learned the librarian had been gone for at least a year and the collection had suffered. As booklovers everywhere believe books belong to the person who loves them, so books had clung to their dearly beloveds, and the shelves, in their solitude, developed large and still larger gaps. Greedy pickers. I came to know who some of them were.

The library door was warped and leaking, but it was not padlocked. Except for Rockwell Kent, I had never seen or read these books or magazines. Daughter of a bookman, from a household that had thousands of volumes. Daughter of a bookman, an editor, who cherished his friendships with American visionaries like Lewis Mumford and Stringfellow Barr. I knew a lot about what my father thought and I had roamed the stacks of Chapel Hill's university library, discovering only far away radicals, French anarchists, Italian surrealists, Russian nihilists. What *was* this other dissident American world that shadowed – that might be able to overwhelm – the liberal world of Lambert?

The library building was not the only one-story white clapboard structure. Black Mountain had four or five of them in use as classrooms or art studios. Charles Olson and Connie lived in one of them and so did John Chamberlain and his wife Elaine. The university campus in Chapel Hill had scores of similar surplus prefabs, along with enormous corrugated tin Quonset huts. We were just ten years from World War Two. In Chapel Hill, Victory Village was a warren of prefab shacks for the families of married students on the G.I. Bill. That summer Black Mountain had eight young men for whom the G.I. Bill paid the tuition.

That summer, Dan Rice and Jorge Fick lived and painted in one of the prefabs down on the lower campus but the rest of the lower campus was closed, to save funds, I was told. The lower campus had those ample buildings that figure in so many of the photographs, the Adirondack-style lodges with porches, beamed ceilings, fieldstone fireplaces. I peered through the glass doors. We were asked to please stay out.

My Black Mountain started further up the hill, just past the swampy upper edge of Lake Eden. There was a turnaround by the Studies Building, and a concrete pit, empty, for storing coal. The long white Studies Building held ample common rooms on the ground floor, plus classrooms and a few faculty apartments at the back end. All the rest of the building was taken up by individual student studies, two floors-full of minimal cells, each with a door, a window, and a plank desk.

"People have fucked in every one of them," Gerry van der Weile said admiringly.

I picked out one that had been completely upholstered in wholesale egg crate dividers, painted rose red on one wall and left as is elsewhere. I liked the look. Some studies were filled with left-behind possessions, rotting mattresses, worn out boots. Those in use were piled with books, reams of typing paper, overflowing ashtrays. There was nothing in mine to supplement the overhead light bulb, so I took a gooseneck lamp from the unused room next door.

On the hill above the Studies Building were the scattered cottages where we all lived. They were winterized summer vacation houses of the same vintage as the big buildings on the lower campus, punctuated, here and there by modern constructions. Student-built experiments in simplicity. Plywood, cinderblock, corrugated metal, transparent plastic, plasterboard. The builders were gone and the materials they used were not new anymore. Minimalism doesn't do dirty very well. A grimy Raphael Soyer cityscape isn't the same order of offense as a Mondrian abstract that needs a good cleaning.

I know some of my descriptions startle and sadden Black Mountainites from earlier times. They remember a campus that worked, new buildings being built, fields that were mowed, the pot shop humming all night, musicians rehearsing in upstairs rooms. They even remember a few black students who braved a hostile world to attend the college.

There were no black people at Black Mountain College that summer. But Miles Davis haunted everyone. I heard him for the first time my first week. Someone, possibly the composer Stefan

Wolpe, had set a record player in a window up the hill – and at night, when the road was so dark you'd blink your eyes to make sure they were still open that spare, long, achingly sad horn split the air. Sections followed one after another, continued and continued. Movement in the face of troubles I couldn't have described; movement, from moment to moment. Miles was everywhere.

Just before summer classes were to begin there was a community party in a faculty apartment in the Studies Building. The room crackled, packed with people. There was homebrew in a vat. It was Tony Landreau's place, someone told me, and that was Tony doing his dirty shag. A skinny man with half-closed eyes and loose blond hair swaying in the middle of the room. His shag was a half squat, butt wiggle and grind, punctuated by wild kicking, and it took a lot of space. He had a collection of thirties and forties jazz on 78's, hard twelve-inch records. As soon as one spun to the end, Tony spun it off the player and across the room like a Frisbee, where most of them crashed and splintered. The whites of his eyes were pink with liquor and exercise.

"You gotta hear this one," he kept yelling, as he and other couples danced. Charles Olson danced with Connie. He bent over from the waist and she tiptoed so their heads connected, cheek to cheek, while his back extended like a tabletop. I figured his legs were three feet away from hers. There was surely nineteen or twenty inches difference in their height, and 120 pounds in weight. Enough for a third person.

Joe Dunn, who had been in the car sent to pick me up at the Black Mountain Trailways stop, told me I'd be awestruck at his size, but I'd had an interview with him the afternoon I arrived in which he remained seated, way way down in a sprung easy chair. He apologized for not getting up, because of bursitis, he'd said. So he has a big head, he's a tall man, I thought. But at that party I got it. The dance was truly impressive as he was when he let go of Connie and stood up.

Tony was stopped by two or three people from toppling an empty baby bassinette, the old wooden kind, a literal basket on tall legs. Then I realized the dark-haired silent woman sitting by a wall was very pregnant and that Tony was to be a father soon.

Tom Field was sick, he said. He hadn't felt well in a week. He looked shamed. He was shamed. He admitted he was having bad dreams. When he was dying of cancer, in East/West House in San Francisco, just a few years ago, he made us promise that we wouldn't worry. "I'll be fine," he said to me and Baz, with that same shamed grin.

At the party Tom showed Tony two blackened puncture holes on the top of his foot, surrounded by an ugly red swelling, and mumbled, "I have these weird marks."

"Man! You're snake bit," Tony hollered. He'd grown up in affluent Washington, D.C. suburbs and knew his snakes. He figured the rattler must have struck something else just shortly before the bite or Tom would have been a great deal sicker.

"But didn't you notice getting bit?"

We all wanted to know.

Tom half whiney, half winsome wasn't sure. Maybe at night? he said. Bashful grin. When he smiled he showed his tiny, ever so slightly pointed teeth. His eyes pale in a broad, bland white-bread Midwestern face. He could have received a rattler's full force and overridden it, ashamed of being in pain. In fact, maybe he did. Ralph Thomas Field, artist.

Black Mountain Golden Gloss

There is no Black Mountain of legend, when everyone present was a famous person, glamorous as the fake spread in *Vogue* magazine that superimposed Jasper Johns' face over a photograph of Lake Eden. (Johns never attended Black Mountain, and to my knowledge never set foot on the property.) But my Black Mountain like every one's from the beginning to the end, had students and teachers who later made amazing contributions. Here is my roster:

Students
Jorge Fick

Tom Field

Gerry van de Weile

Richard Bogart

Grey Stone (really his name)

Terry Burns

Mona (?) later married to Terry Burns

Lorraine Feuer

Harvey Harmon

Bill McNeill (Carolyn Dunn says he came with a wife but I don't think so. Bill, Grey Stone and I cooked suppers together that summer. I never saw a wife.)

Michael Rumaker

Herb (?) - a theater student from Pennsylvania

Joe Dunn - with wife Carolyn

John Chamberlain - with wife Elaine

Resident but of uncertain status

Dan Rice

Ed Dorn - with wife Helene

Robert Hellman

Faculty

Wes Huss - with wife Bea: theatre

Stefan Wolpe: music, composition

Hilda Morley Wolpe: French, classics

Tony Landreau - with wife Anita: weaving, dyeing, Albers color
    theory

Joe Fiore - with wife Mary: painting, life drawing

Charles Olson - with partner Connie: history, mythology, culture
    studies, reading

Robert Creeley: writing – but I recall that he came late that summer and didn't hold classes until the fall, by which time I was back in Chapel Hill.

This totals 31 souls, without counting a small tribe of children: The Huss son was pale, red-haired, freckled, and whiney. Katie Olson at three had a fatally predictive cry as her ultimatum: "My big papa says!" All three of the Dorn kids were blue-eyed and tow-headed. The older ones were Helene's children and only cherub Paul, who was eighteen months old, was actually a Dorn. All them, except Paul, were wily, independent, and in command of an impressive vocabulary of swear words. Especially Freddy Dorn, age six. I had read the word "fuck" in books but had never heard it said by anyone. The children playing outside my window could string together rhythmic sentences, employing "fuck" in all kinds of combinations.

Made sporadic appearances

Jonathan Williams

Fielding Dawson (just released from the Army)

Paul and Nancy Metcalf

Were talked about to the point of seeming present

John Wieners

Robert Duncan (he did come that fall)

Victor Kalos

Basil King.

No gifts, some, or gone to ground in public memory. Amazing gifts, some, now well known or like John Wieners, only now receiving notice. Basil's gifts are the very last ones to surface. And beyond this group subtle influences continue. Black Mountain ideas leave traces, maybe even a reservoir, but never a resurrection. The college was a piece of its time.

I was there the summer before the very last summer.

All golden ages have a lot of dross in them.

I studied theater with Wes Huss; we produced a bare-bones version of Lorca's *Blood Wedding* and worked on scenes from Beckett's *Waiting for Godot*. (This was 1955. I'm not sure where he got the script.) Wes's idea of theater was a world away from the performance-appearance emphasis of the Carolina Playmakers. And different too from Actors Studio psychobabble, which I encountered later in New York, when I studied acting with two Lee Strasberg disciples. Wes said theater was artifice not a recreation of "reality," that the audience was an active cooperator always, that performance began in the imagination and entered a dancing give and take with the situation at hand at that moment. Theater itself proposes a focus, he said. Place an empty chair on stage and the audience will immediately become party to imparting meaning to it because the place is a theater. These ideas were shocking in 1955.

Wes would knot himself up watching rehearsals, his ankles crossed, his long Swiss legs crossed, his long arms so folded up that his body formed a five-pointed star; head, two knees, two elbows.

And somehow he smoked, hunching over to get at the burning cigarette in his hand.

I studied weaving with Tony Landreau, the same drunken Tony of my first BMC party, who, very soberly, gave our small class, Mona, Lorraine, and me, solid introduction to Albers' color theory. We also fooled around trying to dye wool with local plant materials and came up with some squalid grays and lavenders. Like the Native Americans before me, I much preferred using the bright chemical dyes from Germany. The Weaving Lab still had a large stock of supplies and some extremely fine looms as well.

I was supposed to have a weekly painting critique with Joe Fiore but I was too terrified to meet him one-on-one. When it was time for our session, I went on long walks and hid in the bushes. It wasn't him, personally. I was afraid my ideas were childish, or worse, that they were on a forbidden list which I recognized but didn't understand. Oh yes, there was a forbidden list. Had I been more equipped, I might have explored and defended myself per the demands of the Black Mountain ethic. Instead, I was simply frightened. I knew I didn't understand abstraction, although I responded viscerally to paintings by Kline, Rothko, Guston. The source, the thing in itself, why it worked or where it came from eluded me. The things Joe said to students in the life-drawing class where I was the model, confused me even more. But there were many other ideas, new ideas, that did not.

By that time in its history Black Mountain was only about ideas. Almost everything else had been abandoned, lost, broken, fallen in. Ideas crackled across the gaps. I had lived most of my life in an academic society but I'd never encountered people who were as passionate about the play of ideas. Not this way.

Here was a place calling itself a school that seemed always to have lived the primacy of ideas. Throughout all the various Black Mountains, and there were five or six or more of them, most students didn't graduate and didn't work for graduation credits. During their stay they were involved in their own development, not in someone else's conception. School was not to be a supermarket. Education was your personal trip.

While there were certainly teachers who had definite ideas about what to present to their students, and in what order, and others who delighted in responding to the flow a class generated, there were never any set achievement requirements. Working for graduation was a personal choice, and the requirements were negotiated, case-by-case, by the student, the student's advisors, and the head of the school. People who didn't really work at anything were not asked to leave. Instead, they were almost literally driven out by communal disgust.

I was at odds with the school's ethic by skipping out of my painting tutorial. Indeed, quite soon I had no new art to present. I wasn't doing any. But I was working daily – in the weaving lab, in

Wes's theater class, and I was reading and writing look-back essays everyday, but only for myself. Black Mountain left me alone which I seemed to ask for, and so I was without any feedback, without the exchange of teacher/student or lone student/larger class. I have missed out on that my whole life – both deliberate choice and unhappy accident. At Black Mountain I was private, writing for myself; I liked the solitude but I was not confronting or confronted by how deeply my parents' belief in male superiority had stained me. I was passive, soaking up as much as I could of what passed around me, and it was a rich stream.

For Olson, radicalism was not socialism, but rather a willingness to see history as contending forces of wholes – ideas that could be impacted by someone's indigestion in the night, by what the price of turnips did to farmland values, by a person's desire to claim a personal change from the implacable weight of what had come before. History had no beginning. Something had always come before – and clarity was not the goal in the study of it.

Surrealism was distained. Abstraction was king. But I admired Djuna Barnes and Georgia O'Keeffe; my inclination was always to the narrative, and I was overcome that I couldn't support my weak convictions. It seemed one more proof that girls were not capable. We were to cook and clean up. We were to produce babies. Olson valued women's otherness and boasted about it. As if Martha Davis of Chapel Hill was in touch with the Goddess! Olson laughed at me for trying to understand his poem. Did he mean that understanding was men's work? It was easy for me to take it that way.

And yet, Black Mountain style was also a gust of profound expressively female freedom for me. Babies didn't mean exile in a suburban kitchen surrounded by proper equipment. Black Mountain women improvised their clothing, cooked exotic peasant food, tied nursing babies to their waists with Mexican scarves. We've had the hippie era since that time. We've had a relationship revolution. Nursing is no longer scandalously unsanitary, primitive, or immodest. In fact it's the mothers with bottles who have to apologize for themselves. Paying attention to one's children is no longer proof that intellectual, aesthetic, or business-world pursuits have been abandoned. Daddies today, from truck driver to corporate chief, routinely tote their kids, wipe noses, change diapers in the men's room. Oh, but not then. Not 1955! Not only did women do nursing and childcare and household management exclusively, but beyond Black Mountain College, middleclass women did most of these things out of the sight of men.

Surrealism was distained for its adherence to system. For its European-ness. At Black Mountain, system was suspect wherever it could be discerned, as a possible trap, a cut-off, a bulwark against the awesome realm of the imagination. Novels that proceeded on a logical trajectory to resolution or (worse) epiphany were more than boring, they were propagandist and wrong. Back in Chapel Hill, mid-century modernism was Cubism and Le

Corbusier; it was the paintings of Matisse and Picasso; it was confessional poetry that minded norms of rhythm, structure, line breaks and Euro song-sing. The outliers were Randall Jarrell, Elizabeth Bishop, Robert Lowell. And the Great American Novel was still the holy grail in prose. Had Dos Passos done it? Would Steinbeck?

Charles said the novel was over, it was done by Melville, and worth a re-read yearly. Creeley said this was a different time, not a novel time at all. "A quick graph" describes his language. Stripped of sentiment and the beguilements of romance. Process was the issue, not achieving conclusions. While abstraction eluded me, this idea spoke to me then and speaks now; in writing this I try again to practice it.

At Black Mountain people acknowledged there was something new in history. After mid-20th century, and well before recognitions about ecological damage, it was clear that the whole globe could be made uninhabitable by atomic warfare. We students could all remember when we learned this. (It was in August of 1945. I was eight.) What was different from similar acknowledgements in Chapel Hill was Black Mountain's collective understanding that this new planet-wide destructive capability altered a great deal more than politics. One way or another, this recognition was now a visceral part of how any of us did anything anywhere.

It doesn't matter whether Charles Olson was a good teacher to me or not; or that my Black Mountain experience confirmed the personal me in a pattern of withdrawal. It doesn't matter who drank too much or who screwed whom or how. Black Mountain is important because it grew a language – in collision – that is still available for use. A language that works at getting at things, making connections that might be generative, a risky language not focused on defending itself, ranking itself, not devoted excessively to maintaining prestige and position. Black Mountain grew a capacity for essential bravery in some of its members, perhaps in many of them. Bravery is in this language. There's a common willingness to go where the conversation will go, to allow a suspension of control. There's a trace of this bravery in many old Black Mountain students, even today, and more than a trace in the work they have done in the world since.

Black Mountain, just three months of it, brought me into this, and laid a way of speaking and thinking before me. It said connection matters, it said ethos matters. It, they, them, the spirit of the place. Said. Said to ask this:

"What do you mean?"

"Do you mean it?"

The Set Up

I was not at Black Mountain in 1957. I was in San Francisco. I was still shy of 21. Basil King was in San Francisco in 1957. He was 22. In 1956, Black Mountain College closed forever. That finality, the end of that extraordinary school, improbably existing for 23 years in the mountains of western North Carolina, ended Baz's plan to re-order his life by working for graduation with a degree in fine art. The end of Black Mountain had come a year earlier for me; I was forbidden to return in the fall of 1955 for a first full year.

I was trapped at home in Chapel Hill by *in loco parentis*. Again. Failure to act in accord with this institutional obligation was what my father threatened Charles Olson with if Olson, as Rector of Black Mountain, permitted me to return against his expressed wishes. My sense of what school might be had been completely reframed. My ideas about intentions and commitment, the commitment of others if not of mine personally, had been completely reshaped. Black Mountain had the things I wanted to learn. Otherwise not. No.

Olson wrote me about my father's threat and promised to fight for me if I came back. I'm not sure he believed Lambert would actually take the school to court, but I had no doubt of it. Authority was behind him and swelled him with pleasure.

I didn't keep Charles' letter. I threw it away. I thought his offer was majestically hopeless. Black Mountain was scrambling for the money to buy coal for the coming winter. The faculty were being paid in scrip if they were paid at all. Robert Creeley later said they were given baskets of vegetables instead of cash, which sounds almost Victorian, and far cuter than anything I observed. In the fall of 1955 Black Mountain needed everything, and a fight would require lawyers, time, money. I couldn't ask BMC to try it. Advantage Lambert.

If I wouldn't return to the university, UNC at Chapel Hill – and I wouldn't – I would have to learn a trade, Lambert said primly. I had to be able to support myself.

Okay.

For four months, I rode a bus from Chapel Hill to Durham every weekday for a course at a business school for poor white working girls who hoped to stay off the floors of Liggett & Myers' cigarette factories. Their goal was clean white-collar office work. The factories stank up the air nearly as far out of town as Duke University. The stink inside those buildings must have been monumental. They were huge Victorian structures filling street after street, pale orange brick with painted over windows, and fancy brickwork eaves as if the top gutters were the crenellations on a European castle. Their stink was yellowish and sweet, and tiny scraps of tobacco waste, quite like the contents of a bag of Bull Durham, eddied along the gutters and lodged in sidewalk cracks.

We girls all typed in unison while the instructor timed us. Bing. The keys were blacked out, so you couldn't cheat. Bing. Your errors were counted and a chart of the winners was chalked on the blackboard every day. Bing.

With my certificate in hand, I went to the university employment office. Chapel Hill was as much a factory town as Durham, with the university the only real employer. Starting in January, I had a job as the junior subscriptions clerk in the library of the medical school, on the top floor of the new N.C. Memorial Hospital up the Pittsboro Road from the campus proper.

I had no idea how much money it took to leave home. It seemed so big an undertaking I figured $2,000. My salary was $28 a week. My mother refused my father's request to charge me for my room and board so I could save almost all of it. It would take 100 weeks. Almost two years. But suddenly in the early summer of 1957 I got a check for $900, settlement for an automobile accident I'd been in. My leg had been scarred. Three inches of pink scar tissue and I was over the top.

I didn't know before I left that $300 bucks would have been – was! – more than enough to get me on a bus to San Francisco, settled into a basement apartment on Filmore Street, and free. By the time I'd done it all, I realized my remaining stash was halfway to my Big Ticket. Australia. I opened a bank account and obtained another office job.

Australia. I wanted to be as far from Chapel Hill as the earth would provide. I wanted to go the whole damn way west. Farther than the Antipodes would become perversely East, and threaten me with a retrograde seep. I was not thinking of art or poetry or theater – I wanted the otherworldly, upsidedownness of a huge foreign continent, where fall is spring, where English sounds weird, and the trees smell like cough drops. I wanted to see the Great Barrier Reef. (I've still not been to Australia. I still want to go.) I had no plan that would have been deemed serious by sober observers.

I did know by then that the last Black Mountain people had dispersed. I knew that a troupe had followed poet Robert Duncan to San Francisco in 1956, in part because they were involved with a play he had started creating at the school, based on the Medea legend. I knew other people had gone to New York or Chicago. And some had gone on the road. But I'd lost touch. I was so angry. The Black Mountain student I'd slept with that summer had dumped me for a woman with money; he wrote me a letter about how beautiful her pubic hair was but I knew what he loved. Toward the end of his life Robert Creeley denied hating anyone, which was undoubtedly true as time drives most of us to know the value of grace, but back then he was vehemently condemning of him. And Charles Olson wrote one of his great poems taking this young man to task for his faith in control. He would have been perilously like my father and a personal disaster for me had we stayed together. But in 1956 I'd have followed him wherever he asked. Instead he dumped me.

Now I was on my way to Australia. I was not in San Francisco to find lost Black Mountain. It was lost to me anyway. I was in San Francisco because it was on the way west.

Until I saw a sign pointing east.

It was a poster in the window of City Lights Bookshop advertising that members of The Magic Workshop, led by Jack Spicer, were reading their poetry the next night at a branch library. Among names I did not know were two from Black Mountain I knew very well: John Wieners and Joe Dunn.

Most of the library was dark, and there were only a few people sitting among the many empty chairs. There was a heavy wooden lectern, the kind often found in churches, up on a small stage. It was after 7:30, when the reading was meant to begin, and some nervousness emanated from the library lady. She looked a bit green. Then it was 7:50. Then it was going on 8. Two carloads of people burst in, in the kind of manic haze only days of drinking will create. Huge, tall, and tiny. Startling. All talking. And indeed Joe Dunn was among them, sly, flat-footed, voluble, and glad to see me. As he had done the first week of my summer at Black Mountain, he quickly took on the role of guide. He took me to this one and that one, introducing me and beaming. Among them was a young man with a pale skinny face and a mop of dark frizzy hair, wearing mirrored aviator sunglasses with one lens missing. A very bloodshot brown eye looked out through the empty frame. When he heard my name he said I should hang out after. He said they were all going to eat Chinese food and I should come along. He said he wanted to look me up that weekend. I tried to put him off, but he persisted.

Do your thoughts match your legs in a long walk? Do your legs push your thoughts? There's a kind of lope to the walking-thinking, where breathing becomes part of the flow. Hard to say which comes first, or how they interconnect. We didn't mean to go for so long, we just wanted to get away from the Black Mountain campus for a bit, get away from the grounds of exploded grief and pain, the ugly aftermath of a car wreck that was itself an explosion. Tom Field had gunned his car into a stone chimneypiece, to end a protracted session of needling teasing that had been going on for hours over beers at Ma Peeks' bar and had continued as Tom drove his tormenters from the bar down on the highway all the way back up to the school.

No one would sleep much in the nights after, although within a day we knew that no one was going to die and that the rule of Omerta would protect our inside world from cops or lawyers. Bob had been in the hospital with a wrenched shoulder. He'd thrown away the ugly hospital-issue sling and had his arm supported in a soft bandanna.

I don't remember how the two of us left the lighted rooms together, but there we were, walking down the hill past the lake. When we reached the junction of the campus dirt road and the paved road, we turned in the direction away from Peeks, three miles away, which was the usual night-walk destination. I'd never gone the opposite way any further than the turn off to Doyle's farmhouse, empty now. Doyle had managed Black Mountain's farm program, until debt drove him away. Beyond was woodland, then other farmed fields, and a curving ascent along the edge of hills.

It wasn't one of those pitch-black nights. It was starry, and half-lit. It was easy walking in the wet mountain cool, lit by mildly phosphorescent gravel, sparkling with mica shards. The sky was brightened by damp air's capacity to magnify night light. It was easy breathing a spongy smell, mushroomy, pine needley. At least for me it was easy. Twice that night, Bob suggested we sit down, and he smoked a cigarette and leaned back on one elbow. His shoulder probably hurt, but he didn't say. Eventually the road doubled back along the curve of the valley wall opposite the school. I had no fear of getting lost but it seemed to me Bob didn't know any more than I did exactly where the roads went.

We were talking all the way. He told me about his difficult childhood after his father died and how important the boarding school he went to had been for him. He told me about the homing pigeons he had kept there and tried, unsuccessfully, to train. How a teacher who befriended him would patiently drive him to retrieve his birds, again and again, and how the same teacher introduced him to Herbert and Marvell and Donne. I told him I had read them and loved them also. Measuring a measured world, a world that may have offered answers but accepted that answers would not always be understandable. Hence the attraction. Not Christ, but doubt.

I told him about my brother, who was about to be sent off to a boarding school by my parents, and how worried I was about how he would do and how callous my parents were about him, how indifferent to what *he* might want. We walked and talked all night. I don't know if Bob told me then about his father's death, or if it was later that I got that defining image of the two dark tracks from the ambulance wheels that backed across his snow-covered front lawn and carried his dying father away. Tracks that stayed until the spring thaw. That backed across his heart. That stayed for a lifetime.

We were fine when we got back to the campus. We were hungry and pink cheeked and everybody assumed we'd been fucking. Bob went up to his house and came back with a copy of D.H. Lawrence's *Studies in Classic American Literature* for me. We'd been talking about Williams' *In the American Grain,* which I'd read earlier that summer.

It seems to me I didn't see Bob after that. I had to go back to Chapel Hill. Or he left for New York. Or both. It was break time, of course. It was the end of summer.

"Why ever did you ask me for my phone number that night," I asked Baz a long time afterwards. "I was really annoyed."

"Oh, you were a long way from being pleasant."

"Well, yeah, you can't imagine how you looked. And later I looked in your address book where you supposedly wrote down my phone number and all it said was 'Martha Walnut.' Martha Walnut!"

Walnut was my phone exchange. There were names in telephone numbers then.

"How'd ja find me?"

"Information."

"Yeah, but how did you know my name? You wrote down Walnut."

"Bob Creeley told me your name. Creeley and I took a couple of very long walks together that last year at school. He told me one night if I ever came across Martha Davis I should be sure to spend some time with you. He said a whole bunch of things about you. He sure was glad you didn't marry that jerk. He told me he was afraid you would, and if you did you'd marry five more guys before you were through, and it wouldn't do you any good at all. He said I should find you, and stick around."

A Wedding

If we could have done it over, I think we'd have gone off down the beach somewhere, built a small cairn in the dunes, and come back married. Who'd ever dispute us? Who asks to see your actual wedding license? Heirs and their lawyers in some Dickensian legal fight? Same-sex couples, bless 'em. They need that formal paper to stave off humiliation and that's another story.

Baz and I do have an actual wedding license, signed and stamped. It's at the bottom of our safe deposit box. But no landlord, employer, hospital official, passport officer, or IRS auditor (and we've been hit a couple of times) has ever asked for it. We've simply checked the "married" boxes on documents year after year.

So why did we do it?

I wanted to say *we are married.* The public claim of it. I'm not sure why it was so important to Basil. Stability perhaps? He's only said it seemed childish not to. That we were in love was overwhelmingly true. We didn't want to spend a day apart. But getting married in 1958 was one of the very few public positions the two of us were to take for a very long time.

When I think about our wedding, it's like the stuff art's made of. A mess, full of frustration, denial, lies. But when I tell it, even to myself, it comes out comedy: a movie Louis Malle could have made. He'd have kept all the distress just under the bizzaro surface. He'd have let his audience develop affection for each one of us even while everyone laughed.

First: absent parents, Esther and Mark King. Baz wrote his father a letter saying that he loved me, that he wanted to be with me, that we had decided to take this step together. We were going to marry and move from San Francisco to New York City. San Francisco was a fine town for writers, but a painter needed to be in New York, he explained. He wrote this out at our kitchen table on Lombard Street, laboriously, on a lined yellow legal pad. He let me see it before it was mailed, and I cried.

His father replied using his characteristic two-color typewriter ribbon. The letters in all caps were bright red.

"A very interesting letter from you. You couldn't tell me HER NAME?" (Oh migod, I realized, I'd never noticed.) "And yes, we would like to know IS SHE JEWISH?" (Oh migod, I looked at Baz. His father was a Socialist, he'd told me, and variously an agnostic, an atheist, a secularist, or a Reform Jew so radical he could never find a group that met his standards of liberality. Was this an *issue*?)

The letter went on, not getting better. All about Mark and Esther's lack of money, their unsatisfying life. Not once had Baz shown concern in sufficient quantity. The letter brimmed reproof.

One thing was clear. They had no intention of coming to San Francisco for a so-called wedding. Period.

Second absent parent: my father, Lambert.

I telephoned my parents to tell my news. The response was frosty. Lambert didn't get on the phone. Isabella said if I were going to do this, the two of us should come home to Chapel Hill immediately. Basil should meet the whole family there and, she said, "face Lambert." If we were still set on marrying after that, we should have a real wedding at their home on Greenwood Road.

I said no.

I had no intention of using our carefully hoarded "back to New York" money for a trip to Chapel Hill so Baz could be grilled on the hottest fire my parents could kindle. Well, I was told, that's pure cowardice – a sign of immaturity and shaky resolve.

A few days later, my mother called back. If Baz wouldn't come to Chapel Hill to meet Lambert, Lambert was certainly not coming to San Francisco to meet *him*. But she would come.

A movie would let you see Isabella at the San Francisco airport. She is not yet fifty, with an extravagant hardy exterior and uptown socialite manners, surrounding a well of insecurity. A tall ruddy woman, with a throaty voice, given to quick wisecracks, sometimes exactly on and sometimes agonizingly off. Though born in the 20th century, she had completely absorbed Edwardian notions of caste and privilege in her childhood and never really moderated them. It had been ten years since Lambert left New York City and his place in the uptown publishing world for small town Southern academia where he headed the university press, yet Isabella was still struggling to get the two of them established in the in-bred world Chapel Hill was at that time.

This trip to San Francisco was not an offer to stand up for me. She'd promised Lambert she could stop this marriage; her feminine sympathy and worldly persuasion would work far better than his bullying. She gleams with this expectation as she arrives and she is way out on a limb with her boast. She and I had been wary combatants since my childhood. There was no ground of trust or intimacy for her to exploit.

Back in Chapel Hill, from within a cloud of male privilege, Lambert dismissed her scheme, accurately enough. Then he went to the bank to borrow money to pay for her trip. Moving to Chapel Hill had involved a spectacular cut in Lambert's paycheck. They were chronically close to the edge, fudging their upper middleclass appearances from month to month.

I'm not sure if this movie would run chronologically or chop up time, back and forth. There are many threads to this braid. Would you film that movie trope, San Francisco from the air? Show western sunlight streaming into the arrivals area at the airport? Would you cut back for a two-shot to show Isabella, deafened from the plane, and too hyped up to realize how loudly she is shouting "Are you pregnant?" at me.

"I'm sorry, I can't HEAR YOU," she goes on, ignoring my shaking head, oblivious of all the faces turning toward us.

Next person in this cast should be our best man: Tom Field. We both knew him separately from Black Mountain College, where Baz and I had never overlapped. Tom had endeared himself to me my first week there.

I'd arranged with Wes Huss, school treasurer, to model for the life drawing class, as I had no money at all for tuition. The money I'd brought with me would be needed to feed myself, Wes had explained. The dining hall was closed and everyone was on their own to work out cooking food for themselves. The school truck would make a weekly run to the A&P in the town of Black Mountain. The offer of modeling for a life drawing class seemed okay to me, generous of the school, even. I'd modeled for university art classes in Chapel Hill, in a modest bathing suit or wearing my dance-class leotards. This was the middle fifties, remember, when no state university would have tolerated nude models. It wasn't until I walked into the studio where the painter Joe Fiore was holding the class that it dawned on me the eight guys sitting at their drawing boards weren't expecting me to pose in a bathing suit. I retreated to the bathroom, shucked my clothes, took a deep breath and walked out. I didn't even have a cardigan to drape over my shoulders for the march to the platform.

During my first pose Tom ducked out. He returned in a few minutes bringing me his dressing gown. Dark blue. White polka dots. A gift. Somehow letting me know without any embarrassment on his part that a model normally walks to the stand in a robe, takes it off after climbing up, becoming by virtue of the conventions, a "model" not a naked girl.

Tom had endeared himself to Baz as well. A year before he and I met, Baz had fled San Francisco, scared, drunken, exhausted – determined to try mind- suicide. He gave Tom all his brushes, canvases, and paints. It was over, he said. Baz hid out in his parents' house in Detroit for months, and by and by recovered his health and nerve. When he came back West Tom had all his things waiting for him. He'd even cleaned the brushes.

Tom was a brilliant painter, Ralph Thomas Field; Tom was also Black Mountain's village idiot; doughy body, drawling Midwestern speech, keeping his dawdling manner and androgynous persona among all the testosterone addicted zip gunners of Black Mountain College. Here's Tom in his McAllister Street kitchen gently mixing martinis in a large Japanese teapot. Here's Tom taking forever to carefully brush his rabbity teeth, then stopping to crush his morning eggshells for his houseplants, to fuss at his brushes in their cans of turpentine before he'll leave with us for a day of roaming. And here's Tom in front of a canvas almost as big as his apartment wall – the very opposite of epicene, bumbling, or alcoholic. Here he is a masterful, inventive dancer, crackling with energy.

Tom was one of the few young men of North Beach for whom the merchant marine remained a life solution. Briefly at the end of the fifties, shipping out was seen as a brilliant way to make a free life in art possible. Six months out could buy as much as a year on shore. Everyone said.

The poet Michael McClure jumped his first ship after a week, as soon as it got to Hawaii. The painter Paul Alexander stuck out a three-month cruise – and said never again. Reality bit one man after another; and the craze was at its end by the time Baz completed the training needed to qualify. Able seaman didn't take much time, but he'd gone for cook's helper papers. That meant merchant marine cook school.

He had graduated just a few weeks before I met him.

Baz regaled me with descriptions of his classmates. Jailbirds, drifters, down and outers. Under the watchful eyes of a master cook, with forearms big as Popeye's, they all learned how to make radish roses and patterned butterballs. Also meatloaf and mashed potatoes for a hundred people. Five days a week, the cook school students made lunch for administrators of the San Francisco Board of Education.

Then decked out in chef cloches and clean white aprons, they served them in their cafeteria. Baz, no stranger to overnight lock-ups, was actually the only member of his class who wasn't a convicted felon. He should have gotten the message from his fellow students' constant practiced cruelty to each other, but it took an actual ticket for a year-long cruise to wake him up.

He was waiting at the Seamen's Union Hall in Oakland for the bus to take the crew out to their ship, when, he told me later, he looked at the faces up and down the Union Hall bar. The mist cleared. Get out now, because sooner or later someone would push one of his hot buttons, and he'd be killed. So he asked to be scratched and that was the end of his marine career.

But not of Tom's.

In going out to sea, Tom had found a perfect connection for his constant disconnect. He had no difficulty keeping a distance from his unstable shipmates. He was as unplugged as Baz was wired and wasn't provoked by the bullying, prejudice, or blatant self-deception of these uneasy workingmen. In fact he shared many of their sex and identity terrors. Suspension of social norms on the shifting body of the sea worked for all of them; you didn't have to be queer or not queer, you could fuck or be fucked as convenient. All was shifting and transitory. So ship out Tom did, over and over. By the time Baz and I decided to marry, he was already working up the long ladder to his master's papers.

But being Tom, he'd missed two scheduled lifeboat certification days.

We wanted to marry on March 7, the day Baz had arrived in the United States at the age of eleven. We compromised on the 6th, because that year the 7th was a Sunday, when municipal marriages were not performed. Tom's last chance to qualify for the lifeboat certificate was March 6. He had to go.

John Ryan will take his place. Go close-up on John: his bluish white skin, crooked teeth, cig-stained fingers. He is infinitely social, politically savvy, personally miserable. Black-Irish good looks – thick hair, brows, and lashes – setting off dark China-blue eyes. He is gay and exudes a calm acceptance of himself totally rare in those dark times, even in art scenes. But John cannot write. Moreover, two years ago, the love of his life died miserably of infectious hepatitis, and John cannot reconcile his helplessness and rage. He's a nonpracticing Socialist Catholic, who hates church hierarchy too much to ever consider being a priest, but he longs to be of service almost as much as he craves the ecstasy of art. So John is always on the scene. He can tell funny stories for hours at a stretch, sipping whiskey and never seeming drunk. He can listen to everything; he knows everyone. In a blue nimbus of cigarette smoke, John presides as head night bartender at Henri's Vesuvio on Columbus Avenue. Unofficial mayor of the Beach. Of course he wanted to be in on our wedding. I was not well-known, but Baz was. Baz had the imprimatur of Jack Spicer and Robert Duncan – an aura of value. Moreover, he moved easily through the petty criminal demi-monde topped off by outcast poets that was North Beach at the time. Of course, John will fill in for Tom.

There is no maid of honor. There are two ostensible matrons, both of whom helped produce the wedding party but neither of whom will come to the actual wedding. Tense and brilliant dark Sue Rosen (who later, briefly, married the writer Ron Loewinsohn) and Saxon blondy Dora, the motherly, the practical. She would sometime later marry a fabulously odd painter named Russell FitzGerald, friend of Jack Spicer, and become part of a vanguard that left San Francisco for Vancouver after Spicer's death.

Our premarital counseling is provided by John Wieners. The filmmaker should show us meeting on Columbus Avenue. John looked far younger than his age when he was young, and the man we encounter on the street is a delicate bird, with a prominent hook nose, smooth forehead, and curling dancing eyes. He will write all the work in *The Hotel Wentley Poems* three months from now. The book will be published a little later in the year. But we already know what a poet he is. And we're excited. We tell John we're getting married. But instead of smiling he looks worried. Then asks us each for our place and date of birth, which we give him. The time of day? We both guess. He pulls a pocket-sized astrology reference book from his inside jacket pocket.

"You'll be fine," he says after ruffling some pages. "It works." He wreathes in smiles and kisses us solemnly on our foreheads.

I'm not sure how the filmmaker should handle the doppelgangers, the shadow couple who were married with us. They can't be left out, but their appearance is limited to the wedding morning: A furtive looking man with a small, pale, dumpy girl, pudgy for a junkie I was thinking, and showing a bit of pregnant belly. His street name is Hube the Cube. A small-time dealer and big-time creep. I didn't know her name then or now. I suppose I heard their formal names in the course of that morning, but I mostly recall Hube scurrying frantically among the waiting wedding parties, and then spotting Baz. They'd come to the courthouse without a witness.

Before Baz can duck him, which he certainly wants to do, Isabella jumps in all girlish, with "Oh, we'll have a double wedding with your friends."

In the courthouse bathroom Isabella wants to let me know that she can *tell* my friend is pregnant. "Did you know?" she whispers. "I don't really know her," I say.

Double wedding! What made her act so goddamn cute? The Beach is full of this story: Hube is getting paid for this. Her father, some heavy banker or investment broker, is fronting large bills to protect his family's social position. Her parents have been told he's the father. They weren't even lovers, but they both loved their smack, and were pocketing a lot of cash as part of the arrangement. Six months later, after we've left San Francisco, the deal was off. A baby arrived and it was clear that the actual dad was African American.

The movie should certainly show Isabella in the hotel bar. Our friend Ron Loewinsohn had once been a bus boy at this hotel. One of the nice old, then quite inexpensive, small hotels just off Union Square. Isabella had been living in bone-dry Chapel Hill. There, even the "nice" restaurants, which could supply actual wine glasses, required their patrons to stash their shameful unChristian booze in brown paper bags underneath the table. Here, she could sit in a dark wood-paneled bar at a little table with a white tablecloth, order a dry martini, light a cigarette, and lose herself in a lost, older life. Isabella did a lot of bars that week, and restaurants too.

Fortified, she gets right down to business that first afternoon. It's a two-pronged attack. First, why do I want to marry so soon and so young, especially as, she finally absorbs it, no, I wasn't pregnant? Then she plays her ace: Why don't Baz and I just go ahead and move to New York? "You two could live together," she says conspiratorially. "It'll be our secret. I wouldn't tell Lambert."

In deference to the standards of the time, I have packed a little bag and moved in with a girlfriend of Sue's. We've hidden the rest of my stuff at our place on Lombard Street so it can pass as "Basil's apartment."

"Well," I say, "We've already been living together since last October."

It's clear by the blank look on her face that she won't or can't take this in.

We planned a dinner at "Basil's apartment" that night for their introduction. Baz cooked. He made roast chicken with crabmeat stuffing, one of his specialties. He had crusty bread, antipasto snacks from the deli down the street and a good white wine.

"Are you sure he's not a homo?" Isabella asks me in the cab back to her hotel.

She's sincere. The good food, the nice way he poured wine, his manners, his entertaining conversation. It's clear she's been expecting a Marlon Brando straight out of *Streetcar Named Desire*. A wild bull of a beatnik, who sasses civilized behavior.

Much later I will learn what's up. Or some of it. A movie might use flashback techniques. This introductory evening was no blank slate. My old friend Avery had been in New York. Avery from Chapel Hill. My pal and my peer. Another university brat longing for something different. Avery had been in the Cedar Bar while I was in San Francisco, and among other adventures, she had slept with Fielding Dawson. I actually knew about this well before Isabella arrived. Avery and I wrote occasionally and I had been wowed by the world of coincidence that would bring Avery into the Cedar Bar and Basil's roommate from his first year at Black

Mountain College into Avery's bed. The relationship hadn't lasted very long and I was a bit disappointed. I never got sensible details from her, but I knew she was trying out a lot of possibilities in New York at the time, flexing her intellectual and sexual muscles.

It never occurred to me that she was also struggling for position back home in Chapel Hill. I thought she'd left that place behind as definitely as I had. I didn't dream she'd tell tales to my parents. Friends didn't break those rules.

But she had. Lurid stories of Basil King had been floated in my parents' living room at Christmas vacation, when Avery came home to Chapel Hill to visit her parents. Now it was March. She must have pumped Fee Dawson dry and he must have been eager to spill for her, perhaps propelled by the crush he had on Baz. Baz excited him but horrified him too. At Black Mountain College, sixteen-year-old Baz had challenged Olson, argued with him, come up with unexpected ideas, and, at that time, there was no more devoted Charles Olson acolyte than Fee. Baz holding out against the spectacular ire and energy of Olson was fire, was danger incarnate. And Avery must have been burning that I had the jump on her by having as my boyfriend a personage who figured not just in Fee's Black Mountain history but in the Cedar Bar gossip she was avidly soaking up. Avery had been moved by spite, impure and complicated. I don't know how you'd get all that in a movie. It would probably take too long.

On Wednesday Isabella switches ploys. Getting married means a wedding, no matter where or how you're doing it. She insists that we go to I. Magnin, then the fanciest department store in town, and *register* at the bridal counter. I am made to pick out a silver pattern. Mercifully, no single person in the family or among Lambert and Isabella's network of friends and business associates ever gave me a piece of that silver (thank fortune and the power of gossip). But she isn't finished. I need something special to wear. A suit. A *good* suit, she says, because I'll have to get a job once we're in New York City. She's seeing me in pumps and white gloves, a Doris Day heroine, taking dictation from a powerful executive. The image both excites and repels her because she has never supported herself. She thinks she's forcing me to see reality.

I sulk into Better Suits. After a while, though, I actually find one I look good in: it's a nubby off-pink, with a knee-length skirt and a short boxy jacket. It's the kind of suit Jackie Kennedy would wear two or three years in the future.

Isabella absolutely refuses. I couldn't wear a suit like that to "the office." She picks out an olive green creation, with a long skirt and a fitted jacket. It has a scalloped collar and a peplum right across my ample hips. It's the most expensive suit in the store. I wear it on my wedding day. There are no photographs.

A few weeks later, Baz and I will spend an evening together cutting it up into tiny pieces. It really was "well made." I remember getting red welts between my fingers from pressure it took to cut it.

San Francisco is seductive all through this. Civilized and beautiful and photogenic. A slightly milky Pacific light over pastel buildings and dark green trees. Manicured palm trees in Union Square. Crowded sidewalks. Isabella has her borrowed money to spend. She asks us to pick out a nice restaurant, a treat for us and our best man on Thursday night. Tom, Baz and I enter as arranged. It's very French and very quiet, with dark gold curtains and attentive waiters. She's waiting for us drinking a cocktail.

She begins again. We should come to Chapel Hill first to meet the family. I crack. Before we've finished our soup she and I are screaming.

"I'm not marrying Lambert, I'm marrying Baz and I don't care what he does or doesn't think!" I said.

"He's your *father*. How dare you say that."

Then Baz gets in: "I can say worse. Fuck Lambert!"

"I do **not** approve of this marriage!" she shouts, banging the table with both hands. "And I will not attend. I'm going home."

Baz is icy: "You'll come to the wedding or you won't see Martha again."

I'd like to explode at Baz for this, but I won't give my mother such an edge.

She flings her napkin down and is off for the door. Tom jumps up and races after, taking her arm. They vanish.

The dining room is hushed, stunned, and all ears. I grab my napkin and burst into tears.

"He'll take her back to the hotel," Baz says.

I'm not worried about my mother being lost. I'm paralyzed with embarrassment and rage. "Plus she's stuck us with the bill," I snuffle from under the napkin. "We'll have to tell that snooty maître d' we have no way to pay." I want to dissolve like spilt water or disappear in a poof of smoke.

Someone puts a hand on my shoulder.

"Excuse us, please, for butting in, but we'd like to tell you something," I hear.

I free my face enough to see an elegantly dressed middle-aged couple standing by our table.

"You marry him, dear, and be happy," the woman says. "Don't let that old bitch run your life."

Shortly, our waiter pads over with two large brandies. "Your friends have settled the bill and sent these to you," he tells us.

Over the brandies, Baz talks me into going to Isabella's hotel. I say I'll be boiled in oil first, but he says I'll be sorry if she has to make good her threat.

Tom is in the room with her when we arrive. I'm not sure how he has managed this as sophisticated chitchat isn't Tom's thing, but he's sitting in a chair, smoking, and seems quite comfortable. Isabella is resting on the bed. She's ill, she tells me, looking very frightened.

I bring her a glass of water and an aspirin from her kit in the bathroom. We tell her we want her to be at the courthouse on Saturday morning at ten and she promises to do it. She arranges for me to buy a case of wine for the wedding party and gives me an open check. I move back into our apartment that night. Sometime on Friday I buy a pair of sexy black shoes.

Everyone should have a memorable wedding. The sky is deep blue; the municipal building dark and dusty. After marrying Hube the Cube to his partner the city judge is testy. We two had been party to that, with my mother signing as their witness, so what else were we party to? Communist Party, you can see him thinking. (Rotten commies.) Basil's hair curls over the collar of his neat green corduroy suit. (Homo beatniks.) Baz is wearing a tie and a pair of expensive jodhpur boots. (Riding boots with a corduroy suit? Nothing worse than a rich brat.) We had a ring, which I wear still. It cost $3 from a pawnshop in the Mission District, and I'd been wearing it since we bought it the previous week because the pawnbroker had so sweetly asked Baz put it on me. I pull it off my finger and hand it to Baz. (Another sneer from the judge.)

He doesn't get up but sits balefully behind his desk. We stand looking down at him. Isabella develops her church expression, a patently fake pious look, like a five-year-old telling a lie. She clasps her hands and picks at her thumb with her forefinger. Before we went into chambers, she'd opened her silver cigarette case and selected a half-smoked butt. I thought cool John Ryan would wet his pants. "Not what you think, really not," I told him. "She's always trying to cut down." He doesn't believe me.

"Marriage is serious," the judge announces, glaring up at us. "I hope you two have thought this over."

"I've been trying to talk them out of it all week," my mother volunteers.

Cold pause.

I go red and clammy.

"Please get on with it," Baz says.

The language for a civil marriage is bogus, a phony Christian service, leeched of religious reference and larded with bureaucratic terminology. No plighting troths, or "with my body I thee worship": the State of California wanted Baz to say he'd honor the relationship forever and ever.

"Forever and *ever?*"

The judge shuts his book.

"If you don't want to do this, it's fine by me," he says.

"Forever," Baz manages.

"*And* ever," says the judge.

"And," says Baz. And then: "Ever."

I do mine in a fast monotone, and we were married. Back out in the lobby we wait for the signed certificate, and the judge's flunky comes up with an envelope for the judge's tip. "Forget about it," Baz says, his eyes smoking.

The flunky is horrified. "It's customary!"

"Well it isn't customary for me."

It's barely 11:30. My mother shepherds me and Baz, John, Hube, and Hube's bride to a restaurant nearby, barely open. It is filled with empty white tables set with lots of stemware waiting for the lunch crowd. Hube has also caught a glimpse of that silver cigarette case and he's trying to move in on Isabella. John and Baz block his way, which leaves us bunched together on one side of a table with the new wife alone on the other side.

Isabella orders champagne. The waitress looks frightened. Hube's wife quickly says she wants a coke. The waitress asks me for my i.d.

I don't have one. If I had, it would have shown that I was a month and four days short of the magic twenty-one.

"I beg your pardon," my mother announces in her best Westchester contralto. "This is my daughter's wedding day and she's *having* champagne."

The waitress brings it and I do.

Pull back. Long shot of the table. Did anyone say "cheers?"

March 7, 1958.

That's enough movie, but there's always more to a short story. There was more to why my parents were so uptight. Fifteen years after our wedding, over drinks in their Greenwood Road living room, my mother came out with it: Basil's mother Esther had written a letter to them as soon as she'd learned our plans.

Esther's letter said how sorry she was that the Davis's daughter was marrying her son. He was a juvenile delinquent, she wrote. She and Basil's father had tried everything to reform him. And nothing worked.

"What were we to think?" Isabella asked us.

Only then did I understand how brave my cowardly mother had been that crazy week. And what a poor player she was, if a relationship with me was a prize she wanted, and I believe it was. In San Francisco she never told me about Avery, let alone about Esther's letter. She couldn't hear the little I tried to tell her. She had been paralyzed by circumstances that flouted too many of her treasured notions of social behavior. And so she muffed a huge chance to trust herself and me. That was our war, which never really ended.

Esther's war on Baz was something else. It erupted in rare spectacularly sharp attacks. When Baz was four, she smashed his prized toy train, stamping on it until it was a ruin, ostensibly because he had not put on his overcoat when she asked. This marriage letter to my parents was of a piece with that. And soon after our wedding, she gave all his paintings away to a local Salvation Army. She reported this blandly as Baz excitedly led me up the stairs of their house in Detroit to show me the paintings he had done at Black Mountain. Paintings he had managed to ship home before setting out for the coast the fall Black Mountain folded. And also paintings he'd done in high school, one of which had won a statewide prize. Paintings he'd described to me. The upstairs closet where they had been stored was bare and walls in the bedrooms had empty picture hooks still in place. Mute witnesses to her act.

Her knives came out again in Brooklyn, ten years before her death, when she and Mark were living in the garden apartment of our house. One day Baz mentioned how much he loved her fluted silver candlesticks. She lit them every Friday. They had been in her family for generations and had been left to her by her mother. The next week, the candlesticks were gone. Esther told Baz she'd sent them to her brother as a gift. Her half-brother Ken, in California. Annie was "his mother too," she said.

"Someday your nephew Nathan will get those candlesticks instead of your own granddaughters," Baz said, and she went quite white with shock. That effect of her spite had not occurred to her.

My mother's parting message to Baz was different. "You're the best thing that ever happened to our family," she told him from her nursing home bed when she was 91. "I think you're a Christian after all. You've forgiven us everything."

Black Mountain Teens

In 1985, when poet and Olson scholar George Butterick was still assuming he had 12,000 poems to write, he was advising Carrol Terrell on the Charles Olson volume for the University of Maine's series of biographies of contemporary poets. George wanted a Black Mountain reminiscence of Olson from me, from Baz, or from me and Baz. We couldn't do it. I begged off that we had been teenagers, Baz and I. I told George I'd attended BMC just three months, three months in a bad summer when Charles was away much of time. This was true. He was off begging for money to keep the school alive, and failing to get it. He was also trying too to sort out a domestic crisis involving Betty Kaiser, who was pregnant with his son (Charles Peter would be born that fall) and Connie, the mother of his daughter Kate, his partner of many years. Connie was losing; Charles was losing what had been; the school was losing under Charles' watch; Kate was to lose her big poppa; and the seersucker suit Charles wore to his meetings with foundation executives and education patrons in New York and Washington had already lost most of its shape.

The closest I ever came to an actual class with him were some long evenings when he held forth in a booth at Ma Peek's, over pitchers of beer, and my head for beer was weak, so I took in only some of it.

Besides, I was the wrong sex.

I think my relation to Charles might have been deeply qualified even if he had been less gender haunted. I was not engaged and self-protectively I asked for nothing. For different reasons, Basil needed self-protection too. It would be many many years before he recognized how deeply he cared and was cared for. Another much later story. At that time, 1985, what could we possibly write about him I complained to George.

"Just allow yourself whatever narrative play necessary," George wrote back.

And next, "Maybe you and Baz could do Olson in dialogue. Mike Rumaker sent three pages on how he called Olson a whale. It's your narrative-you I want. Don't be burdened by the portentousness of it all. You, the great editor of *The Drizz*." (He meant *Giants Play Well in the Drizzle* – a newsletter poetry zine I was publishing at that time.) We did nothing.

Then it was January 1986, and the book was to go to press that spring: "End on your own narrative," George demanded in an ultimatum letter. "End on Olson and Black Mountain, physically described. Six sentences. Fade Out. There has to be one overwhelming capture of Olson. I am *intent* on having this… "

We did try the double interview approach. What I produced was not at all what George had in mind, not at all what

Terrell would dream of accepting. George sent it back to me, and crossed out my words "bad medicine" at the end.

"You can't end like that!" he scribbled on the page.

Slightly shortened, here it is, as written in 1986. I gave it the title, "Black Mountain Teens."

Basil had arrived at Black Mountain when he was sixteen. He was there off and on again and again until he was twenty-one. That was a whole year after my summer. He was there the fall when the school closed and someone took that sad photograph of the last class.

Baz and I never met there but when I came up from Chapel Hill the previous October to visit the guy I'd gone around with that summer, the two of us passed Baz in the hallway of the Studies Building. Leather jacket, sexy scowl, cocky walk, one shoulder up.

"Who's that!" I asked.

"Just another painter from Detroit. You don't want to know him."

All these things frame me, or what I would talk about if I were talking about me. To talk about Charles, okay, we will interview each other:

M: Charles is my father's age. I always connected them. My father loves Eliot and fears Pound, and Olson the opposite, but politically, I call them both "American-century" jingoists. "For us – and through us – America is coming of age." Hear that Virgil Thomson music? Olson running to Washington to work for F.D.R.? Sure, I'd never met anyone like him, but he was certainly recognizable to me. It's a continuum that stretches from John Jacob Niles to Buckminster Fuller, from the folklore movement to the millennialists. Lambert Davis (my dad) and Charles Olson were peers. No wonder Charles was so itchy-scratchy when they met.

B: He was itchy-scratchy about every dad. He was about mine. He went to work to charm my father the minute he saw that my dad had some understanding of politics and literature.

M: Put you in a funny position, didn't it. It did me, when my parents arrived at Black Mountain. They were driving cross-country for a university press convention in Seattle. Lambert was president of the association that year. So they stopped by to check up on me. Lambert was in the world of academic publishing – and he was looking with real horror at how rundown the school was.

But I believed Charles' vision of the world. There was a war going on, not just between the generations, which there was, but essentially between the intellectuals willing to be radical – "to the root," as Charles would stress – and everyone else who, it seemed to me, more or less did what they were told. It still seems so to me. And it matched emotionally how I viewed the war I was in for my own existence. Then all of a sudden, there Charles was, standing in the driveway in front of the Studies Building, trying to impress my father. I didn't get it. I thought he would ignore my parents, that he'd take one look and know that my dad didn't count for what he thought he counted for. Instead, there was Charles, talking a mile a minute, and trying to overpower them both. Wrong move! Even though Lambert's neck was getting redder by the minute, he could calmly stand on his mainstream authority. He was the editor from Harcourt Brace, with a dozen years of New York publishing behind him. And Olson *cared* about that. I felt betrayed.

B: Well, the bottom came right out for me. I was mad at my dad for his sentimentalism, and at Charles, for giving my father such a welcome. Charles invited him to become the school's fund-raiser. He asked him to leave Michigan and join the Black Mountain community. I could see the next move already – kicking Joe and Mary Fiore out of their place in Minimum House and moving my father and mother in. Now, where the hell could I go? To top it off, everyone was so impressed. I was getting patted on the back. Oh, you've got such a great dad. And my mother, she loved Charles. She whispered to me: "The man's brilliant!"

M: But what did we learn, now that we've got that off our chests?

B: (still angry): Not to drive a car the way he did!

M: I thought it was funny. When he got in that little car, the springs were on the ground and you'd see this great pumpkin head through the window and you couldn't help wondering how the hell was all the rest of him in there. How could he shift? His knees had to be up against his chest.

B: It wasn't the shifting, it was the talking. God knows why he didn't get killed. But I can tell you about what I learned. I don't know if it was in class or at his house, but Charles asked how does one go about putting something together? How do you look at the materials? How do you get to the thing? I said, subtraction. He said, "No, no, no: division!" This is one of the most important things he ever gave me. It hit me between the eyes.

M: You mean the whole is always there?

B: You can keep dividing and dividing. You can keep going. Yes, the whole is still there. Maybe I would have gotten to that myself eventually, but he put the boot in my head.

One of the worst things I ever did to Charles was in a class on Rimbaud. He had talked his heart out about Rimbaud for three hours. Then he asked, "Is there anything anybody here doesn't understand?" We didn't say anything. "Any questions?" And I – and everybody else – shook our heads, no. He looked crushed. I can still see his face.

M: You guys were tired.

B: No. He talked so much you felt you understood everything. But I – we all – knew we really didn't. Sometime after that, I had a huge argument with him. It went on for months. I said that when Rimbaud said, "Women nurse men home from hot countries" he was talking about his father. That nearly everything he talked about was about his father and not about himself. I said I'm seventeen too, and I know what he was doing. Olson said no.

M: I think you were right.

B: But I didn't understand everything. It's a funny connection because Charles himself continues to be an enigma. He started out with a memory, which I have never quite understood – he had a memory instead of himself. He had Melville's memory. His father's memory. Pound's memory. Even civilization's memory. I'm not speaking about knowledge. He internalized other people's memories in such a way that when he spoke in poems, from "Kingfishers" on, or when he spoke in class, you got a sensation of a man going through the thing himself, in person. It was terribly exciting.

M: [interrupting] Olson was writing the second part of the Maximus poems the summer I knew him. If he wasn't writing much, that's what he was intent on doing. I don't think he ever questioned if there really *is* a New World. He wasn't interested in going over European assumptions.

B: I'm not so sure. I suspect Charles was more involved than we like to think in going over all those old European spoons and bones.

M: That's not what he said in the poems. But I guess Europe was closer to him than we think. I mean he was the child of immigrants. He grew up in a household that must have had a European feel – a foreign ambiance among the regular Yankees.

B: He denied it.

M: Did they speak English at home?

B: I don't know.

M: Were both his parents Swedish?

B: I don't know. I suppose it's documented.

M: I take your word that it's documented but it's interesting that we don't know. I mean he was a great storyteller, he talked all the time.

B: He did tell a lot of stories, and you don't necessarily know if they're true or not. Charles didn't actually tell you much. He told me one story nobody else heard. I've told it to Dan (Rice) and (Robert) Duncan and Fee (Dawson) and none of them had ever heard it from him. Charles told me he was living in New York in the same building where I later had my first room – that rooming house on Second Avenue at 6th Street. He was lying on the bed. He said he had been married while he was an actor, and the marriage didn't last very long. (George Butterick was adamant that there is no record Charles was ever married when he was an actor. I'm sure George, careful scholar that he was, is correct. Just the same, Baz is sure Charles referred to a marriage. My thought is that Charles had an intense affair and described it as marriage in the interest of economical storytelling.) He told me he had been having an absolutely miserable time.

The day before, he had been in Union Square and he was the tallest person there. He had shouted out against the speaker and everyone listening had turned on him. "Why don't you fuck off, you big bully!" He was just humiliated. Within the same period of time, maybe thirty-six hours or so, he'd also gone to a party and had a terrible fight with Hart Crane. He was lying on his bed, and going through it all in his head, when somebody knocked on the door. He said the door's open and Marsden Hartley walked in and stood over him. Hartley had a stammer. Hartley took off his hat, very formally, and looked down at Charles – he was another very large man and he said, "You – you – you don't know anything!" And then he left. Walked out the door. Charles said to me, "That's why I hate New York."

It was rare for Charles to tell a story that shows him so vulnerable. He liked to project himself as the Boy Scout, the general...

M: (sourly) He was a leader who didn't always inform his troops about the true goals of the battle.

B: Yeah, was he trying to outdo F.D.R.? Who was he trying to influence?

M: Well...

B: Well. (Pause.) You get to know some people so well there's no doubt about what they want. I don't know what Charles Olson wanted. I hope I'm not being pedantic, but I think that's one reason why his influence hasn't been as strong as we all thought it would be.

M: I don't agree with that. Charles *was* clear about what he wanted – to be an influence on the culture. I'd go further. He'd put it that that ambition was the only one worthy of a great poet. But I think we're talking about something else. We're talking about how he took advantage of the students at Black Mountain. It sounds to me that you were all cannon fodder....

B: I don't know. One thing Charles did in the classroom that was truly remarkable: he didn't stop things. Even when he disapproved of the tack someone was taking, he'd let things go, let them run through whatever kind of confusion, sometimes even mayhem that could ensue. Sometimes he wouldn't answer a question until two classes later. He was never tyrannical in class.

M: There, in the most tyrannical of situations?

B: Basically, Charles was dealing with history, just as he said – more than with poetry, which he didn't say.

M: I think that may be fair. He wanted to be a singer, but he wasn't... umm... wasn't...

B: Song didn't come easily for him, like part of his nature, the way it did for Wieners. He adored John Wieners. To tell you the truth, I envied it and I looked at it with joy, the way the two of them talked to each other. There was a love between them. For whatever reason, Charles didn't compete with John. Not there, at school. I saw him encourage John. And John wasn't competitive with Charles, even though he valued his independence and could be a very difficult man. They had a seriously enviable position with each other at that time.

But Charles was always mad at me. He became mad at me early and he stayed mad. I wasn't doing what I was supposed to do. And that was real. *I wasn't.* Unfortunately. But between John and Charles there was a quietness. When they talked together in class, I'd feel everything is possible. They spoke in a tone that had absolute well-being in it.

In the end, Charles gave me a nightmare definition: he gave me a place without giving me a name. To this day, people who went to Black Mountain don't know what to think of me because of it.

M: (Pause.) Perhaps I was lucky after all, being the wrong gender.

B: But you didn't really need him for anything. You weren't at Black Mountain for ambition...

M: I was there to get away from my dad. And I was met by teasing. Such a terrible weapon. You're diminished before you open your mouth! This is my abiding image of him: I was in my room one night, on the second story of one of the cottages. The hill behind was steep, and all of a sudden his head appeared right in the second-story window and he was going "Ho, Ho, Ho!" I was sitting under a lamp, reading *Maximus*, the blue covered book that Jonathan published.

"Trying to figure it out? Ho, Ho, Ho!" he went.

What could I say? I *was* trying to figure it out. Wasn't I supposed to? And then I thought maybe I *wasn't* supposed to. Maybe it was supposed to come all at once if you were a truly able person. I was absolutely flattened. I could hear him still laughing as he walked away. So I'm suspicious. I think he made your life difficult because he resented your intuition.

B: Not wholly. He admired it and was interested in it, along with being jealous. He wanted intuition badly and he had to fight hard for it. I remember a class uproar about the meaning of wildness and I piped up with "Domesticity is the wildest thing." He pounded on the table and just roared, "Where do you get these things, boy?"

M: You know what Charles did for me? He gave me a reading list on a piece of paper. A terrific list. I started off with *Moby Dick*. That was a good thing. And he laughed at me. That was bad medicine, seriously bad medicine.

Ah, but I was bitter then. Baz was so much clearer, and far more generous. Then as it happened, George Butterick died, and painfully, of throat cancer, before he could make good on intentions he expressed to Baz – to help end Baz's "definition by Olson," to make sure Baz was included in Black Mountain's legends and legacy. This all happened before he was able to finish his contribution to *Charles Olson: Man and Poet*. It was a loss to us both, of a graceful and devoted scholar, a lively mind, a friend.

Basil has much more to say about Charles, then and now. I have only the stories I told in 1985, tempered now of some of my angst. Baz told me about Charles lifting the chair Baz was sitting on in the dining hall, and holding him up in the air, a terrifying act of strength. There was also a day when no one showed up for Saturday work detail and Charles stormed into Basil's room bellowing at him for influencing everyone to shirk. But when he saw Basil's swollen ankle, Charles picked him up, tenderly this time, called him Robin, put him in his car and drove him to a doctor in Asheville. After the ankle was treated for a bad sprain, they went to a bar. Baz says it was the Grove Park Inn, the fanciest place in Asheville at that time, and they sat there drinking for the rest of the afternoon.

Most seriously, in 1956, Charles saved Baz's life. Baz had wrecked a farmer's car and destroyed U.S. Government property, a fence at the front of a Veteran's Administration hospital I think, in a drunken drive back to the school from a drive-in movie somewhere past Oteen. The school had just received the news of Jackson Pollock's death. The movie, Baz remembers, was *Trapeze*. The car was packed with students, all of them drunk. Baz was speeding. At the end of a wild drive up and around the hospital lawn, through the fence, and back onto the road, none of the car's occupants were hurt, but the car crashed into another car and there was a poor man standing on the road with his busted automobile. Who would pay him to fix it? Basil's plan was to let himself go to jail. To plead no contest. He felt terrible about what he'd done.

Charles knew jail could quite literally ruin Basil's life. He had to argue him out of it. It took all night. Then Charles took school money to hire a lawyer and arranged for half the student body to be in the Asheville courtroom, in clean shirts.

"Your honor, we have college student here, got in a little trouble last Saturday night," Baz heard the lawyer say. He was flabbergasted. The fix was in. Charles had transformed a young man's self-destructive rampage into a funny story.

With all of that, Baz is still aware of what he said in 1985, which Butterick did not cross out on my manuscript: Charles gave him a place, without giving him a name – and Charles' influence in that subtle regard followed Baz for fifty years.

Entre Act

Who *are* these people? a young woman asked me after I gave her a few sections of this manuscript to read. She recognized Frank O'Hara; she knew Allen Ginsberg. But Gene (or G.R.) Swenson? John Wieners? Bob Thompson?

Baz and I turned the corner into the Renwick, a red brick Victorian pile on the corner of Pennsylvania Avenue right across from the enormous gray colonnaded Victorian pile that was once, simply, the U.S. War Department. (Imperial America today has no War Department.) There, in a rather indifferent show of African-American art was a dancing Bob Thompson, "The Conversion of Saint Paul," all rushing leaping men and women and horses, a marvelous small work, brimming with Bob's hope. It was painted the year our daughter Hetty was born: 1964.

Just a year or so later, during one of our trips south, Virginia Parker, an old family friend, showed up at my parents' house on Greenwood Road. Invited to meet us, perhaps? Or the visit might have been a coincidence. Virginia lived in Washington but spent her winters on the Gulf Coast of Florida and stopped in Chapel Hill periodically. She was a magnificently independent woman, a slender horse-faced middle-aged beauty, a painter, and one of only two independent woman artists who didn't rate behind-the-back pity or scorn from my parents after the visit was over. (Eudora Welty was the other.)

My parents had two Virginia Parkers in their house. One was really terrible, a stiff life-size portrait of my mother in a white dress, in sticky overly brilliant pigments. My mother's bulging blue eyes are cocked sideways and the faux-Renaissance background is filled with the landscape tropes of Piedmont Virginia – oaks in the meadows, two track dirt roads, brick-red clay in the road cuts and fields, apple blossoms in a distant orchard. But the other picture, hung over the kitchen stove in another of my mother's la-de-dah rejections of providing proper care for mere art works, was a wonderful watercolor. Beach detritus – disheveled shells, straw, sticks, and a blue-clawed crab, which might have been alive or dead to no difference – as the whole painting floated lively and light as watercolor paint itself. As good a piece of art as the other was dreadful.

Virginia Parker supported herself on something. She seemed unencumbered by "family money" burdens; if she worked I don't know at what. She had worked. She had gone to Washington originally during World War Two where she was part of a small team of artists who designed camouflage for war material in all kinds of environments. She loved that job, and liked to talk about the mental exercise the work required and how wonderful it was to feel her talent could be useful to the war effort. Camouflage saved lives, protected resources! She tolerated Washington, which she described as provincial. She had lived in New Orleans and may have lived in France at one time, but during the 1930s, I'm fairly sure she lived in New York City, and for some length of time, she'd had an affair with Gaston Lachaise.

Who *are* these people, my reader asked.

So I asked the plump, pleasant-faced woman at the information desk at the Corcoran, (where we'd gone right after the Renwick) because I could see a Gaston Lachaise at the top of the stairs just above us: "Is Lachaise still a familiar name to art students today?"

Sorry to say she looked a little blank, but it was Sunday morning, and she was probably a volunteer.

Gaston Lachaise isn't exhibited in shows of "Caucasian-Europeans," that's for sure. He comes from a time before ghettoizing by gender or race was done; in his day the ghettoizing was sternly national and by "school." And almost all artists were men. I don't want to sound peevish, but I'd have assumed Lachaise to be a modern icon. It's hard for me to imagine a reader in the subpopulation "culture feeder" not recognizing names like Rosenquist or LeRoi Jones. But icons shake out like so many cards. Only one bears a picture of Lachaise's monumental bronze women with their giant breasts and bellies.

"All his mother," the nearly breastless Virginia Parker remarked with some asperity. "You can see why our affair ended."

That afternoon in North Carolina, Virginia Parker was determined to cultivate Baz and me; she intended to approve of our lives and to identify with who and what we were. She wanted to know where we went to talk. Who were the writers?

Baz and I volunteered some names: Hubert Selby, LeRoi Jones, Gil Sorrentino, Diane DiPrima. Virginia looked blank. We went on out of our immediate neighborhood: Robert Creeley? Robert Duncan? Still nothing. Who had she been expecting? Philip Roth? Susan Sontag?

Even in her generation, the writers *we* considered important – Louis Zukofsky, Basil Bunting, Charles Reznikoff – were barely mentioned by the mainstream. Unknown, or almost worse, treated like William Carlos Williams, who was given a peripheral nod, with a few of his less powerful works regularly anthologized. The wave off, the knowing 'yes, of course, but.' It continues now.

What is this tilt to the wrong side of *what*, that is or becomes the received knowledge of those ever-mysterious cultural arbiters? It was the existence of this barrier that made the international success of the abstract painters such a heady miracle for my generation. They broke through! The rise of rock music for a shivering second or so seemed capable of doing the same thing for poetry, for popular culture. But Bob Dylan and Jim Morrison never were poets like John Wieners, Robin Blaser or Ed Dorn.

Will "radicals" ever shake free of that limiting label, their experimental tendencies forgiven, their work accorded a major place? History isn't consoling. Blake, Whitman, Melville, Dickinson? All waved off as freak lone eagles who had no chicks.

On the other hand, every art scene contains mostly people called hangers on. Not Melville. Not Susan Sontag either. These people are the actual scene of the scene, the minor characters, in Joyce Johnson's phrase. Just as every scene also has major characters who never become or do what had once seemed nearly inevitable.

As any library or art museum proves, there has always been a lot of really bad art. And if ants didn't eat the dead, we'd be over our heads in aphid corpses. If DNA wasn't mostly nonsense, the living world wouldn't work. Could it be essential to our mega-organism that most of what most of us artists do is lost well before the end of our time?

Perhaps it's not the question of who, finally, rises to a place of respect and visibility, or should rise, or should never have risen. Who are these people probably isn't the important question. Process, my dictionary proposes, means a set of facts, circum-stances, or experiences that are observed and described or that can be observed and described throughout each of a series of changes continuously succeeding each other. Passing through, it goes on. A continued onward flow.

Would it help if you could see this man in his spotted yellow shirt, that woman with the curl of black hair she keeps twiddling as she speaks?

The light splashes across the loft floor and gleams on a small stoppered bottle on the table in which the woman of the house stores kosher salt. The brass bed in the corner is covered with a cotton Indian print in buff, tan, brown and daubs of mahogany red. Except when she is in that bed with him, she is removed, as if encased in a dream. The young man says little to her. His unreleased tears clog his chest. They are together in unremarked-on desperation. He leans over, pulls a cigarette out of the package on the table, and lights up. She does the same.

Whitehall Street Brief

In 2002, 33 Whitehall Street was NASDAQ. Huge entryway with reflecting pool and fascist sculpture four stories tall. Clock. Penis. Globe. Somewhere in the space near the lobby ceiling, just above the capitalist prick, is where we lived in 1959. By 2002 on endless floors above the lobby, the cyberbrokers and data analysts of global economy 21 were spending their working hours.

In 1959, 33 Whitehall Street was also an office building, an office building circa film noir. It was three stories high, plus an attic. Mr. Kaplan's menswear occupied the street level. Upstairs, long linoleum covered hallways, pebbled glass doors with faded gold lettering, globe ceiling fixtures with 25-watt light bulbs. You've seen it in old Sam Spade movies.

In 1959, we lived there and people stayed there with us off and on. They moved in by turning up and parking their stuff, by shouting up at our windows in the small hours, and catching the key we'd throw down. Dan Rice, who knew when our paydays were, was one of them. He'd even leave a cab on the street and stumble up the stairs to borrow cab fare on days when he knew we had some money.

But we didn't take everyone in, for reasons that were sometimes obscure to us, or unexamined, or very obvious.

Most of the people we knew were five to fifteen years older, but no one appeared to think of us as babies. Only Max Finstein, a poet, former jazz musician, the prince of thieves I called him, was offered hospitality and never came back. I fed him a cabbage sandwich on a thin Thursday-before-payday night. It was all I had and he was too good a con to waste any more time at such a dry fountain.

Baz and I had Fame and Rejection. We lived in a flow of contradiction.

In order to arrive there

We had some money in 1959. We'd come to New York City prepared. Baz said don't arrive in town without bread, so all through our last months in San Francisco we'd been dedicated savers. He was a box-jockey in a Railway Express warehouse, socking in overtime. His checks were as high as $130 a week. My job was typing property insurance forms from nine to five. I made $42 a week. Our monthly rent was $45. We lived on my salary and saved every penny of his.

Basil's friend Lynn

Baz and I arrived and crashed with his old friend from Detroit, Lynn John St. John. Lynn had completed Cass Tech and been in New York for about four years when we arrived. His first year he had shared a loft on Fulton Street with Baz. It was a bitter cold winter; Baz was half at Black Mountain College and half in New

York and Lynn was working as a counter boy in an underground orange juice stand in the 14th Street subway station. But now he was a studio assistant to the photographer Irving Penn and could pay good rent. He had a very tiny, very right Greenwich Village apartment, up one rickety flight of steps in the tiny street tucked behind Jefferson Market Courthouse.

The lot across the street was filled by the Women's House of Detention, a ten-story tower of ugly Art Nuevo yellow brick. At night, pimps would holler up at their ladies, and when they could manage, the women inside yelled back. Today, that triangle is occupied by a densely planted garden, and the once-dwarfed Victorian courthouse, now refurbished as a public library, looms over Sixth Avenue and 10th. The row of little buildings, one of which held Lynn's apartment, is now exposed but unchanged: small paned windows off plumb, chimney pots askew, flower pots on window sills, cute.

Lynn let us and our baggage in. We had boxes and a big trunk. It wasn't nothing. We struggled all our stuff up his narrow stairs and he gave us the big mattress by the front windows that doubled as his couch. He wedged his sleeping bag behind a narrow counter at the kitchen end of the studio. In the mornings he went to work. We went house hunting. Finding a place to live took us a long time.

What we saw on the hunt

Our hearts were with Rimbaud: *ne travaillez jamais*! But one can't live on the streets and paint. One could, in 1959, obtain space cheap. One could also obtain low-maintenance income with minimum effort by taking blue-collar jobs, the easy hire, easy fire, dirt level, no-care, do-it-for-the money jobs. If willing to live poor one could be free from working at jobs that required too much attention.

We tramped the grey city of New York 1959. It was a scene of loss, that New York, and thus it had all that cheap space. In the fifteen years since victory in the "good war," the industrial base of the city had melted down. Gone South? Gone out of the country? Gone. Had the old walk-up factories ended up too unionized for the fat cats to accept or too small for postwar technology? Whatever the reasons, the tide had gone out and huge swaths of once industrial Manhattan were almost empty. There were blocks of dark coal-smoke-stained 19th century loft buildings, with unwashed windows and tinned over doors.

There were huge swaths of poor residential Manhattan, too, the "new law" tenements with their famous dumbbell shape enclosing narrow airshafts. They were not empty but they had neither been gussied up nor demolished in 1959. In fact, they were only recently promoted from cold-water status. The city ordinance that forced landlords to supply all residential units with heat and hot water had gone into effect just four years earlier, in 1955. These apartments were cheap enough but unthinkable for a painter. Nine feet wide with airshaft light? We wanted a loft.

We tramped through the desolate district west of Fifth Avenue above Union Square, we checked out buildings along Second Avenue, where old factories and tenement buildings were cheek by jowl. We looked at second floors on Allen Street.

The beleaguered landlords were ready to rent to anyone with cash in hand, no questions asked. Spaces not previously used by an artist would have toilets only, one or two tiny hand sinks, no kitchen, no hot water. We saw a lot of enticing raw space. We looked at huge floors piled with abandoned machinery we'd be on our own to haul away before we could even begin building a living/working space. But more to the point, Baz had no more plumbing or electrical skills than I did. Installing a clandestine kitchen or a working bathtub was beyond us. Hiring a pro (unless he was your uncle) was out of the question too because the installation was illegal. We needed a place already pioneered by an artist, which meant paying the artist who wanted to move the cost of the stuff he'd installed, plus something for all his work, plus a taste as a finder's fee, because this was one sweet cave, hand-dug out of the urban barrens. This purchase agreement was totally under the table and way off the books. It had nothing to do with the lease to rent the place, to be signed with the actual owner of the building.

Baz wasn't much moved by the homemade anarchy of those lofts; lofts were simply practical workspaces to him. If they'd been made cute, he was offended. But I loved the tree-house hobo jungle qualities; the salvaged furniture, jury-rigged sinks, ancient second-hand appliances. To me it was all of a piece with the idea that you didn't have to do what *they* said.

How we came to live in an office building

Whitehall Street. That was weird. No one else did that. No one else lived so far downtown either—except for a small knot of artists who had colonized some older, more picturesque buildings on Coenties Slip, just around the corner. Those buildings were so old they had sail-making lofts. They had pitched roofs and fireplaces.

The Coenties Slip group knew each other: Agnes Martin, Jack Youngerman, Ellsworth Kelly. We sometimes saw each other on the street. But even when I was in an acting class with Delphine Seyrig (who starred in *Last Year at Marienbad* when she went back to France) and rode home with her on the back of her Lambretta, we never established real friendships. They were older; to me they were adults. Youngerman was becoming established; Kelly would soon follow. I thought the reason for our avoidance lay there. Now I think that Baz sent out his potent 'don't bother me' vibes because he didn't need yet another tribe of bohemians offering to accept him. We were present but we were not. We had come to the big art world and then moved to the far end, the very bottom of the island.

How is easier to say than why

We had seen a billboard painted on the side of a building

advertising a huge real estate firm. Why in hell did Baz call? And then we went there, to an office building in the Wall Street area. Walter was a big deal, with real estate holdings all over the city. Walter was behind a big desk in an inner private office. Why did he even see us? He got up and walked us over to 33 Whitehall, showed us around the building and then walked us around the corner to an army surplus store on South Street so we could all talk to Gertie. Dirty Gertie was her street name. She owned 33 Whitehall and how many other nearby buildings we'll never know, but Walter knew, and he knew he'd never turn a buck on her property if he didn't do it her way. She was a widow and she was used to being on her own. Soon, but not yet, she would turn it all over, take her money, and move off to the suburbs or Florida. But for now, no. Not yet. Her dusty store catered to a dwindling bunch of alcoholic ex-seamen. Little Gertie was so used to talking to the brain-damaged and mendacious that she characteristically tipped back her head and rasped into your face very loudly, syllable by syllable. And so generous that she actually returned our rent money one month when I had to see a dentist and we were short.

Number 33 was virtually empty. Neither she nor Walter were really trying to rent any of it. It was a waiting game between them. And thus it was a deal for us: we were to be "caretakers." We were to sweep the halls once a week, keep the hall lights in working order, and do a few other trivial things. We didn't tend the furnace. And as we learned one bad night when the sprinklers went off soaking Mr. Kaplan's coats and suits, we didn't even know where the water main was or how to cut it off. We were really there to make sure no derelicts got inside to piss or sleep, and we were also asked to look out for the one remaining upstairs tenant. Ferguson's had been a travel agency when both Fergusons were alive, but now the widow came once or twice a week. She'd sit in the office under the fading cruise ship posters and drink down a pint of bourbon. Mr. Kaplan, the guys in the candy stand across the street, and later on Baz, would help her into a cab when she was ready to go home.

For these responsibilities, Walter said we could have the whole third floor for $50 a month. At one end of this floor, for some odd reason, there was a small domestic apartment: a kitchen, bathroom, bedroom and living room. For Basil's workspace, we could remove as many wallboard partitions as we cared to take down. The third-floor offices were quite simply built and many partitions didn't go all the way to the ceiling. I think we ultimately combined three large offices. There was terrific light; the windows, pivot-hung windows that rotate on a central rod, were almost floor to ceiling. And the buildings opposite were also low rise.

There was one down side. Pigeons had gotten in through a broken window. We did some truly miserable cleaning – with chisels followed by disinfectant – to make the place habitable. And all the while we worked at this, we went back each night, filthy and exhausted, to Lynn's place. It was hot mid-summer before we finally moved.

And soon thereafter…

We might have twigged. Thirty-three Whitehall was just one block up the street from the Lower Manhattan Army Induction Center and while we were at work cleaning we got used to seeing hangdog young men in handcuffs being loaded onto army buses headed for Fort Dix.

We'd only just had our telephone connected when there came a terse long-distance phone call from Detroit. "Don't write," Basil's father said. "Don't phone. The FBI is looking for you." Click. Baz had liberated an item or two from the Railway Express warehouse in San Francisco, including the wonderful wooden office chair that I'm sitting on right now. But surely the FBI wouldn't be involved in that.

Don't write. Don't phone. So we didn't.

I'm not sure where I'd gone that Saturday afternoon, but when I walked in the door, Baz was sitting at our table with a middle-aged man wearing a brown suit. A buyer? I wondered.

"You must be Martha," he said.

Baz told me later he had not mentioned my name. The man had given his name, and showed Baz a badge. He had this to offer: "Be at the army induction center day after tomorrow or we'll come back with arrest papers. Understand?"

Baz had not been in touch with his Michigan draft board

since leaving for Black Mountain College. In 1959 the draft was not then the deadly threat it would soon become. The Korean War was over except for the endless "truce"; Vietnam involved only "advisors." Nevertheless all men were required to register when they reached age 18, and the draft was a menace. Getting drafted in that eerie "peacetime" would mean two years of total boredom, of "parking tanks in Kansas," as my sister's husband put it. *He* was exempt by virtue of a baby son. Baz had nothing to protect himself with and only twenty-four hours to get ready.

The experience of our peers was not reassuring. Jorge Fick had tried to flunk the I.Q. test and was drafted. Fielding Dawson had equipped himself with a letter from his bishop, relying on his once regular church membership back in Missouri to support a conscientious objector claim. He was drafted. Then because of his C.O. claim he was required to salute the flag while his fellow inductees received rifle training. Claiming to be homosexual, whether it was true or not, was a crapshoot based totally on the outlook of a local draft board. In New York City it was hardly worth the effort. The story was that openly gay men drafted in New York were shunted off to units in Alaska. Someone Baz knew got exempted by simply scribbling NO over all the blanks on all his tests and intake forms. He was a soulful looking young man, with big eyeglasses and a sweet face, and he didn't have a record of failing to report. "They'd never take that from me," Baz predicted.

We sat up all night. We walked all day Sunday.

Somewhere along the way we got to Thomas Mann and *The Confessions of Felix Krull.* A charming movie from the book had recently played in one of the movie theaters on 42nd Street. I sent Baz off that Monday morning, down the block. He'd been told to bring a bag as he'd be leaving for Fort Dix immediately. He didn't. Five hours later he walked back in the door, out of breath and starving for lunch.

"I lost my piss bottle," he said.

"Well that's not much," I said.

"When you're in a hallway with forty, fifty stark naked men and you go up and down the line, all worried because I lost my piss bottle, what should I do, you get noticed," he said. He'd kept it up all through the physical, telling the guys in line with him, Felix-Krull-like, "They gotta let me in!" When the army doc asked him to bend over, he said he'd been too short to play basketball in high school. "You gotta let me in. I want to kill Germans." He told other examiners, "Look what they did to my people! I want to kill me some Germans."

By the time his cohort was allowed to dress again, he was called to report to a room upstairs. The army psychiatrist asked a few mundane questions and then told Baz to walk across the room. Halfway across, he barked, "Halt." Here's the part no one could fake. Apparently Baz didn't pause a half second. He just kept on walking. "Why didn't you stop," the army shrink asked.

"I don't stop for anybody."

Then he waited. While he stood there the shrink wrote and wrote in tiny handwriting all over a form. And then he was handed a subway token – fare to get home.

But it wasn't quite over. About ten days later he got official papers in the mail stating that his draft status was 4-D. By then all his cool had melted. He was petrified. I told him to call to find out what 4-D means. He was unhinged. He said the call would be monitored, he would be traced, that no matter what 4-D meant, calling the draft officials to ask would mess up his narrow escape. Finally Lynn made a call for him. "4-D is the exemption for divinity students," Lynn told us trying not to break up. "Don't argue!" And that was that. We heard nothing further, ever.

A postscript

Well, not quite ever. He was still 4-D in 1963, by which time getting drafted had truly ugly implications. We'd become parents that February, and Baz wrote his draft board to report this change. He got a form letter saying he was now listed 4-A. No panic this time; he sent another note asking under what circumstances he'd be called up. This time a personal letter arrived from a lieutenant general, ret., head of the Mt. Clemens, Michigan draft board: "In the event of a national emergency serious enough to require calling 4-A's there would not be time. Sincerely yours...."

Below the Deadline

By the sea. By the estuary and harbor. By the sludge water, the pulse of tides, the Atlantic Ocean, the braided strands of Hudson, Passaic, Bayonne. Only the giant Customs Building (which is now the Museum of the American Indian) one block over lay between our block on Whitehall Street, and Battery Park. The daytime streets were noisy, smelly, crammed with restless life. The print shop opposite us clanged and clattered nonstop. The smells of street food mingled with car exhaust. When the weather was warm and the windows were open, there was constant low roar: people talking, shoes hitting pavement, cars, trucks, busses, exhaust fans, hand trucks, the unlistable human mechanicals of big city motion.

A human tide into or out of the Staten Island ferry terminal set the weekday rhythm. A little after eight in the morning and again as it neared five, footfall sounds would begin rising. At its peak it was peppered with shouts and car horns, but in thirty or forty minutes the crescendo would dwindle. Mornings it was followed by the ongoing work roar; evenings by a cool almost liquid silence.

Everything shifted. Sea wind blew. Cold in winter, cool in summer. Down our street, beyond the ferry terminal the harbor was large and dark. Behind us, buildings were large and blazing light. Office lights burned all night but not for office workers. Wall

Street high achievers all went home in those days and waited for their data to be crunched by clerks and typists who would be back in the morning. The only people we'd see were cleaners or security guards, scattered groups of Eastern European women in white uniforms heading for the Bowling Green subway station or bored guards in uniform smoking together in the ground floor doorways. There were no cars. The streets were ours.

There was a resident population – a handful of drifters, the Coenties Slip gang, feral cats, an old poet named Oscar Williams. Maybe a hundred people lived below City Hall. The Manhattan that never sleeps was way north, in the Village, in midtown and beyond. Cops used to call Fulton Street the Deadline. The restaurants, stores, and sandwich shops were locked tight by nine except for a short row of businesses just by the ferry terminal. There, the Bean Pot Bar & Grill harbored Gertie's customers, alongside a poverty late-night liquor store, and a place selling sex magazines and cigarettes.

We were all to ourselves in the middle of an enormous city, silent and windswept. We might have been living on the floor of the Grand Canyon I used to say, as we walked among the towers. It was endlessly amazing but it was also isolated from normal city services.

We had to wheel our bulging laundry cart a mile north to the housing projects on Chatham above the Brooklyn Bridge for the closest laundromat. We shopped there too, or went further into

Chinatown. Slowly we discovered other shopping oddities our haven afforded. The nearest one lay inside the ferry terminal. We didn't need greeting cards or flowers, but one of the shops was an expensive, beautifully stocked fruit and vegetable store catering to upscale commuters. Baz got into conversation with the owner one night while he was bagging up cauliflower.

"Eh, my family's sick a cauliflower," he remarked. "The customers want 'em spotless – everything in this store," gesturing at a few brownish stains on the cauliflower heads.

It was true. Not a bruise, not a nick, not a stray imperfection discolored his artichokes, his apples, his mahogany red cherries. No wonder they cost the earth. It turned out he culled his stock for aesthetics every single night. He took to saving bags of rejects for us, which he'd happily hand us for a dollar.

"Enjoy," he'd say, often repeating resentfully how his customers couldn't tolerate a tiny spot.

The other shopping was offered by what was left of the old Washington Markets, a short walk to the west side of the island, the area eventually torn down for the World Trade Center buildings. By 1959, most of the city's food wholesalers had decamped for bigger modern terminals in the Bronx – but even the remaining fraction of what had once been there was panoramic. Coffee and tea merchants, jobbers of canned goods, meat packers, wheat dealers, spice merchants. Their scale was city-wide and the sidewalks were pitted with crates, barrels and packing cases. None of these merchants would sell retail except for the place I called "Whitman's Supermarket." Old Walt would have found it quite familiar: A huge high ceilinged space with creaking wooden floors chockablock with retail counters. There was a butcher who sold mutton, another who specialized in blood puddings, a condiments shop filled with jarred chutneys and mustard pickles, and the bonanza store where you bought unlabeled dented cans, two for a nickel. Adventures in eating. Each counter was an individual enterprise and there was an arcane system for cooperative retailing.

At each counter, your purchase was wrapped in white butcher paper and tied up with string. Your name was scribbled on the outside with a black crayon, and you were given a paper receipt. When you were finished shopping you'd take your fistful of receipts to a black iron filigree cage at the very back of the store. There sat the teller who handled the money. She pushed change out in a wooden tray with fantastically well-worn sections for each type of coin. As you paid, she solemnly stamped the receipts and placed them in a little bullet-like container that was released to roll itself up a thin cable and away across the store's ceiling. I think this contraption ran on compressed air because the bullets made a soft whooshing sound as they rolled along the wires. There were always several crisscrossing the ceiling. It was like a huge model railroad layout, without toy trees or papier mâché mountains. When the bullet reached the front counter by the exit door, a bell clanged two or thee times. You walked up there and waited until your packages were delivered to the front by runners, mostly teenage boys in white coats. The front doorkeep solemnly asked your name, matched up receipts, and handed over your packages.

Mutton, I learned, if trimmed and pricked to release the old fat, and roasted slowly, with copious hunks of garlic poked into the meat, is delicious. Blood pudding I left to Baz.

We were in other far less pleasant places in our hearts and minds while we lived on Whitehall, but we lived sequestered, even privileged by the weird terrain. Once the office partitions had been removed, Baz began painting furiously: ab ex paintings and drawings. And we both got part-time money jobs, but our lives seemed suspended. Great changes had taken place during Basil's absence from the city and we were not welcomed into the new dispensation.

Down on Whitehall our empty building creaked and released 19th century dust. Our romance blew around our building like the sea breeze. Because we went to the ferry terminal shops so often the ferry people got to know us, and waved us to duck under the turnstiles. A free boat ride was our summer night cool-off. We'd sit on the open end with our feet up on the railing, listening to the dark hiss of bubbles, watching bits of the city dance on their own reflections, and eating Frosty Freezes from the terminal's ice cream store. On the other side, we'd walk around, back up the ramp and be waved under the turnstile for our trip home. Regardless of the wider world, a free life could be scavenged from the city's excess, from the edges, the ignored, the overlooked, in the middle of our life in the city where we found so much confusion.

Whitehall Street Brief, Two

It's wrong to imply we were always alone. Dan Rice stayed with us on Whitehall Street, often and for days. He was beautiful, tiny and large headed, strong but not muscular. "I'd a been a full-blown dwarf if I'd stayed in the womb a bit longer," Dan said. His arms and hands were wiry and seasoned. His chest tight, his movements quick and competent. He was California's golden Celt, a cool jazzman with long sea-blue battle eyes. That was the Dan Rice Charles Olson adored.

Black Mountain's towering Charles Olson was also clumsy Charles, Charles the nerd, the scholarship boy trying to crack Brahmin Boston with his brains. Dan Rice, American, not a Brahmin in the slightest, never (before alcohol destroyed his nerves) made an awkward move. He received Olson's adoration smoothly, as if it were his natural right.

Kicks. A haymaker. Dan was a master at hiding. No one knew. His small dots, his tiny paint smears interrupt the plane of a blank white canvas so underlying forms can be discerned in muted points, intense as the notes in a Chet Baker solo. But not that many were ever painted. All his life it was exquisitely difficult for Dan to work; *work*, the engine and gyroscope of artists. No one could see the delicate web Dan wove for himself. No one knew. Least of all

Charles. He adored Dan, the exemplary student-monitor of Black Mountain College.

Baz adored Dan's older brother Jack. Jack was red where Dan was light brown, and, if possible, more glamorous, more tightly strung. If Dan exuded intellectual and artistic intensity, Jack exuded intense material mastery. Baz didn't crave an American archetype as Charles did. He needed a big brother, and tough Jack was his model of male sweetness.

Jack never became an architect or a designer. He lived out his life in southern California, where he married, raised kids, and turned his talents to building – houses, fireplaces, terraced gardens, retaining walls. They were sculptures of earth, stone, and brick. There were, occasionally, movie stars among his well-heeled clients. Jack himself always worked alongside his crew, faithful to a crafts ethic much promoted but not invented by Black Mountain. He died in 2002. I met him just once, but I know the brother he was to Baz.

There's a photograph of the Rice brothers, taken early summer in 1945 on a street in Honolulu. Jack, marine, and sailor Dan are striding in step. They are 23 and 19 respectively. They are the boys that Truman saved with our terrible atomic bombs. Both brothers expected invasion duty and both had already seen enough fighting to be fatalistic about their chances. With Ricean adroitness they had wangled simultaneous shore leaves. There in Honolulu, the impending invasion not to think about, they swung down the sidewalk together, into the street photographer's lens: caps crooked, eyes sparkling, cocks on the ready. Jack, the taller, is five feet five. Even a little bomb would have killed him. Bombs easily kill humans. But don't provoke Jack Rice in a bar. You'll wake up beaten up.

Why did Dan take up with us or us with Dan on Whitehall Street? In the hermetic Black Mountain College circle, Basil King was a renegade. He had argued with Olson and turned down his prescriptions. No, it was Baz, the others said, who didn't like *them.* It would be fifty years before Baz allowed, and they could see, that liking them was not the issue. Baz was not *like* them but he was unable to absorb that fact, to live it, or to offer others some all-important reassuring ease.

 Back in 1959, the approval of Dan Rice meant a share of Dan's golden aura, a share of the blessing Olson bestowed when he declared Rice to be "the finest painter of his generation." So why did Dan take up with Baz who wasn't impressed by what Olson said? With Baz who flatly stated Olson was brilliant in history and literature, but about visual art, a real stumblebum?

 A New York art world, wider than Black Mountain, congregating nightly in the Cedar Bar, had disliked Dan for the way he aligned himself with Kline and de Kooning. He wasn't just their friend. Dan's posture said he was the Abstract Expressionists' peer. Even worse, in some of the Cedar regulars' eyes, the old guys clearly *liked* Dan and cultivated his company. He was sparkling smart, a fearless maker of combinations in talk, with a fine ability to listen and to smell out bullshit in talk, with great patience in talk, great inventiveness, and with a font of intelligent elfish wit.

The Bar. The Cedars. Technically, of course, the Cedar Street Tavern. But the name was usually given as a plural. When everybody was there it was as crowded as a mosh pit but everybody was there. Everybody. The entire downtown art world fit into one medium-sized garden-variety bar room.

The Cedars was stock exchange, pawnshop, rental office, squat, and psycho ward. It was the village post office. Messages were posted and delivered. It was a small-town city hall where reputations could be created and destroyed in a day's time.

The Cedars was peaceful in the afternoons. People would read the newspaper, revise their play scripts, correct school papers, unwind after a shift, chat. If there was a TV it was so unobtrusive I don't remember it. In the late afternoons there was always a mix: postmen, union organizers, college professors from NYU down the street, New School activists, firemen, here a painter of houses, there a painter of art. Mostly men. They wanted to eat hamburgers or cheese sandwiches with a shot of rye, water back. They wanted a couple of draft beers and familiarity. Unaccompanied young women could sit at this bar and do the same without harassment – and that was a very rare thing at the time.

In the evening, every evening, the downtown art world would file in, a crowd that grew less quiet and more extravagant as the night continued. Then the bar would be thick with blue-grey cigarette smoke and the energies of 75 or 100 people topping each other and jostling for position.

The attitude of many Cedar regulars was that Baz had not mastered bar manners, that Baz was provoking, self-destructive, and his problems were his own fault. That reputation of having no bar manners was of long standing. I had come to town married to a very young man, a 23-year-old who nevertheless had years of past – all the way back to an earlier era, seven years earlier and already the stuff of legend, when 16-year-old Baz first hitchhiked up to New York City from Black Mountain College.

I never knew that young man. He was part of a Black Mountain invasion, a small shock troop of older but also still young mostly men most of whom believed that Black Mountain, particularly in the person of Charles Olson, possessed the vision for a whole new world.

"Olson says," Joel Oppenheimer or Fielding Dawson would intone, with all the certainty of converts. Have you *listened* to Ives, to Cage? Do you understand what William Carlos Williams has really *done* for prosody? Are you following Zukofsky? The social reforms of Dennison and Goodman? The American focus of Perry Miller? Don't talk to me about Paris! Fuck France and all those European perspectives. Black Mountain has the inside edge.

But, as Frank O'Hara said to me and Baz a bit later, "We were already here. We didn't need to be told."

During that past, the equivocally credentialed teenage Baz had become a pet. Grace Hartigan liked him. De Kooning befriended him. Even crazed Jackson Pollock talked to him. Joan Mitchell bought him beer. They had treated him with affection and familiarity in the Cedars of seven years before, and the rest of the bar, the striving wannabees and neverbeens, the starstruck, and the discouraged, all held this image of him.

Now, "Second Generation" abstract expressionists were also showing and not on 10th Street but uptown on 57th. In this new scene, money was a definite possibility not a distant scent. A gallery dealer was no longer co-conspirator with an artist in a wily plot to subvert established aesthetics. The art world was becoming one in which art reputations meant opportunities to juggle investment profits and build society ambitions. The change was actually visible, if you wanted to observe it. Smart operators at uptown parties were sipping Coca-Cola instead of slugging down bourbon. Every move could have corporate implications.

Baz was rejected and rejecting. I was his silent sidekick. Baz lived in a state of anxious energy always close to spinning out of control, and it never took much to provoke him. A careless word, a lazy assumption, and Baz would launch one of his furious condem-nations. The status or potential power of his target meant beans to him. A defense or request for restraint based on the offender's status only upped his stake in the contest. Baz would be off. Hot coals. High winds. A crown fire.

Worse, he was sometimes bone-chillingly accurate in his rages. In his own way he was as dazzling as Dan in his free flow of connections. He was no brilliantly armed academician, but he knew what matters in debate from his British schooling and from a crazy missionary teacher he'd had in Detroit public school, Grade 9. Even so and all too often, emotions would overwhelm him and he'd grow inarticulate with passion. He'd tangle syntax, garble references, fly into nonsense. His pupils would expand until his eyes sprayed black light. Even in that state he was likely to hurl at least one unforgivably accurate insight. He could be one scary guy, this delicate young man of 135 pounds, with his spastic right hand, his half-paralyzed right leg. There were people in the Cedars who acted as if he could or would or actually *had* physically beaten them up.

A climate of powerful protection and tolerance for Baz, which would have covered me as well, was absent when he and I entered this world. Instead, I too was glared at and insulted by people Baz knew but I didn't. The city edging toward 1960 was absent the regular presence of the old Ab-Ex gang. Pollock was dead. DeKooning was in the Hamptons. Joan Mitchell was married and living in Canada. Kline, whom Baz had angered by flouting his advice not to go back to Black Mountain three years earlier, was living with Betsy Zogbaum and had become a sporadic rather than nightly presence in the bar.

"You back?" a man said to Baz on a typical night in the Cedars. "I thought you were dead," he sneered.

So why did Dan seek us out?

Dan still had Kline and to a lesser extent Bob Rauschenberg as his backstops. And he was a politician, as Baz was not. Even so, it must have been payback time for him as well. Is that why Dan sought us out?

Dan needed meals and we usually had food; he often needed a place to stay, and we had a living room furnished with several mattresses. He needed a loan. So did we. A hundred dollars passed back and forth between him and us so many times, we finally lost track of who owed who. We needed conversation, and Dan sharpened his wits with Baz, always a fountain of the bent and unexpected. Talk. Talk. Talk. Oh we needed talk. We needed acceptance. Dan accepted us. He did better than that. Dan could see worth in what Baz struggled for in his studio. Way faster than me. Sometimes faster than Baz. Dan wasn't worried by the lumpiness or wild disdain for conventions that emerged as Baz wrestled with space, against balance. Dan loved Baz for being an artist, around, beyond and through the competition for dominance that always rocked between two of them. And we both loved him back.

Our first bleak Christmas in New York included one of those trips back to Whitehall when suddenly our subway train was clanking. Clanking meant we were up on Manhattan Bridge with the dark river below; it meant we'd taken a "Bridge" instead of a "Tunnel" train, and now there'd be a cold wait at yellow DeKalb Avenue in Brooklyn and then another wait back uptown at Union Square, to get us onto the right goddamn poky "Tunnel" local to Whitehall that we should have caught the first time.

At our door at the end of the third floor hallway sat a small newspaper nest knotted together with intricate string. I cautiously scissored off the bindings and discovered six pretty highball glasses, the kind with heavy bottoms, each one also wrapped in rolled newspapers tied by yet more spider-web string. How could the package have gotten there? The building was locked. No note, no tag, no nothing. Just the nest in front of our unmarked door.

Dan didn't fess up for almost three years, though god knows I asked. In fact I was certain that the gift *wasn't* from him. He'd been at the Cedar's when we left that night, thoroughly plastered, and looking mysterious about his plans. It wasn't until we moved uptown to the Rose Building on Delancey Street that Dan admitted he'd copied our key.

Among the rejects

American llamas are reluctant beasts of burden. They can't be ridden; they won't pull carts. But they do carry. The Inca and the

119

Aztec wove saddlebags for llamas and had no need of wheels. The wheel was a toy for children and the grownups made them out of clay and wood. But couldn't buffalo have pulled carts of goods? hauled grain into town and manure away? Aztec and Inca children played with toy wheeled carts. Apparently no one built big ones for work.

Freud said: "Anyone turning biographer commits himself to lies, to concealment, to hypocrisy, to flattery, and even to hiding his own lack of understanding for the biographical truth is not to be had, and even if it were, it couldn't be used. Truth is unobtainable."

Knowledge of bits and bridles is also elusive. If domestication were logical, zebras would have been prized as steeds for upscale children.

John Wieners arrived; another young man living on wits, but this one was engaged in the systematic ruination of his senses, in derangement of everyday life, in determined romantic quest for poetry's authenticity. As seemed utterly reasonable to me and Baz. Destroy to make a world. Destroy to make a self. How else? Brilliant John, a poet of crazed lyricism, invention, and song. Baz loved him. He'd known him since they were both students at Black Mountain. Baz said he'd never seen a person work so hard to make his art, or worked so hard to make himself a master.

Did John crack under the strain? Or was it the strain of social intrigue? Or simply the effect of viciously inept treatment for mental illness furnished to the poor by state hospitals? After the Black Mountain years, a complicated rivalry with Charles Olson developed that cost John in his core. But there was more. He cracked and he mended many times, mending each time less perfectly, cracking and mending until it seemed the mends were everything and the original entity nearly gone.

But not the poems. He said that himself: the words go on. Perhaps he wrote his best early: "The Hotel Wentley Poems," "Ace of Pentacles." They stand. But so too do some of the later works. You learn to always look again.

John was ferret-faced, and then elegant; loving, then haughtily disapproving, runty and illcomplected; and then, on some days, as beautiful as a young John Gielgud – the chameleon survival of homosexuality. At one time, forty years ago, he and young Frank O'Hara looked like hawk-nosed brothers.

When I met him, late 1950s San Francisco, he was a virgin as far as women were concerned but wanted desperately to be in love with one of us. He wanted desperately to have a woman love *him*, more perfectly to be a woman himself. This would have been a part of the alchemy, the reorganization that the poem could give him, and that he could give to poems.

"Does it hurt you?" he asked me.

"No. It feels great!"

"I can't imagine how, going *in* that way!"

I was too shy to reverse the question. Perhaps he was never the receiver, I thought blushing, thinking about the pain implicit in buggery. "I don't explain it well," I said. That was lame.

"I felt so sorry for my mother," John said. He knew her as raised on guilt and duty, raised in Catholic Boston where pleasure was forbidden to women. He'd have felt differently about his mother if this hadn't been true for her, whether he grew up straight or gay. This understanding is the knowledge of auras, which very small children know, and it has nothing to do with mental understanding.

"I fell in love with other boys as far back as I can remember," John told me dreamily. "What's earlier than kindergarten? Nursery school? Then, back then. The first other boys I was ever with."

When he arrived at Whitehall Street, he had a woman with him. And her friends, two other guys and one more woman. He was on the mend, John said. He had a chance, again, he said, after the disasters in California, and after the hospitalization, his first. Later there were many more shock treatments, but this was long before it was clear to everyone, including John, that he had not courted disarrangement of his senses but had fallen under a boulder of mental illness.

He had returned to his home turf in Boston, and in this woman had found, he told us, a refuge, a family, a place to spring from. It was methedrine, I think, that she and her friends shot; but it might have been heroin or maybe a mixture of the two. A bit of grass always useful, when coming down. Beer in gallons for the thirst. We shared these last two with them. How much injectable John did, I can't be sure. My guess is none at that time. My guess is he sniffed.

She had a hard androgynous body, and a beat face. She might have been beautiful. She might have been brilliant. Who'd know? Junk does that. She might have been forty. She might have been seventeen. Her life was well organized. Junk does that. I think of that when people spout that disgusting cliché about not sweating small stuff. Like any junkie, this woman knew exactly what she needed, what was essential. It was always time to get some, and scoring was the guys' job. She'd stopped turning tricks to please John.

She sweated. A lot. Junk does that too.

Within an hour of arrival our place was their nest. Swirls of clothing, bottles, paperback books, plastic pouches, tins of weed, ashtrays with tiny matchstick teepees. Like winter camp. Sleeping bags and pillowcases full of dirty laundry doing duty as berms in a mattress land. The group was mammal-friendly, easy, but without much conversation. Whoever was there squidged over to make room whenever someone else entered the room; and sprawled to take up the vacant space whenever someone left.

How our friend John loved her, that she sucked his dick, that she held his dick and guided it for him, that she needed him and whatever he promised her, that she promised him Peter-Panhood. It wasn't clear to me and it didn't matter. There was some reason they'd all left Boston. Some problem, some scam unglued. Not the point. John offered them **us**. We were the bent home, the warm nonjudgmental haven. We could take them all in and offer shelter. It would be our gang against the world.

The two men might have been brothers. I sat with the two women while all three men were out one night and watched as they lovingly, sexually, shot up together. The other woman used a vein above her eyelid. It was bloody.

Days went by. Slowly. Was it a week? Two? More? Baz and I had day jobs we had to go to. We had to arrive more or less on time, in clothing more or less clean and appropriate.

We were fraying.

Baz came out with it: It was time for the group to move on.

"You're making her turn tricks again! What else can she *do?*" John screamed at Baz. You of all people, said his eyes.

Tears, a scuffle. The lumbering men friends, one of whom had never said more than 'yes' and 'no' made a flailing attack and not so ineffectually. Kicks. A haymaker. These two were butch guys, once upon a time. An arc of nose blood spotted the Chinese newspaper we'd pasted on our windows, for a modicum of daytime privacy. Weekdays the printers in the shop directly across the street sat in their open windows, legs over the wide sills, smoking or eating chips and drinking coffee while their machines clattered through a run.

One of the men howled "Fucking squares!" Flared at John, "Why'ja bring us here!"

The eyelid woman demanded money from me. In exchange for her derision. You hopeless bourgeoisie, her face said. Baz gave her some. We left. They left. He left. She left. They left and did not stay. Then they were gone, we cleaned up, and John Wieners didn't forgive us.

Long after, Baz and John did speak again, when he came to our house in Brooklyn. He wore a fluffy red organdy apron that he'd purchased at the Waldorf Astoria, and he danced for our children, explaining his desire to be Joan Crawford, to be Bette Davis.

"Are you English?" six-year-old Hetty asked.

"I certainly *hope* so," he said.

He was there when seven-year-old Mallory came home crying because she hadn't been elected president of the second grade. Another poet was at the house, the son of a high-powered pediatric surgeon. His eyes welled up and he told her how hard it had always been for him to be the shortest kid in class. John held Mallory on his lap and listened as she said she got only one vote, her own. Her eyes were red behind her eyeglasses. She couldn't believe her position. John told her he'd never fit in at school and he wept. I suppose Basil fought tears. Or maybe they flowed. I was away at work and know all this from what they told me later. Reports of my oldest child's first painful skirmishes in the life-long social war.

It was a wonderful visit. Baz and John spent three days interviewing each other for an article to be featured in *Mulch*, the literary magazine Baz had started that year. But it turned out that the mike was crummy, the tape was shot, the volume had not been properly set – or something. When I sat down to transcribe the tapes, all I could hear was mumbling, punctuated by great loud gusts of laugher, and shouts like "Oh, SHIT, nooo!" followed by more mumbling, up and down the scale. Six tapes, all the same. No one had checked the machine beforehand or reviewed any tapes while John was still with us in Brooklyn. Instead, evenings of his visit, after I got home from work, we would eat and put the kids in bed and talk on till late at night.

All of us left the subject of his visit to Whitehall Street carefully unexplored.

Rose, Possible

Baz and I left the land below the deadline and moved up, up into "downtown" when we took up an offer to live in the Rose Building on Delancey Street for a year. This is the building that was painted more than once by Edward Hopper. One painting shows the edge of Williamsburg Bridge, our top windows, and, large in the upper center of the frame, the building's lintel spanning the top floor. This space was often embellished in the 19th century with a name, the name of the builder or the firm carved or cast in cement or metal.

In Hopper's painting the lintel says firmly: ROSE

Names are carved into collective family imagination too. Were yours? My parents believed a family name carried great weight. Not simply your personal tag. But your word, your honor, your bond, your family name. Your brand? No, it was deeper than that; it was profound identity. You *are* a Symmers from the South Carolina Symmerses; a Shuey from the Valley, a Lambert, or "just like a Davis"; you are this name. And thus you are your ancestors, or at least all ancestors fit to brag about: That would include the Reverend Maes of the Jamestown Colony, William Davis of the Lynchburg Quakers, Thomas Mifflin, General Washington's Quartermaster General, and Gabriella, Eugene, and Celestine

Garth of Birdwood Plantation, Charlottesville, Virginia. My ancestors.

Basil's family names are all invention, translation, or possibly subterfuge. His father's name was Cohen in England but family legend had it that Cohen was simply assigned when the first family members arrived in Britain from somewhere in Poland with a name that was too much for the immigration official. He asked instead for the tribe, hence "Cohen." Or maybe. And now it's King, the translation of Cohen, ostensibly because Basil's dad's younger brother, the first to move to America, had made that change when he arrived. Or maybe. Basil's mother's family name is even less transparent: Board. What kind of name is that for a Jewish family from middle Europe? Was it shortened from something else? There is no family legend to explain, nothing of family history at all any further back than grandparents. Except for candlesticks. The silver ones Esther gave away were way older than Esther's mother. I know the bright feel of old silver, and these were much softer than even 19th century blends. Another pair of heavy brass candlesticks was dated to the 17th century by an expert at the Detroit Institute of Arts. But were they always in his mother's family?

The name ROSE was on the lintel of the building on Delancey Street. The name of a family? a woman? a flower? a color? a firm? a brand? Was it the name of a firm rose?

In the window, Edward painted a woman in a white dress, sitting where I sat, looking over the unchanged bridge plaza, a wide expanse of dun-yellow concrete. The young woman in white was not Jo Hopper, Baz said, dating the painting. Too early. The bridge plaza is wide and sloping and I'd watch kids play hopscotch there or idly ride bicycles in circles.

Baz and I sublet the top floor for a year while the regular tenants went to Europe. The tenants were both artists – Robert Beauchamp, painter, and Jackie Ferrara, sculptor.

Bob Beauchamp, the beautiful French countryside, pronounced BEEch-um Brit style, had a face marked by Oklahoma poverty and squinty with desire. A scrawny body, a delicate feminine voice. Bob worked in the same frame shop Baz did. He gilded frames with a soft precision Baz imitated for me because he loved it so: how Bob deftly swiped the fragile gold square across the side of his head so the static charge would make it leap from his fingers exactly as he intended. Though he held this frame-shop day job, Bob was known in the downtown art scene. At that time, Walter P. Chrysler had an agent named Al who visited studios and bought art by truckload for the Chrysler art collection. The prices were pretty low. Bob may have sold twenty or thirty canvases to Chrysler for the $6,000 he was paid. And then a fellowship came through for him, a Guggenheim or a Fulbright.

However it was managed, it seemed unreal to me. I expected very little. Bob and Jackie had money in hand and were simply going to wander – to France, Spain, Italy. They didn't have to do anything or go anywhere in particular. They were just going to take it in. It seemed unreal.

Jackie has since achieved some status as a minimalist sculptor, greatly helped by the general change in the status of women artists that began to take hold in the 1970s and 80s. The same machinery that once stamped her as irredeemably marginal later worked to assure the world that her work has significance. Once that was in place, good galleries (no longer carefully designated "downtown") could exhibit and sell her silent stacked pyramids and oblongs, beautifully crafted in layers of dark wood or cast resins. Back in old Delancey Street days her pyramids were dark wax, awkward and irregular, filled with rows of small black women. Odd ersatz-African fetish objects. They were not minimalist pieces at all. They were portraits of Jackie, I thought. Who was Jewish, not black. A large and seemingly motherly woman, brimming with determination. A Mediterranean woman with a triangle of densely curling dark hair and heavy Coptic eyes. She had large hands and was an avid poker player. She was lush flesh for thin, driven Bob.

She really fixed him up, their friends said.

One of the people who said this was Bob Thompson.

Bob was a condition of our sublease. We were to permit access to the shower in the top floor hallway to Bob, who lived and painted two blocks away in a loft on Clinton Street, and to Bill and Sven, artists living on the third and fourth floors. The shower, the only one in the building, had been installed in one of the two box-like hall johns from sweatshop days. Neither was actually a room. On one side you opened a door and stepped into the shower, leaving clothes and towels on the wall hooks outside. On the other, you kind of backed in, if you were female, sat down, and the closed door hit your knees.

It was a public hallway. Bob – or anyone in the building – could have showered there without our permission. I don't remember that we kept a lock on either door. Nothing would have been farther from our ethic. Not that we were free and easy about the street: we were all concerned about the integrity of the street door lock six flights below, and grateful that anyone who entered could be seen through a glassed side door by people in the bar on the ground floor. The bar was run by the building's owner, who had a good street reputation, and his barkeeps did doorman duty, even occasionally admitting friends who didn't have copies of the door key.

So Bob became a regular presence at our big round table, bringing gossip and dope, bottles of beer, and stories of his childhood in the racial interstices of St. Louis, stories brimming with the complexities of Black life in America. Bob said his family members had skin colors ranging the human rainbow, having collected genes from all over Europe, Africa, Asia and indigenous North America. White Louisville considered the entire family "colored" but there were a few things about some Thompson family members that they didn't know. Moreover, Bob's parents didn't fit their expected categories. They were educated and well off. His mother owned a string of beauty parlors. His father was a chemist for DuPont, rewarded with company stock for his numerous innovations. Though Bob was not light-skinned, he had learned to slide along the margins of many intersecting worlds long before he came to live in the New York art world.

He slid into our lives too, toting his bathrobe, clean clothes, soaps and combs over from Clinton Street in a brown paper shopping bag. He loved Poussin and Jan Müller, who had only recently died, with an almost equal reverence and he had no patience for the raging ideological battle between the abstract and the figurative in art. Old stuff. Let the art magazine esthetes have all those ideas.

On his canvases Bob housed figured action in brightly colored landscapes lush with lollipop trees. They were flattened figures, often females, fucking horses or being fucked by men. Battle scenes of love not war, of nymphs and satyrs transmigrated through the traditions of American folk art or "plain" painting. It was integration. He wanted to blur distinctions between European and Native American myth and ease people of color into a general everyone's mythology. He adored the subject matter as well as the space of Europe's Baroque masters, and appropriated their compositions for new purposes.

A silhouette of a black man in a black hat occasionally and unremarkably appears in many of his pictures. It might be a self-portrait or it might not, but it is surely there as an indication of participation. But less poignantly than the civil rights placard of the 1950s: "I am a man." It simply said, "I am here." The sexuality in his paintings, like the politics, was decorative and only rarely disturbing. I found it easy joy, appealing but maybe a little too sweet.

Because he was around so much Bob fell under Basil's influence. Baz used to bawl him out for his poor technique – for his jerrybuilt stretcher bars, for using pre-primed canvas. Short cuts! More to the point, Bob touched the devils, the monsters, and then made them palatable, Baz said, urging him to more violence. I think I thought then but know I didn't say that he overestimated Bob's confidence. Bob was nervous and Baz's high demands for art, echoes of the Black Mountain brainwash, put Bob on edge.

He was a fine young athlete then, eight years before a major drug habit killed him, with an athlete's concern for body care. He cut his hair in front of the mirror over our kitchen sink, catching the clippings on an opened newspaper. He showed me how they could be rolled into springy little sausages and ping-pong balls. He tended his fingernails, cleaned his teeth, and stood at our sink to methodically drink down five glasses of cold water. His mother had told him hydration was essential to health. Because of the people who depended on the shower we had sublet part of Jackie and Bob's social life as well as their loft, a soothing solution as Basil's welcome in New York City had evaporated. The first generation abstractionists' regular presence at the Cedar Bar had ended with the exception of Franz Kline's and the bar was far from the friendly center it had once been. But 168½ Delancey was another story. The building had been arty for a very long time. We were told Walker Evans had lived on this top floor briefly, after Hopper moved on. Evans had in turn given the place to Robert and Mary Frank, the photographer and the sculptor, when he moved on. When Robert and Mary were still together. When Bob and Jackie were still together. When LeRoi Jones and Hettie Cohen Jones held all-weekend parties at their place on West 20th Street and jazzmen Archie Shepp and Wayne Shorter and Cecil Taylor would drop by. When Bob Thompson was still alive. When another gang of artists, all Bob Thompson's friends, led by Red Grooms, started The Delancey Street Museum just up the street. When Red Grooms and Mimi Gross were a new couple. When happenings were put on in scruffy lofts, and Jay Milder, Mimi, Bob, and other friends performed Red's joyous "Magic Train Ride." The performance was complete with an elaborate cardboard locomotive that caromed the length of the loft down a wire track suspended from the ceiling while everyone shouted.

That year 1960 had begun but "the sixties" had not. Cuba and Castro were the big news. Vietnam a distant blip. Living in a loft meant having a floor greasy from a machine-shop past. Amenities were impromptu, second-hand, scrabbled together. There were no lofts with Jacuzzis, new hardwood floors, stainless steel sinks, well-insulated windows. There were no lofts that were legal dwelling places. We lived with the ghosts of small factory workers, workers who were neighbors, family members, and friends and who worked at machines set so close together they felt each other's sweat in summer and jostled knees as they stamped their feet for warmth in January.

But by the late 1960s Manhattan artland began to fill vacant lofts on the other side of town, down West Broadway, and eventually south of Houston Street. The boom years took the scene across Canal and all the way through the old Washington Market area on the west side of the financial district. NoHo, SoHo, Tribeca, home of megalofts, borne on money and the spirit of real estate entrepreneurs. The Lower East Side where we lived a bit later was tarted up as Alphabet City first, then Loiesida, and finally as The East Village. But some areas were backwash. They festered and were hit hard in the crack wars of the 1980s. In those corners, owners and real estate interests took to arson, and by the 1990s, there were blocks on blocks of open space on the far East side – just flattened out rubble dotted with weeds and ailanthus trees.

In 1960, lofts in the Rose Building, like most lofts then, were zoned for light manufacturing or storage. Use as residences was illegal. Our top floor was two loft spaces, connected by a wasp waist section fitted as a kitchen. The back room was cool and remote from the action, a sanctuary, where the light was even most of the day. North light. Beauchamp painted there and so did Baz.

The front room was raked with sun, warm in winter and frankly hot in summer. Jackie had put up reed window shades but we usually kept them rolled all the way up even when it was hot, so as not to block the river breeze.

When we moved in, a forest of houseplants lived around the left-hand front window, including Jackie's special pet, a giant avocado. In addition to the shower arrangements, we had one other instruction: we were to try to keep Jackie's plants alive. We were generously forgiven in advance if we could not, Jackie told me, woman to woman, so of course it was a challenge I took very hard. I was desperate in February when the big avocado began to yellow and drop leaves. In fact, none of the plants looked good by then.

"My great-aunt grew the best house plants in Seattle," Dan Rice said. This was the childless great-aunt to whom he had been sent as an orphan boy of two. His father was dead and his mother hospitalized with a nervous breakdown. His four-year-old brother had been sent to live with a relative who had children, but no one in the family had much money, and two extra children on one household would have been too large a burden. Dan was exiled to a fussy elderly apartment, where a good-hearted virgin spinster did, as Dan loyally said, "her best."

I believe her best must have been terrible but I'd never heard him say much more than "She tried. She just wasn't used to children," to describe the years he lived with her. This houseplant news was a revelation.

All her friends were terribly envious, he told us that night, and nagged for her secret. Finally she confessed – water once a week with three parts water, one part urine. Then he unzipped, wavered to the plant corner, and let fly.

"This is three parts beer, one part urine, but it oughta work," he said, basting everything, as our door opened and in walked Avery, my friend from back home in Chapel Hill. Avery was already scandalized by my defiance of my parents' expectations (at least as she saw them) though she had copied me by dropping out of college too and moving to New York soon after I left Chapel Hill for San Francisco. I got a glimpse of Avery's shocked moon-white face as she closed the door and went away. I suppose she heard me yelling down the stairs to come on back, but she didn't. Everyone around the table was roaring.

The treatment worked. The plants recovered.

For years I believed what Avery did: that I was defying my parents' expectations. But obedience was my problem, not defiance. I am here on this page as I was then: smudged, out of focus, aided by thick glasses in transparent pink plastic frames; unruly hair, not red-black or blue but a mop-like shoulder-length of brown so dark it was black, with skin pale enough to burn and freckle and never tan. I was slender but believing I was fat, of medium height but believing I was oversized; clumsy, athletic, awkward, competent, asleep but sexually alert: I was twenty-three. I was an observer waiting to see the next scene unfold. I was in a species of shock, a low-keyed, long-term condition like someone who can't recover from the war but can accommodate to altering circumstances and move along as long as I could stay on the surface.

Small surprise that what I remember is so indistinguishable from what I was told. Swarms of detail easily wrap themselves in clouds of false emotion. Memoir is always, you understand, a re-vision, a form of fiction, a portion of the Rose Building.

Ferry Year

Bob Beauchamp and Jackie Ferrara were tan and full of stories. Italy was the best they said, and gabbled on about peering at great paintings in churches lit for brief interludes by metered spotlights. Perugino, Pontormo, Uccello. They had traveled in Spain and France as well, slept in youth hostels and once in a whorehouse. They had had encounters with other roaming eccentrics. Now they were back, to digest, to settle in, to change their work.

Baz and I were pale, short of money, paranoid – and we had to move quickly. It was only fair. We'd shaken hands on the sublet deal and now they were back. They were back even though I'd dreamed they would decide to stay away forever, and we'd have their place for our own.

The painter Jay Milder turned up and wanted a couple of hundred bucks for a loft he had down on Ferry Street. His wife was pregnant and they were moving to a more residential part of town, where domestic amenities, like supermarkets and laundromats, would be nearer than a long hike up to Chinatown. Ferry Street took us back into the deep downtown below the Deadline, though it was a good bit further north than Whitehall Street. Ferry Street had once led to the Manhattan-Brooklyn ferry landing, transport made obsolete when the Brooklyn Bridge was opened.

We went down to take a look.

The huge stone base of the bridge formed the uptown side of the street. But number 48, a three-story building with a steeply pitched roof, was far enough up the hill to have beautiful light and low enough for the bridge noise to float away far above. Jay explained that a long-ago resident had wired and piped around the building's main utility meters. At 48 Ferry Street, care of Overbrook Associates, gas and electricity would be forever free.

Our stupidity, on that warm September morning, we never asked Jay for a demonstration of the gas space heater, a giant blackened contraption hanging from one of the beams. On the first crisp October night we watched in awe as it roared into life and sent out two-foot-long tongues of flame through multiple rusted holes. We snapped it off fast. Free gas for a heater we were afraid to use wasn't such a bargain, but whatever else happened in that building, Con Edison never came gunning for theft of services. Not even when Jean Cartier, the artist on the second floor, flew a big blue Con Ed flag he'd stolen from a construction site out of one of his front windows. "Dig We Must, for Growing New York."

It was fire inspectors who got us. We were evicted the next spring in a citywide hunt for artists living in illegal factory spaces.

The disaster had started far away and initially involved no one we knew. There had been a bad fire in a building on lower Broadway, a dangerous multi-alarm blaze that had threatened other buildings and injured some firemen. It caused a hue and cry about fire inspections as it was soon clear the burned building had been full of violations – rubbish clogged stairwells, broken fire alarms. There were newspaper editorials and accusations of pay-offs.

Abruptly the scandal shifted. Fire inspectors discovered that artists – families! some with children! – were living not in the building that burned but in nearby lofts zoned light manufacturing. The tabloids ran shrieking headlines. No one knew that people were living there. Suddenly focus shifted from corruption in the fire department to something suspect in the department of buildings.

And a witch-hunt was on. Artists were to be hunted out from where we were hiding and saved from ourselves.

No one was being disappeared. No one was being put into boxcars. But the evictions were swift, unfightable, and terrifying. There would be pounding at the door, sometimes at night. Uniformed police accompanied the building inspectors. Seventy-two hours to clear out. Boom. No appeal. Every week we'd hear that more poor bastards got it.

Jean Cartier, downstairs, went underground. He was about the same age as Baz and had lived in Paris as a boy during the war. He wasn't Jewish but the habit of avoiding official notice was strong in him and he was excited by what he could improvise to accomplish it. He built a false wall to hide his kitchen, and another into which his bed could vanish. He packed up his books, threw out his houseplants, took down his curtains. All of us knew the hot buttons signaling residence to the inspectors: TVs and hot plates were okay, and so were couches if shabby, and sinks or refrigerators, especially if they were grubby and old. Normal manufacturing lofts might have such things. But kitchen stoves were red flags. Other tips offs were pantries, kitchenware, baby cribs, toys, bureau drawers full of socks and underwear, closets with clothes, beds with sheets.

We didn't prepare. "I can't live like Anne Frank," Baz said. So we trusted to the whatever and the whatever didn't work. Jean's preparations did. That spring, he survived the probably inevitable flash inspection of our building. He hung in. We blew it with our big brass bed and the shelves full of pots, pans and grocery stuff.

When our summons was served, the Ferry Street landlord did as all the other landlords did and saved himself a fine by giving us two days to find living quarters. Baz could keep the loft for working purposes, but only if we moved our household out. The landlord acted mad. He'd *no* idea the two of us lived there, he let us know. And, he let us know, he could have called in the lease, demanded all the rent to the end of the term, *and* thrown us out. But, hey, he was a nice guy. Baz could keep the place for his artwork if we got our domestic possessions the hell out by day after tomorrow. We were to appreciate that.

So Baz and I moved our household goods to three rooms on Avenue D between 5th and 6th Street, a cat-piss and cabbage-smelling tenement, miles from our friends in the civilized Lower East Side many blocks to the west. It was dangerous and bleak.

Angry young men roamed the streets after dark, looking for anyone they could roll or torment. It was slums unredeemed by any hint of bohemian presence. The apartment itself was the smallest, foulest place I ever lived.

To manage paying two rents, Baz sublet half of Ferry Street to Marian Zazeela, who was then a painter. But soon, too soon for us, Marian took up with the composer La Monte Young and gave up the space for painting to devote herself to creating light/color and music/sound environments with him. When that happened Baz said Ferry Street was a lost cause. The whole area was slated for demolition anyway. A painter who had occupied the front half of the fourth floor in the Rose Building was leaving town, defeated and beat. Baz and I couldn't live there, the space was smaller than the front half of Bob and Jackie's place upstairs, but the guy said oh hell and simply gave Baz the place, no key money at all. That price was right, but the space was not. It was stuffy and roared with traffic noise from the bridge just outside the windows, noise that had been only a distant hum when we lived on the top floor. The deal was done.

Not so long after our moves, we heard that artists were squatting at 48 Ferry. Using that beautiful huge space free. Why were we always so legal, so rent-paying? I wailed. Baz could have, should have, stayed on and just not paid!

He was stern: I can't handle a sudden eviction. I could get

tossed out on my ass, with no notice at all! Then what would happen to my work?

Flash to the Cohen family in England. Wartime. Sometime in the 1940s. Thrown out. Boxes and possessions piled on the curb. Esther taking young Baz to a bargain hotel to sleep for the night. Mark sitting up on a chair overnight to guard their things.

What did you do? What happened then?

Flash to the Cohens out on the street somewhere. The same street? Or a different time? In this story they are waiting for money that is on the way from an old friend of Mark's. Was this Symie the rag-picker who had made a fortune in the First World War making military buttons? Surely it wasn't sweet Symie, about whom Esther always spoke so fondly, who had a candy store and Socialist dreams, volumes of Spinoza or Proudhon always under the counter?

Here's the part Baz loved to retell: Mark shows his wife and son his hand. "This is all the money we have while we wait. It's enough to buy a box of strawberries or get us tickets to a movie." The three of them decided on the movies because that would last much longer than strawberries.

Lifeboat talk. We can handle it. If you're thirsty or tired, don't discuss it. Pass the time. Worse things could happen. Baz used to say that to me often. Just don't *say* it. Don't complain.

Tossed out on the street.

When Baz was sixteen he hitchhiked to New York from

Black Mountain College to look up his heroes. And just knocked on studio doors. It was like that then.

"I'm Basil King. I have greetings from Black Mountain," he'd say.

He found Franz Kline on the curb of 10th Street just off Third, with boxes and possessions tossed out on the street. Paintings, the black and white Kline's that Baz had come to see, were leaning against the walls. Evicted. This would have been 1952. Franz didn't bother to sit up on a chair all night to guard his work. He left the pile as it was and walked Baz over to the Cedars, where beer was still a nickel.

"Don't worry about it, kid," he'd said. He had a friend who was coming with money. He'd get everything inside before the end of next day.

Tossed out on the street isn't the worst thing that can happen.

So it gnawed on me. If getting tossed out isn't so bad why didn't *we* risk it? Why are these guys squatting on Ferry Street, having the use of that great space without paying while Baz is squeezed into the hot front loft on the fourth floor of Delancey and we're paying rent for a shithole on Avenue D? Quality squatting, they have. They're free to use the shiny new second-hand space heater we'd put in. All that winter, from October to February, we'd lived at 48 Ferry Street without any heat. No pot bellied stove. Nothing. Tenement tricks like running the oven with the door open, or keeping two or three pots of water boiling on the stove, had no effect on that great high space.

Just do the next thing. And then the next. So we did. We even threw a couple of epic parties that winter, and crowds trooped in, liquored up, smoked, danced in their coats, filled the dark ceiling with puffs of warm breath. But Basil's temper was bad: he was painting enormous abstractions, dark with fury and energy, and behaving like a flayed cat, all nerves exposed. It wasn't the cold. That is the cold didn't cool him off. Paintings filled up the studio. He worked and worked.

Despite my pledge to never work a job, I did. I worked a whole series of off-the-edge jobs, never at any one for very long. I worked at a club that sold blocks of tickets for Broadway shows, shows in trouble, of course. And Baz and I scored tickets to some epic stinkers. I worked at a knitting yarn company writing letters refusing to compensate heartbroken knitters whose yarn had "pilled" or faded or failed to match a previous batch. The boss told me these were called bed-bug letters after a U.S. senator who complained to the Pennsylvania Railroad and received his own letter back with "send this nut the bed-bug letter" scrawled on the face. I worked at a Mad Ave agency that sold ad space for out-of-town newspapers, and covered for a boss who was always ducking out. That no-heat winter I always had some sort of office job and I defrosted every weekday.

Baz stayed in the loft and painted. Night and day he fought

everything. He argued with the walls, the floor and the ceilings. He snipped the fingers off a pair of leather gloves to better hold his brushes. His fierce abstracts were envied by many, and condemned by some.

We warmed up together some evenings at the Cedars but I had come to dread being there. Money and fame were pooling into a place that had once been a kind of refuge. Almost without anyone noticing, "making it" wasn't about making one's art do something, or even about finding someone exciting to sleep with. "Making it" was money and it was stars. Movie stars came to the Cedars to be around the art stars. Tourists came to say they'd been there. Now when we went out, we often just went to the movies. We saw a new movie every time the neighborhood theatre changed its bill – and sometimes we went up to 42nd Street, which was then a solid line of movie theaters from Times Square to 8th Avenue, half of them legit and the rest porn. Some of the legit ones showed foreign movies; others relics from the thirties or forties and reams of B westerns.

Once in a long while, because our money was tight, we'd splurge on an evening at the Five Spot which was intoxicating, and made our heads ring. The Five Spot was hosting Coltrane or Coleman and we didn't come to talk.

That Christmas, I had declined my parents' invitation to Chapel Hill. What I said must have sounded an alarm because my father suddenly appeared in New York, ostensibly on a business trip. I still had a Christmas tree up. He sat at our big round table, wearing his overcoat and scarf, and promised not to tell Isabella. He was even sort of funny eating dinner on our mismatched plates and chatting on about baronial dining halls, site of elegant British life, which were not much warmer than this, he was sure.

Soon after his visit, we chopped the Christmas tree up and burned it little bit by little bit, right on the floor in the middle of the room. There was a storm the night we did it, and the wind was rattling steel shutters and howling up Pearl Street. I had hoped a fire might cut the edge off, might even somehow heat the interior air for an hour, but no. Nothing we did did. Later I was oddly proud of the dark scorched spot on the floor.

In January, in the deep chill, George Stanley came to live with us. We had met George in San Francisco, a skinny eager Irish guy, bursting with smarts and contrarian humor, in love with writing: a poet. He adored Jack Spicer and at the same time loved to brag about his policemen relatives. Worse, in San Francisco he worked as a typist for the police department and there were people on North Beach who thought he might be a spy. He even had a police department badge, which he was known to use for himself and his friends when the paddy wagons came around scouting for Beatniks to arrest. Baz, the contradictory, defended him on that. George was perverse! Yes, he was, but he was also loyal to himself in a curious and admirable way. Being public with his contradictions. He was openly homosexual which was perhaps easier in San Francisco than in New York in those times. But even so. Here in New York, he was without a place among poets he admired or trusted and in a crisis about writing and love and identity, about which he said very little. Money was a problem too, I suppose, though he had some kind of office day job. He fit well into our "slog ahead, just do the next thing" ethos. We certainly had *space* for him if he was willing to share our non-amenities. He was. He chipped in for food and drink.

We had two electric heaters. We put one heater under our big round table, to thaw feet. We gave George the other, to position right by his pallet at the far end of the painting side of the loft. After all, Baz and I slept together. And we all shared one advantage: glorious hot water, tons of it, thanks to the free gas. Steam from the hot shower would pour out of the little bathroom and into the wide loft like a San Francisco fog. Pink from hot water, we'd all sit around the table in hats and coats and drink hot tea with whiskey in it, and never feel particularly drunk.

Sometime before the end of February, though, George moved out. Someone with heat took him in; I think it might have been the poet Marilyn Hacker. Whoever, he had scored a warm place and more privacy. The cold was worse without his company but that same month we were at a big party where Allen Ginsberg told Baz he'd just received a check, a windfall from the outer blue. Came home and found this grant or gift or whatever it was, in an envelope in his mailbox. A thousand dollars. It was beginning to be clear that Allen's life would be different.

Baz promptly asked him to lend us some money for a heater. He gave Baz cash the next day. It was like that then. Baz went to LeeSam, a famous Lower East Side purveyor of second-hand everything, and shortly we could snap on the switch for a huge space heater and the shiny pipes would pulse out a strong warm breeze. It made a dull rumble, and emitted a very faint blue gas smell. It was heaven. But that was also when the search for loft-dwellers began in earnest. The witch-hunt.

Now it was summer. Goodbye to crazy space and the specialness of living on an edge. We were on foul Avenue D, watching bags of garbage, what Cubby Selby called airmail, tumble down the airshaft. That was the view from our living room window. Meanwhile sunlight was pouring through the two huge skylights for *them*, the squatters. On the stuffiest of summer nights, when our open windows admitted the reek of poverty cooking, mold and rotting trash, they would smell the salt harbor air as breeze stirred in the steep roof peaks. And when the next October came, *they* would be taking off their coats and hats and sitting around in sock feet while the new heater ripped off Con Edison.

Years later, I saw our place on Ferry Street as it was after we left. My mother gave me a book of photographs by Danny Lyon called *The Destruction of Lower Manhattan* and there it is – the photograph shows just the back part, the jerry-built chest-high partition between what had been our kitchen and where we'd had our big round table. Some dope had doodled huge heads on it. Danny Lyon must have liked that. It's the center of his photograph. I'd have turned the camera around to take in the beautiful slant-ceilinged painting space, fourteen feet high at the peak, nine at the low end, with its two great skylights and twelve little windows, six on each side. There were huge wooden crossbeams and angular rabbiting to support the roof slats. It was built like the hull of a ship. When we first moved in we'd paid a guy with a commercial paint sprayer fifty bucks to make the whole place white and even at winter's worst, it had been like living inside a giant Louise Nevelson. Baz wouldn't have a studio as luxurious as Ferry Street until the 1980s, when he took space in a factory building on 39th Street, Brooklyn. Thirty-ninth Street was 1905 reinforced concrete industrial. Ferry Street was older than Crane, older than Whitman. Everything in it had been chopped and planed and hammered by hand.

In the photograph, our stove and refrigerator are visible, although domestic living arrangements were what had gotten us evicted. Beautiful Ferry Street. I was right. The squatters had had everything. Until everything reversed again.

Moving Money

Picasso wadded up a painting and jammed it behind a sink to sop up a leak. Not in the war years, when he was thin and cold in Paris, but in the lush years post war, in the south of France, when every scribble he made could have paid three plumbers for a year.

Artists like rock stars endure reversals that bugger the middle-class imagination. Keeps the middle class safely in the middle class, doesn't it? Marsden Hartley burning paintings because he can't afford to store them? Hans Richter showing "Dreams That Money Can Buy" to an audience of eight people? Fourteen-year-old Basil King and his two best buddies from high school were one third of his audience. What was Richter paid for that appearance at the Detroit Art Institute in 1950?

Garrets are passé. Middle-class parents pay for clean art schools and MFA programs that have good cafeterias and health services. Career ladders and fellowship systems grind up the young and, every June, schools duly pump out a paste of beautifully trained 'artists' and 'poets' with high expectations.

What does an artist do?

Baz was nearly the age Hans Richter was the night Baz caught his film when Baz took a job running a freight elevator every morning.

It has always been hard to sell art.

It has always been hard to get paid.

Here is an anxious, overweight, carefully coiffed daughter and wife of Jewish millionaires. Jewels on her ears, fingers, neck. Gold dyed hair. Tits displayed like the trophy vegetables in a gourmet deli. Money gleams on her skin but it never gives her leave. Maybe anti-Semitism and class barriers in her parents' time derailed her from the start. Maybe an uncle took her cherry when she was twelve. She radiates unease. Does she know that 25-year-old me with no assets and no social support can walk into her giant Park Avenue apartment and feel a small twinge of pity for her?

Lita Hornick won a doctorate in contemporary literature. She wasn't dumb. It must have been some battle to get her dissertation accepted, to get herself all the way through the academic hurdles in those hostile days. She'd had epic family fights just to go to Columbia in the first place, she told me, before she ever faced her first caustic academic advisor. She got through. She got hooded. But then she went to her interview for a teaching assistantship in glitter-green eye shadow, wearing a cocktail dress, a full-length mink, and carrying a designer handbag. In 1954. This regalia would probably work just fine today.

By 1960 she has begun acquiring an entourage of gay men

who recognize her desperation. She has money to purchase top adult playthings, and she chooses paintings, sculptures, literary magazines. Her family believes indulgence will cheer her up. Today, a bright warm day in early fall 1961, she is going to give some money to a young artist for two of his abstract paintings. To her great surprise, her husband actually likes these pictures and has taken one of them to hang in his company's board room.

She asks the artist to meet her at a private banking firm, one of those banks with mahogany desks and leather chairs and the sanctified hush of...oh yes...and he stands alone on the wide marble floor in his corduroy jacket and khakis while she is given new one hundred dollar bills. She doesn't give them to him.

They are to eat lunch at the Carlyle, she says. After their first martini, she pulls bills out of her bag and counts them out to him, watching him turn pink over his ears and down into his shirt collar. The Carlyle's a classy place. Other diners conceal their delight. The lunch drags on until it's after three, which means, in those days before ATMs, that the money can't be banked until the next business day.

It's four when the young man reaches the Villard Houses on Madison which Random House then shared with the Archdiocese. That's where Martha has a job in the fourth floor garret, for a boss humane enough to have given her the afternoon off even though she has only been on the job a few weeks. The afternoon is almost gone by the time he gets there, filled with martinis, wine, and fancy food. Half year's worth of cash is in his inside jacket pocket beating away over his heart, with knowledge that he was exactly what the Carlyle diners saw, because his person had been purchased for performance value, and money buys it. Half a year's worth of money! A sale. A reprieve. A taste of fame.

A month or so before that day I had finally accepted an invitation from my parents to their summer place in the mountains. A sweet interlude in that seductive western North Carolina rain forest. That same Ur place, so well known to us both, on the western side of the Black Moutain range. Isabella and Lambert rented a cottage in a place called Celo, in the Toe River Valley, north of Burnsville, five miles from Micaville, behind a high hemlock hedge on the far side of Rhonda Westall's cornfield. Across the cornfield was a rise of mowed weeds and a white clapboard country church, Sandy Bottom Baptist. From the porch of the cottage at Celo, six mountains were in view: Mt. Mitchell farthest north, Mt. Craig, Balsam Cone, Potato Hill, Big Tom, Cattail Peak. Celo Knob was out of sight. We spent mornings with our coffee watching mist rising first over the corn, rolling up over Sandy Bottom's little steeple, and forming itself into clouds that moved up the mountains beyond becoming firm white puffs in the high blue to the east.

In those brief weeks there was a reasonable peace among us.

At least my mother had stopped telling me how easy it would be to divorce in North Carolina. We had eight whole days to sleep and eat, walk and swim, chunk rocks in the river, read, look for mushrooms, talk and drink at night.

We returned to New York in the midst of a vicious August heatwave – it was 80 degrees at 6 a.m. when we stepped off the Greyhound at Port Authority. Our cab driver regaled us with tales of the murders that had taken place the previous week in the projects on Avenue D just opposite our 6th Street tenement. We trudged up the tinned over stairs to find our apartment ransacked. The front door was loose on its hinges. It had been crowbarred. The floor was ankle deep in books and papers tossed in a search for money or dope. TV and typewriter departed. Even the refrigerator had been raided. And all our winter clothing gone.

I had a new job starting the first week of September. I'd bagged that job at Random House before we left for the South and now I had only a few things to wear to an uptown office as long as the weather wasn't obviously fall. Then what? Cool weather was due in twenty days. Or maybe thirty. Thirty-five?

Money! A rising tide. A hint of fame. Lita and Morty Hornick had taken two paintings "to consider" the previous spring. In early September they bought *both* of them! Not just jackets, sweaters, winter coats. The sum meant we could get the hell out of Avenue D.

This will make Baz more at ease with himself, more sure. I

was sure. Not a one-time thing, that sale. I was sure. It was shocking how quickly things could change. Jim Rosenquist and his wife were already moving to a house they'd bought in East Hampton, building a studio in the side yard, putting a nursery together. Mary Lou had quit her day job at the textile firm. Art world fame was bubbling up a list of entirely new names and Jim's was one of them.

I thought we might join the people who were organizing an end to the witch hunts and lobbying to make loft living legal. A first step had already been negotiated: it involved fire department registration. Small A.I.R. signs meaning "artist in residence" were beginning to sprout in the dark warehouse district just south of Houston Street. It would be a few years before all the codes, tax abatements, and zoning rules were in place, but groups of artists were already forming themselves up to rent collectively or even to buy loft buildings. Could we join something like that?

Some people said the A.I.R. system would simply get your name on the master hit list. You'll be that much easier to find when they decide to clear everyone out. My mother was more astute about the forces that might eventually get us all out. In 1960, she had visited us when we lived in Bob and Jackie's place in the Rose Building. She had sat in our orange butterfly chair with a drink in her hand, and looked around approvingly.

"When rich people find out how much space you can have living in a loft, they'll all want one," she said.

Baz wasn't influenced by paranoia or real estate opportunism. He said he didn't want to live in a loft again. He wanted to live away from his workplace. To leave it and come home at the end of a day. "Domesticity is the wildest," he repeated. He had a fit of fury one night that our arrangements were all impromptu. It was my fault: I relished improvisation, a milk crate coffee table, lamps held together with electrical tape, book shelves of planks and bricks I'd scavenged in empty lots. He wanted a home, he said. He'd been bounced around since he was four. When would he have a real god damn *home?*

It was true. The London Blitz had forced his parents out of the Basil House apartments, beginning forty years of dissolution for his father, a collapse composed of many streams, often somehow blamed on Baz. Baz said he wanted respite. No more unfinished paintings just a few feet from where he was supposed eat or sleep. He would keep his studio on in the fourth floor of Rose and we would use the Hornick money to move into a regular apartment.

Which is how we came to live at 57-59 Second Avenue. Two largish rooms, a small kitchen, a bath and two tiny bedrooms. No closets at all. But it was an elevator building! It turned out the elevator left a lot to be desired. The tiny self-service unit worked erratically and swayed as it moved up and down its big shaft way. I learned later that there had once been a large open iron-scrolled conveyance run by an actual elevator operator. Back when Second

Avenue was the Yiddish Broadway. No one we knew at this point had access to an elevator, no matter how unreliable. Moreover Second Avenue at 4th Street was in the heart of what had become our world. We could reach everything we used and find everyone we knew on foot. It was a wonderfully bustling world, with shops piled high with lovely foods, with restaurants, bars, coffee shops and a big movie theater. The contrast with Avenue D was stunning.

The building itself was also a contrast. It was nine stories high, towering over the six-floor tenements. The apartment we took was on the eighth floor, in the back. Never mind that the bathroom tiles were terminally stained, the toilet was not in the hall and the bathtub was not in the kitchen. Never mind the once fancy plaster picture moldings were clumsily repaired, that generations of substandard paint had made permanent alligator skin on all the walls, that all the windows rattled when wind blew. Pretty French doors separated the living and dining rooms and two big back windows had a view over rooftops all the way west to Broadway. Sky. Sunshine. Cross ventilation. The two little rooms would be bedroom and study, we said. This was a real building, not a tenement. Plus no hauling groceries up endless stairs.

Baz was about to return the keys to Max the landlord, who was in his restaurant on the building's ground floor, when he saw Gil Sorrentino passing. Baz was so excited he ran after him and dragged him up to show off our new place. Later he told me several times: Gil had looked at the second little room and said "bambino."

Boxed

We had domestic space in Max Thau's building while Baz worked in the cramped studio on the 4th floor of Rose. His compositions grew tighter, more linear, more minimal. The new works were small, brighter colored, hard-edged. Other painters went this way too, out from expressionist urgency into a reconsideration of Supremacist control and the Theosophists' belief in ideal shape. They used pure industrial color straight from the tube and the thin line that declares a definite division exists between A and B. What happened optically and emotionally when strong color blocks were laid next to each other was apparently quite new to younger painters just moving to the city, but Baz had been raised on Josef Albers' color theories. He got them even before he was sixteen – at Cass Technical High School in Detroit where a 10th grade art class was taught by a former Black Mountain student.

We heard about a young painter just graduating from Princeton who used the motifs from the *Book of Kells* – not the fantastic animals or the tumbling animated Celts, but the banners and pencil-thin column edges. He imported these devices to solve the 'problem' of the picture edge. He brought edge all the way to the middle, obliterating its meaning.

"What a bookkeeper this guy Frank Stella is," said Baz.

In Basil's hands the positive is never all positive and divides from the negative to confound and alter itself. Often his straight lines trembled, his almost geometrical shapes flirted with awkwardness. He divided his canvas and the picture plane cascaded into boxes within boxes within boxes, doors opening into giddying deep space, box tops that jutted aggressively forward. Nothing was ever tranquil. Problems were not solved! Color straight from the tube bent too — his pinks acquired browns, oranges got green, greens turned gray. He tightened down and worked on a still smaller scale and called the new pictures he was making "School Figures." He was trying to teach himself. Subtraction isn't division. What is "minimal" art? And where can this go?

Into a flat box on canvas titled:

Black Maria

Black Box

Brown Boxes

Sisyphus

School Figures

School Figures

School Figures

Thinner. Smaller. Pull down the lid.

But Baz loved minimalist art. Then and now. The true conservators, he calls them, seeing not theoretical arguments but the flat farmland of Michigan or Iowa, the clarity of Shaker furniture, the ideals of American Puritanism. Baz loves Dan

Flavin's altruistic fluorescent light. Loves it now, loved it then, but he could not live there and thrive.

At a noisy loft party on Canal Street, someone Baz knew from high school in Detroit had introduced us to Jim Rosenquist who was working in a loft on Coenties Slip, around the corner from where we had lived on Whitehall. Jim and his wife Mary Lou had a tiny apartment way uptown on East 96th Street, so far east it was almost on FDR Drive. With split living/working spaces they had never faced the building inspectors' witch-hunt that cost us our Ferry Street loft.

Jim was painting in a third way; this was exciting. Not expressionist, not minimal, and not theoretical. True his paintings were flat and thin and hard-edged, but they faithfully reproduced kitsch advertising images from the 1930s and 40s. What made them remarkable was their absurdly exaggerated scale. As collages they were as unsubtle as those Rebus puzzles where the picture of an eye represents "I" and a heart shape means "love." Jim was unsubtle too. He loved the crazy scale of billboards. He loved the Sunbeam girl and Chef Boyardee of his childhood. He was exactly, authentically, what he showed in his work back then: a mid-western American, proud of his family, of having a Jewish grandmother, of his father's success in business, of his own practical approach to the business of being an artist. His was not the America of Charles Olson or Paul Metcalf, that wild amalgam of clan pride, agrarian ethics, and millennial vision. Not Cotton Mather. Not Doc Holliday either. Jim was the American mercantile middle. He was a modern man. And if the energy in American art uncorked in mid-century by the Allied victory had begun to peter out, if the expectations engendered by that victory which so stirred black people, Jews, the nonwhite world, were beginning to crash against a rock-hard mainstream, well, Jim's work offered everyone optimism again. A beautiful good time could be had in our rich, rich country. And a life in art could be had by clean-cut normal Americans, if they were willing to work hard.

Jim and Mary Lou worked hard; they had a budget, and savings. They kept a little Volkswagen on the strict condition that they use it for absolutely every trip they took unless they walked. Only if no money at all went for subway tokens or taxicabs could the cost of the car justify itself and their delicate budget balance out. Thus Jim drove Mary Lou every morning to her job as a textile designer somewhere in Queens and left his studio promptly every afternoon in time to pick her up again.

Her job required her to turn out designs to be used for children's nightclothes. Specialized, trite, repetitive. She was completely untroubled at spending her day painting yellow school buses with smiling faces or lavender rabbits holding roses. I think she had fun with it. Anyway she was gently tolerant. It was a good job, and she told me she planned to hang onto it until Jim was established. Then they would start a family. For now, with her salary, which was far better than what I earned in offices, and their prudent management, Jim didn't have to work at anything but his art.

They did supplement themselves with an odd enterprise. They were scavengers. They invited us to come along. The old Lower Manhattan was indeed being dismantled, as Danny Lyon's photographs documented, and the Rosenquists told us they combed the rubble for junked cornices and figureheads and decorative moldings – all of which could be sold to decorators, garden designers, and, for really choice pieces, to specialized collectors. They said they combed the rubble. But a bit later, Jim told Baz that he and his friends scoped out buildings marked for demo and did preemptive retrievals. It was exciting work.

Henry Geldzahler, already a junior curator at the Met, was one of the partners. Another principal was Ivan Karp, who worked for Leo Castelli but later had his own gallery, OK Harris. They were the connection to the connoisseur buyers. Jim, athletic and fearless of heights, was chief conveyor. Drawing on his scaffold experience (he'd painted billboards for two or three years) he'd rig and rope himself to get at tempting prizes. They were raiders in the night, with gunnysacks heavy with loot. Plump Henry played lookout. Mary Lou was sometimes Jim and Ivan's assistant up on the scaffold. They were also forging alliances. Baz didn't join in.

Geldzahler and Karp, along with Dick Bellamy, were working together by day as well. Ivan and Henry were putting the backers together who would soon underwrite the Green, Dick Bellamy's 57th Street gallery. They were making some space for themselves, their friends, their ideas.

Jim thought Baz declined to scavenge because of moral rectitude.

I thought Baz was afraid. His unreliable body can do everything and nothing. Just a few years after this, he worked on scaffolds, painting building exteriors for a Mafia-connected contractor in the November wind, but I was already used to him suddenly going white and refusing to do something as unchallenging as leaning out of a window to fix a screen. It seemed to depend on his kinesthetic sensation of the moment. Or he simply had to be in the mood? Baz never explained, even in private. He just said no.

If he'd wanted to do it, *I'd* have been afraid. This was hairy stuff, climbing through abandoned buildings at night, inching out onto ledges with chisels and flashlights, while minding the threat of cops or security men. Mary Lou was not worried. Nothing fazed her, really nothing. Baz joked to me that he'd want to rent her as his wife if he were to have a big opening in a 57th Street gallery. And when Jim did open at Dick Bellamy's Green Gallery and people surged in to see the ten-foot-long red lips and huge Wheaties boxes, there she was, calm and cheerfully social. She greeted people and accepted introductions as if she were at a country-club dance in her own hometown. Baz and I got drunk. Mary Lou seemed quite like the pictures Jim painted. The metaphor was as flat as it looked, although soon critics were writing reams describing Rosenquist's art as loaded with social and aesthetic meaning.

Baz declined to join the pirates, but we had fun with the Rosenquists. If more complicated people were wondering what Baz could be used for, and if Jim was mined for information, nothing Jim said to anyone at that time answered the questions.

"What do you want?" John Chamberlain demanded, perhaps on behest of the Karp-Geldzahler-Bellamy triumvirate or maybe because the question was in the air. "What do you *want*, Baz?"

We were spending the weekend at John's house in the country, a house that gallery dealer Martha Jackson had helped him buy. John was probably seeking allies. The hardline Black Mountaineers were shunning him as he moved purposefully into the uptown art world. There was a kind of sniff campaign: "lax," "hasty," "pandering to fashion" was the orthodox BMC view of his sculpture back then.

Chamberlain turned crushed automobile parts into pure de Koonings, big, jubilantly three dimensional, with just a hint of dada clinging to them, mostly because of the source of the color. Taxicab-yellow came from junked taxicabs. Streaks of silver were recognizable as bumpers or door strips. On an oblong of bright white, one could see, upside down, a chrome Kelvinator logo. The brilliance was in the execution, not the innovation. Abstract

Expressionism was the true faith, per Black Mountain College, and Chamberlain was a sure practitioner. So what did his breach really consist of? Was he disrupting a preordained BMC hierarchy by gaining prominence when other artists with more Black Mountain virtu were unshown or unheralded? Or were the nasty sniffs just an obvious outwash of a triangle involving John's wife Elaine and another BMC artist? The rift might even have been helpful to John in a city that at that time had no intention of making room for Black Mountain's assertions.

BMC connections or not, John offered Baz a generous hand. He counseled him. Getting into the gallery dealers' debt, as he was doing, was a smart move, he told us both, not just because we all need money but because once in debt, the dealers will need to protect their assets. They'll have a stake in getting work shown and sold. When I wasn't present, he advised Baz to tom-cat around, the traditional courtiers' route to position. This too was a smart move, he said, and fun too. Baz shrugged him off on both counts. More to the point, out in the country that Saturday afternoon, Baz couldn't answer when John pressed: "Is it Fame? Money? Influence? What do you want?" I burst into tears because I thought Baz was being picked on and John's wife Elaine dragged me into the kitchen.

But it was a fair question. What did he want?

For years he and I talked around these questions or left them unsaid, gathering dust. You could say we both shrugged. I wasn't sure enough of myself to go public with my ideas about him

– or to say anything much. The notion of talking about Baz's work the way Elaine talked about John's – which she advised me to do – made my mouth dry and my throat close up. Baz wasn't able to say to me what he knew. Life in public as an artist is a rickety proposition. He wasn't ready. His boxes were closing in on him. Where would this minimal work lead him? He knew that his art could die if he were hurt or pressured into moves that could short-circuit his development. He wanted protection from that risk. But he also wanted reassurance from me and from others that his work was worthy. In hindsight, it's obvious an aesthetic crisis was coming. Just when he needed more from me, the public/private pressure pushed me deeper into silence.

Though it clearly wasn't going to do Baz any career good, we met Leo Castelli that same weekend. He arrived late on Sunday afternoon. We were all hung-over and looked it. While Elaine had taken good care of the Chamberlains' two small boys in the midst of all the adult shenanigans, they were grubby and over stimulated. We tried to control our headaches and behave. In the living room dust mites danced in the afternoon sunrays. The men exchanged small talk. I could hear the kids babbling and Elaine rattling things as she fed them in the kitchen. Leo perched on a beaten-down upholstered chair, a truly nervous perch, to protect an impeccable suit that was worth more money than all the furniture in that living room. Then Angus, age three, ploughed in, carrying a banana. He was a sturdy kid with a big head and a mop of black hair just like his dad's. He peeled his banana beautifully, with great concentration. Did we all stop talking and just watch? Were we stoned? With the bare banana held in his mouth, Angus dangled the skin by its stem, crossed the room through the slanting sunlight, and placed it carefully, gummy side down, on Leo's knee.

The Last of the Cedar Bar

John, the bartender, was one of the two owners of the Cedars. John was the city's World War II generation looking out with threatened eyes at who was coming next. The "kids," young men with hair just long enough to curl over shirt collars wearing engineer boots and tight Levis. Their duds didn't just spell sexual prowess to the guys with paunches and drooping hopes. They broadcast attitude. These kids didn't give a shit about the self-sacrifices of Depression families, the achievements of a newly respectable middle class, the rules of church and neighborhood. Their very bodies bragged that blind patriotism was a tainted faith, foisted on the obedient by the powers that stood to benefit.

"You punk! Take a haircut," the forty-year-olds brayed. They leaned out of their truck cabs to shout and gesture. They staffed police stations, night courts, employment offices. *They* had had to obey. *They* had had to pay – and the next generation would damn well do the same.

The Cedars both was and was not an ordinary neighborhood bar. It had a different life, and demanded more. Everyone knew John was never quite able to keep up with the city-sophisticate working-class pizzazz of his partner, Sam, but it was the style of the place to put up with him. John worked the bar most weekend evenings. His dour humor and hangdog resentment was expected by the evening regulars.

John and Sam probably pulled a fortune out of that bar, but not nearly as large as what they would have had they traded bar bills for certain paintings. At the time when that would have been possible, the paintings didn't look like much of a bet to either of them, regardless of the rapport they cultivated with the rough men and women who painted them. Even if they had known more, bartering paintings just wouldn't have been their style. The ponies were Sam and John's bet of choice, and the numbers.

Baz aroused John's latent tension, he was almost a lightning rod for it. Rather than protect himself by taking a few steps back, offering a change of subject or a brief retreat when John's authoritarian anger threatened to break through, Baz couldn't stop himself from taking the bait. "Fuck you," said his body and his eyes, even when his mouth did not.

A threat of being stopped, of being bombed by Nazis, thrown into a horse trough by school bullies, taunted by Jew-baiters, or balked in his then inchoate ambition to make challenging art warranted push-back big time. 'Don't stop me' was a deep interior mantra which had saved him as often as it had put him in harm's way. Whatever the cause, an explosion with John was almost inevitable, and one night it occurred. I saw John suddenly grabbing Baz and pulling him through the crowd toward the street door. Bad boys need to be beaten, and John's pecker was up with the thrill of it. He was undoubtedly drunk although most evenings John's drunkenness simply made him sullen.

John had a helper, or maybe two, because when I reached the sidewalk, someone had Baz's arms pinned and John standing in front was throwing punches at him. Baz had both feet off the ground to kick off the haymakers and his twisting body was all but impossible for the other man to hold. The ruckus was noticed immediately. I was probably yelling. I know I was knocked to the side, my glasses flew off, and then I was on all fours patting the sidewalk to find them. Other people in the bar streamed out onto the sidewalk and stopped John and his ally.

It was over. My eyeglasses were miraculously unbroken. Baz's shirt was not ripped. In fact not a punch had landed. But he and I were humiliated beyond comfort. We refused several suggestions that we come back in for a drink and a cool off. We couldn't. It seemed to us both that no one was sufficiently outraged on our behalf. Did we want John denounced? Did we want people to leave the Cedars en masse and patronize another bar? I'm not sure, but we both understood that the Cedar regulars were not really outraged at all: The conflict was not unexpected. Baz should have known how to control John. And himself.

And yes he should have. That made our feelings all the more raw. We walked away down University Place, and made our way across Cooper Square to Second Avenue. We needed some way to recuperate in our own eyes. The Cedars was still the hub of the art world's social network until the scene morphed and splintered, spinning off to centers from Slugs on Avenue C to Max's Kansas City on Park Avenue South.

But after that night in 1962, neither Baz nor I stepped into the Cedar Bar again. We chose exile. Self-imposed. Baz did continue as a regular in the then men-only McSorley's during our years on Second Avenue, but a bar scene with a social art-world function was over for us.

At Random

Remember me? I was once accepted to serve on a jury because the defense lawyer asked if I could distinguish fact from fiction and I snapped that I wouldn't be much of a poet if I couldn't.

Remember 1961? Baz and I moved into our domestic apartment on Second Avenue, between 3rd and 4th Streets. Remember me? I didn't remember myself back then. I remained detached even while I was working at Random House, where aspirants for mainstream cultural power jockeyed. Like my other job changes, this one was an accident too. I'd had a fight with the office manager at the ad agency – who wanted me to get a better haircut and wear a girdle! I grabbed at the first likely want ad, did some mild lying, and there I was.

Remember Paul Blackburn? Paul should be remembered. He was always on the telephone playing tapes of poetry readings for Baz. Beautiful bandy-legged Paul, with his dark hair and his white skin: his Celtic 'battle-eyes' were so long he looked almost Asian. Were his legs bowed from rickets? Wouldn't surprise me. He had survived a nightmare childhood, half as a hip Village kid, son of a free-spirit poet, and half as a farm-boy waif, an indentured slave to his rural grandmother who systematically abused his body and soul.

Paul was no flaneur, despite his city ease: he was vying for the Socialist dream, trying to invent a public culture – oral, aural, for everybody. A cafe culture where high poetry would make a direct appeal to open ears, barriers removed. He imagined poetry flying free of class or cultural constraints. A poetry as direct as song. He would ride the subway and read aloud to his car's occupants. Sometimes people clapped.

Baz would meet Paul on the street, cowboy hat, squinty eyes, maybe half-toked, almost always brandy-breathed, and sometimes they would talk, and sometimes they would walk. They would do the city talking, the day open before them – a city of bars, bookstores, lunch counters, park benches, chance encounters. Manhattan. Endless home. I would hear the epics later.

A walk with Paul Blackburn in New York City was like a walk in a North Florida palmetto swamp with John James Audubon or a day-trip up Mt. Katahdin with Winslow Homer. There's a pace to this kind of hanging out that I so admire. It rings in my imagination but in practice it eludes me – maybe most women? I can read about it and get lost in the language. I can write it out, word by invented word. But an actual day with time dripped out this way makes me deeply nervous. I keep needing the next thing. Come-on-let's-go, I'm always thinking about "next" not just being. Perhaps I need to be picking at something to enter that flow state. A cultural anthropologist might posit something about women's work – doing hair or nails, picking seeds, peeling food. Or shopping. I don't know. I do none of those things as a source of pleasure with women or with men. Except that now I write, picking and rearranging. And I garden. But then I did not.

Then I lived a life not unlike that of women who have domestic abuse at home. When they show up at work their makeup is perfect, their clothing is cared for. They leave unspeakable chaos at home and go to jobs where no one knows about their other life. I left Second Avenue every weekday with my lunch in a paper bag, and went to work uptown. Fancy land. Random House. I wore no makeup and my clothes were passable, barely. My husband never hit me. *He* had the bruises. He had the fights with other men, shouting or shoving matches mostly, but sometimes punches were thrown. He was an artist with no art he wanted to show; he was systematically tearing away the labels of promise and expectation that had been given him. And what replaced those labels? Now he was a target for all the people he had eclipsed during his reign as the Cedar Bar's very own rebel teenager. He had less and less to say and he wanted it that way. He believed work within would lead to his own self and to his own work, which after a great many years has turned out to be true.

I, on the other hand, had fallen accidentally into socially approved employment, if not by downtown's standards. I had left marginal jobs behind and was now an assistant in the publicity department at Random House – among beautifully groomed A-list darlings with names like Robin and Brooke and Kimberly. Plus the wonderful Sophia Duckworth who was not like the rest. A brilliant misplaced ugly duckling. Nearly six feet tall, contralto voice, floundering for room, for a way to move, she was Sophia Duckworth of, she told me, bass notes booming, the Duckworth Duckworths. The Duck in *Alice in Wonderland* was a Duckworth, the original being a friend of the Reverend Dodgson, and a Duckworth, she said, had fucked up in every notable naval battle in British history, both the victories and the defeats.

Her mother had tired of Duckworthania, his dank British castle, the requirements of Duckworth history, and the gloom of its owner. After a divorce, she had married Benny Goodman.

"A strict dad," Sophia said. She admired Goodman, but she was mostly grown by the time of the marriage and he was her mother's business.

Random House had the uptown half of the twinned Vuillard Houses on Madison Avenue just behind St. Patrick's. The Archdiocese was housed in the downtown half where today the Municipal Art Society shares space with a glitzy hotel. On the Random House side, in what had once been main floor parlors and reception rooms were the offices of the star editors. Albert Erskine, for example, who had been one of Lambert's colleagues. But Lambert never told Albert that his daughter labored in the tiny fourth floor suite of maids' rooms, where the publicity department was. Lambert never gave me leave to introduce myself either. I actually didn't know how close he'd been to Erskine until much later. Lambert never asked me if I wanted anything from that job.

Still I wonder if he told people in Chapel Hill, "Oh yes, she works at Random House." Did he bask a moment in their interest and then change the subject? Was he really so ashamed that I'd dropped out of college? Or was he silent because I worked in publicity, the prostitutes' part of publishing? My mother would easily stumble on such obstacles. She always needed a powerful outside authority to vet any claim of importance for herself or her daughters that went beyond our family history. But my father, I suspect, simply feared he'd be exposed. He was afraid of all his children. His son frightened him as much as his two daughters. Would we become more successful or more well-known than he? He even dreaded the fact that we would in the course of things live longer than he and know another world. He feared his death, he feared the future, he feared discovery. He kept silent. Small wonder I did too, imitating the very fault that bound me.

Silent I was. In smaller rooms on the second or third floors of the mansion, Random House's young Turks had space. This was the epicenter of the uptown New York literary mafia: Jason Epstein who'd been pivotal in the "quality paperback" revolution was there. And some women. And some men.

I passed their offices where telephones were always ringing and sometimes laughter was loud, but I never met any of them. Their books didn't require publicity parties. Their publication press releases were written by the editors themselves and aimed at the authors' literary peers. These books would be discussed in highbrow magazines; their authors wouldn't have to submit to publicity tours in the provinces.

In a tiny cubby under the main staircase was a woman who later became a well-known literary agent; she flashed her red hair and bragged that she'd been the girl in Philip Roth's first novel, *Goodbye, Columbus.*

I didn't think of any these people as stars. I thought of them as hacks. Their skill lay in extracting the easy stuff, in knowing what to take, and how to make it palatable so it could be furnished as embellishment for the comfort of the educated. Perhaps my father was right not to pave a way for me (although he was very wrong). I didn't want these people. Not even if I had been able to compete in their "do you know this person, do you know that person" world. After all if I had wanted to be part of it, I would have worked full tilt to compensate for my lack of social connections, money, and Seven Sisters education. I would have mined my father ruthlessly and probably gotten out of him what little he had to give. Women with far fewer advantages than mine have done this ever, especially in New York City.

Instead, I worked at Random House as an alien. My job *was* silly, it gave me a paycheck every month, and beyond that I didn't really care.

What I did all day was write letters. Not that different from the bedbug letter days. Star authors might not have been required to battle for a place in the mass market, but Bennett Cerf, head of Random House at the time, was a canny marketer who had no qualms about milking popular tastes. He appeared weekly on a national TV game show, and I answered his many fan letters. The author Ayn Rand was a house perennial – it was shocking to me how popular she was with her cultish clumsy right-wing ideology. *The Fountainhead* and *Atlas Shrugged* sold and sold and so did big books of her ridiculous essays solemnly labeled "philosophy." The intellectual elite who dismissed her hysterical "market is all" theories were just as shortsighted as I was. These ideas have come to run the country, cosset the oligarchy, win acclaim, fuel media empires.

I handled all the letters sent to Rand and there were piles of them. For Random House, publicity meant providing troubled star-struck letter-writers, no matter if psychotic or incoherent, with prompt, polite replies. I always started by thanking them for taking the time to let us hear their opinions. I didn't get to answer fan mail for Jane Jacobs, whose *The Death and Life of Great American Cities* came out that year. I think her editor handled them and I would have liked to read and answer them.

I also attended the stunt parties, developed to get press attention for the celebrity books. Geisha work, I called it. Sophia wrote these press releases. Robin, Brooke, and the others cut their society teeth by doing the party arrangements, work that was very like what their duties would be once they made their expected society marriages.

Baz always wanted to come with me to these parties because Random House was having a run of as-told-to life stories by elderly boxers. Baz would tell me who they were. He got a huge kick out of meeting Jake LaMotta, Mickey Walker, and Rocky Graziano. Jean, the head of the department, liked Baz and flirted with him when he showed up.

This was a bad time for Paul Blackburn. He was drinking heavily, philandering everywhere, and his marriage to Sara, a junior editor at Knopf, was going, going, gone. Like me, Sara left a bohemian apartment every weekday to work among the people who steered New York's public literary life. She was not anonymous and aloof as I was. Her editorial acumen was respected and her colleagues knew of Paul Blackburn: they knew of him as 'promising poet'; 'brilliant translator'; 'isn't he one of M. L. Rosenthal's protégés?' There are many knobs and niches to contain or explain 'alcoholic intellectual' – and to contain or explain Sara's pain.

Sara's suffering seemed endless. Then she and Paul ended it. I remember feeling relieved. I suspected then that she felt the same pressure about me, that my situation, married to 'dead beat' 'self-destructive' Basil seemed just as endless to her. I felt she would have been relieved if she had heard that Baz and I had split, and I didn't want to talk to her. She didn't feel like a peer or a friend. She felt like an older, superior, judgmental force who would treat me as my mother would had I given her any room.

Remember me? People who met me and Baz in those years actually don't. I must have been faceless, totally withdrawn. What story can I remember from that time that shows how badly I misread things? Well, in 1962 I was fired from Random House and I hadn't seen it coming. Knopf and Random House merged and the two publicity departments were being consolidated.

"And you see," said the head of PR for Knopf, "we think you really belong in editorial." But he didn't offer to move me there. I didn't ask either. It was all the same to me. Or it was better – because I was being *legally laid off* and thus eligible for unemployment. Unemployment was the holy grail to us downtown folks. With a bit of part-time work for unreported cash I could just about match the money I'd been earning for working all week. And I'd be free of the stockings, office shoes, subway rides; the insufferable dailyness of office work, of living on their time, under their rules, with their niggardly vacations, their airless rewards. Unemployment was better than recess. I was happy to jump off.

One can't say I was having a breakdown. I had broken down as a girl when I was tutored in my parents' belief that a talented woman's ambition should be to marry a superior man. To be a superior kind of pet had been my maternal grandparents' dream for my mother, and it was my mother's for me. She described it to me explicitly: I shouldn't have to drive or shop or do housework. Because I was artistic, I should have a studio in a spacious suburban backyard – a superior kind of dog run, I shouted at her once – and be allowed to paint and write my poetry, she continued, undeterred, and I would be the finest kind of ornament for him.

I didn't believe I had swallowed her instruction as I ran like hell. By the time I was 19, in San Francisco, I was thinking I'd gotten well away, but the prescriptions trailed across the country after me. In fact, out on North Beach, there was nothing seriously on my mind about me. And now, with Random's gift of unemployment money, I wasn't having serious thoughts about myself either, let alone a breakdown. Like many other young women in such a limbo, I was about to become pregnant.

Births and Breakdowns

Mallory weighed in at just two ounces over five pounds but she was pronounced physically mature. She had exquisite blonde eyelashes and binocular coordination both of which normally occur three or four weeks after birth.

"She was probably carried too long," a young resident said, wowed by her ability to follow his finger with both eyes. He also assured me her small size hadn't anything to do with her tumor, the round aberration, poking out of her mouth. It was attached by a thick stem coming out of the ridge in her mouth where her bottom teeth would be.

They'd been very clever in the delivery room; I realized only later that I had heard the OB kick aside the standing mirror positioned so a laboring mom could see her vagina. It hadn't mattered to me: New York Hospital insisted I couldn't have my eyeglasses in the delivery room. Without them I could barely see to the end of my arm, let alone anything in a standing mirror three feet from the end of the table. Basil wasn't there either. A partner in the delivery room was something only private patients could have negotiated back in 1963.

I heard a thunderous crash of water on the delivery room tiles, "It's a girl," and a round of applause. But immediately the nurses had me concentrate on expelling the placenta, which I took to be standard procedure. The OB had Mallory on a side table, his back between us and I didn't twig to anything. Consultants had been surreptitiously summoned and by the time a nurse handed Mallory over to me, the delivery room had many people in it.

She was obviously breathing. In fact she was howling and kicking, very definitely awake, and highly annoyed. The little tumor was so alien I couldn't take it in. She looked as if she had tried to eat a flesh-colored walnut that had become wedged in her open mouth. Her lips were stretched thin around it. In a few minutes she was pronounced hale and vigorous by New York Hospital's head pediatrician. He introduced himself to me. I was lying flat, but he was very courtly and shook my hand. I could almost see him.

An anomaly, he said.

Later, when Baz phoned my parents, my mother gasped, "I've never heard of a baby born with cancer!"

My parents offered to help if we needed it. They'd get a loan they said. But I was a clinic patient, rated for maximum assistance. I had paid $5 at every prenatal visit and I think a final $50 was all we owed. Mallory's extra care would cost a great deal more, but the United States was generous about health care back then. Or New York Hospital was. It cheerfully shifted costs from low-income folks into the accounts that could afford to absorb them.

A team of the hospital's top pediatric docs agreed: Remove

it now before feeding difficulties damage her good health. Fine by me, I thought, holding her. I didn't need to talk this one over with Baz. Snip it off! Toss it in the trash! She's beautiful. She's perfect. She's mine. I could not entertain the idea, very gently offered to me by one of the specialists, that there might be more to this alien thing than what we could see.

Out in the hallway, Baz was trapped by a different expert who detailed to him the large number of other things that might be involved. He was one of those doctors-in-training who is totally oblivious to anything but the medical puzzle a patient presents, plus his own marvelous knowledge of the problems, and his exciting opportunity to be in on it.

Why Baz didn't hit him I don't know. He was probably too stressed and too hurt. It was two o'clock on Saturday afternoon.

The ice storm that had started Friday afternoon was finally over – the sun was out and the glaze on streets and sidewalks was beginning to disappear. Although my actual labor had lasted less than four hours, I'd been at this since Friday morning when I'd had a gush of blood. I was told to come up to the hospital for a checkup. I'd phoned Baz at work, told him not to worry, but to meet me up at the New York Hospital clinic just in case. I got my little bag and took the First Avenue bus.

We'd been held hostage ever since. The clinic had pronounced my gush unimpressive and I clearly wasn't in labor yet, but by the time Baz arrived the weather was rapidly worsening. I was certain to be in labor sometime in the next twelve hours they said. By Friday evening, the city, hammered by sleet, high winds, and snow, had come to a near standstill. At midnight bus service was cut to a minimum; sidewalks were skating rinks. The hospital was far too humane to think of sending me home.

"Walk!" said the clinic resident. "It'll get you started."

Baz and I walked. For hours. Through the network of underground tunnels that connect New York Hospital to Payne Whitney Psychiatric to Memorial Sloan-Kettering to Cornell Medical School. I came to know those halls by heart eighteen years later, when I worked at Sloan-Kettering. We went through the passageways that ensured privacy for high-profile patients, like Hubert Humphrey or the Shah of Iran. We trotted through the short cuts to emergency evacuation routes, and the back alley delivery routes to three institutional cafeterias. Nothing happened. The best cafeteria was Payne Whitney's. The scent of their lasagna and spiced meatballs made me nuts. I'd been forbidden to eat anything. Baz, who was just as starved, didn't want to leave me.

"Walk some more," another resident insisted when we turned up at the clinic a third time. But finally, they gave in. I was admitted, given a bed on a Gyn floor below Maternity. I slept then but Baz slipped and slid through the storm to our old friend Lynn. He was living with his wife Irmgard in a flossy 72nd Street apartment just a few blocks away. They talked and ate and drank through most of what was left of the night.

Mallory's growth was excised early Sunday morning. It was a wad of squamous cells run amok, the pathologist said. Just anarchic skin cells, nothing worse. To this day I don't like to think too much about how it was removed as anesthesia for newborns was medically dicey in those days. I do know it was done with miniaturized surgical instruments, under a large magnifying glass – and much later I learned that the father of poet Paul Pines, who lived in our building on Second Avenue, had pioneered some of the miniaturized instruments and techniques for successful neonatal surgeries.

Well, it was over and there was Mallory. Her shirtsleeves were fastened to the side of her shirt with two large safety pins to keep her from touching her mouth. Just for a day or two, I was assured. The mouth heals amazingly fast. They were giving her glucose by mouth with a dropper. She didn't even have an IV line.

Even so I didn't want Baz to see her that way. I didn't want Baz to visit the neonatal ICU at all. It was a small ward at the back of the maternity floor, where white cribs sheltered ghastly infants. There were some with huge heads or mottled scarlet growths. The crib next to Mallory's held a marble-white three-month old on a respirator.

But of course Baz came, white-faced and swathed in a sterile blue gown. Mallory was newborn yellow, a rich Devonshire cream color, with a long sloping forehead from pressure in the birth canal. Only the safety pins indicated her ordeal plus a small blob of scarlet where her bottom front teeth would be. She was Northern, delicate, like something Memling would have painted. Her lower lip had been stretched by the growth and it pouched out even when her mouth was shut. It was almost cute. The hospital staff were calling her Jiggs.

After twelve months, Mallory had some perfect teeth, top and bottom, a brilliant smile, and had tripled her birth weight exactly, just as baby books said was normal. That made her at one year, a shade over fifteen pounds, smaller than most six-month-olds. There were no fat rings around her legs. There was no excess anywhere. She began standing at nine months, and by her second summer, she had muscles on her legs like a much older child.

She was mature about Hetty, too, who arrived that second summer. I offered Mallory my other tit. It seemed more than reasonable to me. Have some, I beckoned smiling. She'd been so cheated by that tumor. She had not been allowed to suck on anything for two weeks. For her first two days at home, Baz and I took turns feeding her with an eyedropper. She did more screaming than eating because the eyedropper ran out after six drops. In the time it took to refill, she'd be purple with frustration. We were all in a haze of exhaustion.

"To hell with it. Let's try the turkey baster," Baz said. "They don't know everything."

This method got formula splashed everywhere, but we managed not to drown her and to get enough milk into her stomach to calm her down. Enough for her to sleep about two hours before she was howling again. She was healthy all right. When I finally got the medical okay to give her a bottle, which had to have a large x slashed in the nipple so she wouldn't suck very hard, it was heaven.

After that, we gave her bottles all the time. In the books I was reading, "deprived of sucking" sounded like a major a crime against her psyche. With Hetty's arrival there was a magical second chance. Mallory was only seventeen months old. If she'd taken to nursing for a while, no one would call it regression. "Come on," I smiled, offering a tit.

Mallory was completely disgusted. If I'd picked my nose at my mother's dinner table I couldn't have been given a deeper look of social disapproval. Instead, she set herself to her new work – folding diapers for her dolls, and stacking clothing for them in cardboard boxes for elaborate wordless games. She took her place standing on the back axle of what had been her stroller and hanging on expertly with both hands while Hetty lay on the flattened seat.

While I was pregnant with Mallory, Baz had a regular job painting buckeyes, buckeyes, "a naively flamboyant or corny illustration." This definition is way down the dictionary paragraph from basic information about horse chestnuts. The buckeyes Baz did were for a company that supplied art to the "hospitality industry" a.k.a. hotels and motels. "Corny" was right enough, but this firm was too high-class to turn out "naively flamboyant" junk. It had several targeted product lines and upscale hotels and motels on its client list. Painting the early American primitives paid the best. The A.P. painters kept their positions for years, and they were allowed to work at a slower pace than anyone else. Their wooden panels were oven-baked to crackle and age them, and the results sold to fancy law firms as well as blue-ribbon hotels.

Baz liked the grimacing cats and the little girls with green hair ribbons and longed to do them but he was assigned to French Impressionist streetscapes for the mid-range motel trade. The color schemes and general designs were all preplanned. First he copied the sketch. Then, he daubed houses with shutters on cobbled streets usually with a small tree and some street lamps. Frenchie. If you stayed in nice motels in the 1970s, you may have seen his work. He must have done thousands. He had to turn out twelve or fifteen at a time, moving quickly around his cubicle to plop on each color in turn. Then, before the paint was dry, each one had to be artistically smeared to make it "individual" and "authentic."

I was still pregnant when the buckeye job dried up and Baz went to work at the Kulicke frame shop, another place where other artists labored. As it happened, Baz was pink-slipped at Kulicke's the morning of my warning gush. Nothing personal, just a normal downturn. The post-Christmas slump. Our friend Dominic Capobianco very sweetly begged the boss to let him go in Basil's place, he knew a baby was imminent, but the shop had a firm last-in, first-out policy. Baz didn't mention the pink slip to me for days, not until we were home and I asked why he didn't go to work. I don't remember being worried. He'd always worked at a lot of short-time jobs. I knew we could float.

Baz explained our finances to a social worker at New York Hospital, an earnest, well-educated black man. After a while, Baz told me, he was just gaping. Then he told Baz that he should be giving poor people lessons. The hospital forgave us all the extra charges for surgery and special care.

So there we were: a family. We had a baby, then babies, we had daughters, we had Mallory Lambert and quite soon Hetty Malke. Why ever did we give Mallory my father's name as her middle one? Because it rolled so mellifluously with Mallory? It would take deep shrinkage to get to the bottom of that. But joyously when Baz phoned Roi (LeRoi, later Amiri Baraka) about our new kid, Roi promptly announced he was taking a bath by way of welcome. And he did. He and Hettie came over from their place on Cooper Square with infusions of courage. And others visited, painter friends from all over with flowers, liquor, and goofy gifts. She and we were warmly welcomed.

My model for mothering was always Hettie Jones. The old Southern adage, "clean enough to be healthy, dirty enough to be fun" was Hettie's mantra and thinking back on it I suspect she learned a great deal from LeRoi's family. This was surely not wisdom from her anxious middleclass Laurelton, Long Island upbringing. But it exactly fit the dirty floors and diverse company of our Lower East Side life. When our Hetty came along and we wanted to honor her we altered the spelling – Hettie became Hetty – so as not to offend the Jewish tradition of naming children after dead relatives only. We added Malke as her middle name because we believed that was Basil's grandmother's name. Not true we learned many years later in London. Family legend via Baz's parents was often free of restraints.

I worked nights the spring Mallory was a newborn. My unemployment insurance was over and a baby was here. I worked with Paul Blackburn's friend, Bob Reardon, and his wife Eunice. The three of us typed manuscripts for a Catholic high-school textbook publisher. The texts were cobbled together during the day by a team of copywriters and editors, and because the type was to be set in Portugal by typesetters who didn't read English, the masters had to be letter perfect.

The texts were mind numbing but the race to get them down and done was wonderfully soothing. Baz would come home from his after-work visit to McSorley's in time for me to leave Mallory with him. The Reardons who lived the next block over and I walked down to 100 Sixth Avenue together. The Gray Building. Bob signed us in at 5:30 and out at 11:30 – accounting for six hours pay – but all three of us were demon typists and could churn out all the manuscript that had been copy edited during the day well before nine p.m.

Then we'd go for beer. I'd get home a little after ten because I never stayed with them for more than one or two. Bob was alcoholic, and, as it turned out, in the final year of his life. Twenty minutes in a bar would get him into maudlin stories about how he'd been squeezed out at the *Village Voice* which he claimed he'd helped to found, then how his first wife had left him because she was a worthlessly ambitious bitch, which made me squirm for Eunice, and then on and on about the five garbage cans he had at home, holding five mega-novels, unread, unbought, unpublished.

But I loved that job. All women with infants, in poverty, with troubled husbands and misty selfhoods, should have a job like it. Bob Reardon wasn't my problem. He was even funny in a mordant buckeye way before he went under the booze. Loyal, skinny drought-stricken Eunice had a wry black humor. We all got along. Plus I had a respectable reason to leave our shabby apartment, to leave anxiety, responsibility, mess, and undone chores, to change my milky-smelling shirt and baggy pants for actual clothes. To comb my hair. And to bring home actual money, payment for my guilt-free escape.

Mallory who was often screaming when I left her with Baz would be sweetly sleeping by the time I got home and when she woke up for her late night feed I really wanted to see her. I had the chance new mothers crave to actively miss their infant.

But then without telling me, Eunice convinced the textbook company that we should type the work at home. This was so much better, she said. It was an awful change for me. It was painfully difficult to concentrate on typing in the odd hours when Mallory was asleep. I'm not sure it was better for the Reardons either. Bob probably needed the regular exit from their apartment as badly as I did. But maybe he had already become so alcohol-ill that Eunice needed to hide him. The work petered out, or she was keeping all of it herself. I couldn't tell which but soon enough I got the message to stop calling her. And though they lived just one block down 2nd Avenue from our place, I almost never saw them after that. Eunice didn't even phone to tell me he had died. Months later Baz heard that when he asked about Bob Reardon in McSorley's.

Hetty's arrival day could not have been more of a contrast to Mallory's. It was mid-summer, just 17 months after Mallory's birth and Baz's parents had taken her out to Long Island where Esther and some of her relatives could dote on her while we waited to deliver her sib. We two had gone up the street for Chinese food to celebrate a child-free evening and very late that night it took me more than a few minutes on the toilet to recognize that this was a baby coming, not over-indulgence in hot Szechwan. Yikes! But Baz was a tower of calmness. He proceeded to shave, to shave! while I was barely able to pull on some clothing.

"I mean it. The baby's coming!" I gasped.

A fellow park mother and good friend who lived around the corner on Great Jones Street had an actual car and had offered me something priceless. "Call," Delores had said. "You know how taxis are."

"Not in my cab, lady" canny drivers were likely to calculate when waved at by a bulging pregnant woman accompanied by someone holding that telltale overnight bag. Baz woke Delores up. He might have been sure we had loads of time, but Delores took one look at me as we got in the car and gunned her engine. It was not quite dawn. Then Baz got it. Not one of the three of us realized we were going the wrong way on Second Avenue – uptown not downtown – until a cop car with a siren pulled us over. "There's a woman in here having a baby," Dolores managed. I'd begun to do the noisy breathing she recognized.

It was sweet. "Follow us," the lead cop said. We had a police escort all the rest of the way up to New York Hospital and no ticket, and not even a scolding. Dolores, still in her nightgown, was allowed to drive home.

A little later was sweet for Baz too. He no sooner arrived in the tension-drenched 'father's waiting room' than he was paged. He told me how the haggard dads-to-be glared at him as he rushed out. And there she was: perfect and plump, with a mop of black curls, and looking so like her father I wanted to pencil in a mustache like the one Baz wore in those days.

After seeing me settle down for sleep, he walked all the way to West 42nd Street and Grant's Cafeteria, a now long-gone landmark, where piles of the best hot dogs, a raw bar with clams and oysters, huge cold pickles, and tubs of spicy yellow mustard awaited. A camera crew was there, shooting something. B roll? A documentary? Baz happily signed a release, he told me, and the crew treated him to dogs while they filmed. Somewhere, maybe still, there's film of Basil welcoming Hetty on July 10, 1964.

At a time when Baz was throwing everything he had in the art world overboard, he wanted a domestic apartment and a wife and children in a little boat with him. Our babies, our children! Fascinating, funky, infuriating, exhausting, loving, smart, changeable. We were parents, and we were making up a new way to do it. I was waking up too. I was intent on making that new way to do it. I had all that.

Baz had all that and more. He had babies and he had a breakdown. His work was in tatters, his motivations shredded. But he stayed. He provided baby care, cooking, and housework along with the proceeds of a whole string of little jobs. Our friends, both male and female, our bohemian radical friends, were horrified at the easy way Baz took to women's work. In 1963-64, even in our circles, women carried the babies, made the soup, mopped the floor. Roi Jones and Gil Sorrentino kissed their children, but one didn't see either of them spooning in the strained plums. What Baz did was taken by some as a sign of degeneration. His image, his contacts, his place among other artists – he needed to shed them all. Abstraction had come to an end for him, and indeed publicly it was folding up after its Second Generation artists. Other movements were starting up, minimalism, pop, conceptualism. They offered nothing he could connect to personally, even if he admired some of the works. What to do?

He not only spooned the strained plums, he provided them too.

I'd heard the tales of him being the booster among boosters of Black Mountain College – how he could tuck a T-bone steak into the small of his back, how he could make off with a roast, a turkey, a lemon meringue pie. How he didn't even need a raincoat as Dan Rice always did. Baz said that was quite untrue. He *always* wore a raincoat, and he'd never came back to school with a lemon meringue pie. But shoplifting by hungry Black Mountaineers was not a legend. The Black Mountain A&P moved all the coffee to a rack behind the checkout register because students made off with so much of it. And in the 1960s, on Second Avenue, Baz was a master lifter of little jars of baby food. Especially by late 1964 when Hetty was eating three or four of them a day.

By then we were profoundly out of the scene. Baz was thought of as a brilliant has-been if he was thought of at all. The stream of people who had come to visit us when Mallory was newborn were gone. The phone hardly rang. We lived in a permanent winter. Gil Sorrentino's term was the "neverbeens." The neverbeen shown, neverbeen published, neverbeen understood.

After the collapse of the Reardon gig, I was an at-home typist, scrounging for work. In between baby chores, I typed lengthy legal descriptions of cigarette filters for a low-rent patent lawyer. I typed lengthy descriptions of Catskill real estate for a low-rent real estate agent. For Roi's friend, the poet A.B. Spellman, I typed speeches by Malcolm X, recorded by him on reel to reel tapes – riveting and the very devil to transcribe as I had to stop and start the tape by hand. For Eila Kokkenin, an art historian who was a friend of Ginsberg's and who at Allen's insistence had volunteered as Hubert Huncke's editor, I worked my way though Huncke's journal, a sprawling mass of half-typed, half hand-written pages, covered with Eila's attempted editorial corrections. That job took months. Far worse for my sense of self, I typed manuscripts for three or four downtown poets who had grants or money from home. And slowly I began to think of writing myself.

Remember me? None of the poetry people I typed for did. I had become the typist who lives around the corner. The one who'll type your poems without messing up your spacing. But I was not a person in their world. So they spoke to me, and so I answered. It was shocking. I had become completely invisible. If I ever mentioned this to Baz, I don't remember it. I probably did not.

Social workers often hear the great shame-lowering refrains of the involuntary poor: Oh, it's much worse down the street. You should see what it's like on the 10th floor. My girl friend's got a kitchen with *four* rat holes!

I hope the social workers know it's pride they're hearing.

Ours was voluntary poverty. We were not trapped by color, class, or lack of skills. We were mired just the same. A snow-colored poverty dogged us. In winter not enough. In summer not enough. The make-do. The wait. The quietly do without. The sudden unexpected surge of salty bitterness. The blank stare and the white scape. No purchase no matter how small without a pressured calculation: Can I go around? Use a substitute? Invent a dodge? Do without? Do without? Do without?

Stick feet into plastic bags before putting on leaky winter boots. Trim hairs from the shedding overcoat. Mend the buttonholes. Reverse the collars and make sleeveless shirts when the elbows go. A snowfall of unspoken never rules: Never leave the house carrying money that you haven't planned to spend. Never buy food that has been prepared or processed (your labor's free). Never buy presents; make them. Never buy snacks, candy, or coffee on the street. Never give in to impulses. Select fruit and vegetables from the on-sale bins. And keep your mouth shut.

Poverty is always a secret, even among friends. That we shared with the involuntary poor. When one is really without money one doesn't say I can't afford it, I don't have the money.

That's for the folks who do have some. One says, I'll think about it. One says, oh I've changed my mind.

We never had rats. Pride. Our diet wasn't bad. Pride. Some of our never-buy rules actually meant healthier food. Beans from scratch. Home-baked corn bread. Beef bone soup. Pride, pride. We never fed ourselves or our kids soda, chips, or snack foods. Piles of hot popovers from the government surplus food program were my specialty.

Ah, the surplus food program! It was designed to prop prices for farmers and was run by the federal agriculture department with no thought of nutrition. But it was free, unlike food stamps which had to be purchased in set amounts with cash we might not have, and then used in stores where clerks and customers were free to glare and comment contemptuously. Which they did.

Surplus food distribution took place once a month at the projects down on Avenue D. The lines were long but there was a circus-like atmosphere. Strangers and friends chatted and giggled as we heaved bags of cornmeal and flour into our bunged up shopping carts or shoved them into the strollers in and around babies. Lots of kids at the Tompkins Square playground had homemade sand buckets fashioned from the big government surplus peanut butter tubs.

To keep butter prices up we got a pound of butter, per person, per month. Infant Hetty was counted as a person as soon as she was born. Four pounds of fresh butter every month! The powdered eggs were a puzzle until I discovered the foul powdered-egg smell vanished in a hot oven. Popovers! Of course we could slaver butter on them till it ran down our chins. The powdered milk and powdered eggs together could be persuaded into huge baked custards. I even made pound cakes following the colonial Virginia recipe (take a pound of butter and two dozen eggs).

Still we were not so unlike the involuntary poor. The longer we stayed on this thin thin edge the more likely it became that we would never recover. The longer Baz hung in his painful limbo the odder our life became. He was not doing any art at all. Rent on the 4th floor of Delancey was beyond our means. Or beyond reason.

Baz had painted dozens of abstract "minimal" paintings – "School Figures" he called them – on the 4th floor, and his studio visitors had included Henry Geldzahler. Baz's minimal work was a long way from the pared down ideal of the moment, but Henry pointed to one of them and made the offer. "Paint me ten more like that one using a different color in each, and I'll get you a show."

"I can't live in a box," Baz told me.

When he visited Henry's office at the Metropolitan to decline the offer he was told, "Never say you weren't asked."

Stasis. The wall. Baz was doing more walking than odd jobs. Soon he had no studio, he had no steady job. Except for playing penny-ante poker and boosting it was all at a standstill. Except for Mallory and Hetty and me.

Springing the Trap

Baz walked down the hallway into our Second Avenue living room carrying two reams of 8 x 10 sixty-pound bond paper.

"Picked it up at the stationery store," he said. "She's having a sale. One thousand sheets for less than a buck."

He sat on the day bed and put a stack of paper on the coffee table, got out a brush, a glass of water, and a bottle of black Higgins ink.

He drew a circle. One circle a page, circle after circle. Thick black ink. A circle, a circle, a circle. Soon there were dozens of them. There were no greys, no drips, no deliberate variation. Just dense black lines. The feeling of circle. The circle-shape wavered, never perfect. No two were, could be, exactly the same. The world. The void. The Black. The White. Swing around – and close. Start another.

He did this that day. He did it the next. He did it while the kids were sleeping, and during the hours when I was out with them. He did it at night, even ignoring the barrage of TV programs we drugged ourselves with night after night.

Now he's really lost it, I thought.

He let these drawings dry and stacked them up. He spread them out over the big round table in our dining room, across the tops of the two bookshelves, over the record player. When the kids were in bed he covered the floors of the two connecting rooms that formed the heart of our apartment and looked at them. He picked the papers up and threw them all away. Then he started over.

Was I too frightened to think? I just waited. I would have been a proper creature of my time if I'd packed up the kids and split – then or during all the months earlier when he did almost nothing day after day. I didn't. I just watched, wondering what would happen next.

I remembered the story about William Carlos Williams and his father-in-law. Flossie's dad gave young Bill 5,000 sheets of 'second' paper, or was it 10,000? Second sheets were made of cheap spongy yellow stuff and were used in offices for carbon copies. The idea might have been that this ample supply would take care of young Doctor Bill's poetry writing tendencies. Indeed, I understand the supply did last him years, and the rare manuscript curators up at SUNY Buffalo have probably cursed that gift many times.

Basil's paper wasn't yellow, it was white and not spongy. The edges of his wet ink lines stayed clear. His stack of clean sheets grew shorter every day. He bought another ream. Okay.

Then one day a circle grew two small triangular wings. Wings move. Wings insist on it. It (he?) (they?) will move. Then they were birds, they were eye shapes, they were cunts, they were leaves. The circles were smaller and supported large and larger petals. They were man-flowers, black ink on white paper.

The trap Baz had been in was sprung. Why or how is the stuff of "recovery" literature, but recovery was not what I witnessed. Baz simply needed some bigger paper. And then some more. Very soon he needed to paint!

Out of the blue, and for one of the few times in my life, my father came to the rescue. I don't know what brought Lambert up to New York City in the spring of 1965, possibly University of North Carolina Press business. He came alone, and stayed in a hotel somewhere uptown. Long before he retired as director of the university press at Chapel Hill, he had come to hate visiting the city where the gap between the high dreams of his youth and his actual accomplishments was so palpable. His glory days had passed. Did he get those sidelong looks that say, "It's sad, he really wasn't what we thought he was"? Did he have to sit in a waiting room until old colleagues could "fit him in"? Whatever else went on, he said he wanted to see his granddaughters.

Our "big" five-room apartment was actually small, dirty, full of broken toys, saggy furniture. The once lovely maroon paint we had put on the floors when we moved in had chipped and bubbled. The fancy rocking chair had splintered one night into a pile of kindling. The lampshades were spotted, the ceiling had leaked, I'd taken down the water-stained curtains and not replaced them. But what worried Lambert most about our environment was Basil's lack of studio space. He'd long left the 4th floor of the Rose Building and we lacked funds for a security deposit, key money, everything.

The angel of just-enough must have been at work. Lambert's worry came just as Baz was once again able to need studio space. In fact, he was now desperately eager to paint, to take on size, to move the now vibrating black and white organic shapes out onto canvas and into color.

Using cheap construction paper, he had already made one of his flowers into a sculpture, gluing the curved forms together at our dining room table. It was secured inside a Plexiglas box. He boxed it in order to enter a juried show somewhere downtown, and it was hung, although it didn't sell or attract any comment that I ever heard. We have it still, now quite sun faded. Dust has entered the box, as you'd expect, but the bloom of the petal shapes lifting off the flat vertical of the upright page still says "spring" says "hope" says "life" to me.

When Lambert got home, he sent us a check for $500. My father, noted for his inability to spend or give money, the master of the "you don't need this" approach to funds, sent us this check unsolicited. From junior high school on, requests for financial aid, even petty ones, from any of his three children, had to be buttressed with a logical argument and precisely delineated promises regarding the repayment plan. It always was an ordeal. This check just arrived. The sum was not enough to pay for moving us into what *I* really wanted, a living/working loft, but it was quite enough for Baz to rent the large back room, second floor rear, of the empty Anderson Theater, right across Second Avenue from our building.

It was a large high-ceilinged space but it was totally dark, a cave. It had been built for storing theatrical flats. There were six or seven windows across the back, coated with seventy-five years worth of greasy New York grime. They let onto a steep airshaft about two feet wide. Even when open, the windows admitted a very dim grey light, so there was no point struggling to clean the glass. Instead, Baz contrived to light the place artificially. Our downstairs neighbor, poet Frank Lima, who was working at the time as a photographer's assistant, brought him two professional photographer's lamps. The quartz bulbs they used cost the earth and didn't last very long, but the light they gave was daylight pure.

Mother's belly with diamond lights.

Baz began to work on a large painting he called "Venus."

Another Summer of Poverty

G.R. Swenson burst into Gavin Douglas's apartment and
announced breathlessly he'd just taken his very first tab of LSD.
Gavin said, "Oh, you've been there before."

G.R. said, "You're right. I'm disappointed."

Baz and I were introduced to him.

G.R. and Gavin had met at the Yale Institute for Better
Living. (That's what they both called it.) It was the university
nuthouse. Thorazine had turned G.R.'s skin yellow and he had
added to his personal decor by dying his hair bright orange.
Naturally Gavin befriended him. G.R. was a rising art critic, a
major promoter of our old friend Jim Rosenquist.

In Gavin's apartment, G.R. glared at Baz. They were not
having a good hit. I gathered up our kids for a getaway. It was a
sunny May afternoon and Gavin's apartment was not big. Baz and I
had been taking a long walk with Mallory and Hetty packed in the
stroller. We were in the West Village when a snazzy sports car
suddenly stopped on the street beside us, and there was Gavin.

I'd heard about him. Baz had met him in a Village bar some
years before. At the bar Baz had said he was a student and Gavin
had been rude about it. "What kind of school would a guy like you
go to?" I guess Baz already liked Gavin's feel because he didn't lash

out in response. Instead he described Black Mountain. A few weeks later, Gavin appeared in the turnaround in front of the BMC Studies building asking for Baz. He was driving a fancy little Italian motor scooter and he had one leg in a cast. He stayed around for several months. Black Mountain had always been permeable like that, easy about people of uncertain status.

"I live up there," Gavin said, pointing to the fourth floor of the building we were in front of. Gavin was with a woman, a tawny blonde with a classic nose and thin ascetic lips. "We got married this spring," he said. He introduced us to Athena. Up we all went to their apartment.

Gavin should have been handsome. He should have been perfect American WASP, even-featured, brown-hair, grey-eyes handsome. A crop of odd white hair on one side of his head was an accent not a disfigurement. I soon discovered he looked different every time I saw him. His face was like water, shifting, sly, wickedly clever, bored, tired, calculating, puffy with petulance, dazzling with sudden, manic glee.

Gavin was the child of Robert Douglas and Jean Stewart, a middle-class Scot with major ambitions. She had come down to London equipped to work as a secretary, and, as Gavin told it, with heavy plans to marry up. Which she did. Gavin was born in the early 1930s when his father was almost eighty; he was never quite sure if Uncle Eddie, his father's silent partner, wasn't his actual dad. The public and unsilent partner in their enterprise had been Lord

Joe Duveen, and the business was an art gallery, the one that made a small fortune selling Quattrocento paintings to American millionaires in the twenties.

Father Douglas was an art historian, and Gavin said his great uncle Bosie Douglas was the one who had been the downfall of Oscar Wilde. He was from *that* Douglas family – which traced its way back, said Gavin, to Gavin Douglas, his namesake, the translator of the Aeneid, in the 16th century. That Gavin was a pre-Reformation bishop as well as a poet and thus had no business having a family, not one he could give his name to, but I believed the tale just the same. When it came to name dropping, Gavin was always boss.

The family tradition was continuing nicely. Gavin had a sister Claire: she was a model for Phoebe in *The Catcher in the Rye*, and grew up to marry J. D. Salinger. If you're a quick reader, you've just clicked on that crop of white hair on one side of Holden Caulfield's head. Gavin and Salinger had met somewhere. Prep school maybe? Or when Salinger was courting Claire?

G.R. Swenson, on the other hand, was connected to no one; he was a gawky effeminate Midwestern schoolboy, a child of Topeka, Kansas. After our first bad meeting at Gavin's, I ran into G.R. on the street, again with the kids in the stroller. He lived just around the corner from our Second Avenue apartment. I asked him to come home for lunch with us. Baz came in from his studio in the Anderson Theater across the street, and after eating, took G.R.

back to the Anderson with him. Basil's organic abstract-figure works were beginning to blossom. Suspicion changed to fascination. For both of them.

Unlike Gavin, G.R. always looked exactly the same. He was the kind of boy praised for handsomeness by all the women in his mother's church. Handsome being a code word for well-behaved. Too well-behaved. Handsome a code word for momma's boy, a code word for, well you know. He knew exactly who *his* father was: a gas station attendant, patient, quiet, almost inert in G.R.'s telling. A noble boob, whom G.R. adored. But after G.R.'s death, his father was full of rage. He publicly washed his hands of his son and railed at G.R.'s friend Ann who had come out to Topeka for the two funerals. What we called suicide, G.R.'s father called murder. His son had taken his wife away and if G.R. hadn't died in the event, the dad would have moved to have him jailed. Hard to square this with G.R.'s tender picture of him. Hard to match it with what little I know about the woman in the middle. The mother G.R. killed.

Did his mother actually go to a church? I don't know. Was she as smart as he was? I don't know. Did she respond to art? Did she read him books? I do know she had chronic migraines and G.R. had to sit in the darkened bedroom with her, and massage her head and cut her toenails while she lay across the big brass bed, honey. And I do know she made his father find a new place for the family to live every two, three years in order to be in an ever better school district for the sake of her boy G.R.

G.R. had a brother, but I don't know his name, only that he existed, and that he was never in his mother's place of honor, never the focus of her ambition. His brother was in the marines. He'd done well. He was a major or a colonel, and he did go to church. He had a wife and some children and was stationed in Viet Nam.

"He's queerer than I am," G.R. said. "War is his country. The crease in his britches is the proof of his worthiness," G.R. said. "A stone nut-case."

We were well met that summer, Gavin, us Kings, and G.R. but circumstance never again put us all together in the same spot. Athena was expecting a baby in the fall. She and Gavin were looking for a larger apartment. They were in redemption mode, both of them. He from chronic nihilism and despair, she from drugs and lack of place. She'd fled to New York City from a nomadic childhood with a mother who may have been as loony as G.R.'s. But she was not the focus of a mother's transferred ambition. She was accessory after the fact, and even a partner, as her mother converted to a new religion every few years. Athena told charming stories of child life under Theosophy, Baha'i, spiritual vegetarianism. Presently, mom was a Parsi, or some hybrid American approximation thereof. Every conversion had brought a new persona, new diets, and often a new more precarious way of living. Athena had ended up in the Village doing heroin.

Gavin got her out of it. And she in turn got Gavin settled,

although Gavin had been married twice before and the baby to come wasn't his first child. Never mind. This was new. They were not just looking for a larger apartment. Gavin was enthusiastically working for his mother in what was by then called the Duveen Brothers Gallery. It was housed in a large limestone townhouse on East 79th Street right off the park.

His mother had married Uncle Eddie after the death of Robert Douglas. Now Eddie, in his turn, was fragile, deaf, and in his eighties. Not unlike her first husband when Gavin and his sister were children. The day-to-day gallery administration was up to Gavin; his mother was mostly in the country, at the house in Mt. Kisco which she and Eddie shared.

There was energy and purpose in Gavin's plans. Old Master trade is cutthroat, but he was inheriting from masters. He took the two of us on a tour of the building one day. When the gallery was finally, formally his, he would continue the old master business on the top floors, but the parlor floor, with its mahogany show easels and swags of dark drapery, would be focused on the new surrealism. I think he was the first to call Basil's post-abstract work "new surrealism." And in the dark English basement, Gavin planned to sell books, fine rare editions, and small press poetry. That floor was a born literary haven, with fruitwood wainscoting, low ceilings and a slightly clandestine feel. Eventually, Gavin said, he'd add publishing to the mix.

There was a future after all. A Douglas art empire, in which

Baz was promised a fiefdom. There was a way to live, a place where one might be safe from boredom and craziness, where one might hold high purposes while simultaneously profiting from intrigue and connections. One might not have to be ruined by the knowledge that corruption and duplicity are so ubiquitous. There would be ways to use corruption as knowledge and not sink in the swamp of it. Holden Caulfield – home at last.

Athena too would be home with certified gentility and a bloody big bank account. Her diction was so elegant she sometimes sounded as if she'd learned English at a snooty school in Switzerland. She was going to look wonderful at uptown openings.

Gavin was mercurial, full of references, mentally international. We were both cheerfully in love with him and he with us. We spent weekends the summer of 1966 going up to Connecticut with him and Athena. It was a ritual. Gavin had a dark green MG and a Saturday morning appointment with a shrink at Better Living in New Haven. They'd swing by early and pick the four of us up out on Second Avenue. He and Athena sat in front. Barry, their dog, a black standard poodle with a doting disposition, crammed himself over Athena's feet and traveled with his head on her legs. Baz and I, knees to chins, fitted into the MG's half-size back seat. Mallory (aged three) and Hetty (two) were wedged into the storage hole right behind the back seat, along with all the beach bags and towels. We kept the breakable food and drink around our feet.

Not a helmet, not a safety belt among us. With the top down, our six heads were almost at the same level. Only Barry's was out of sight. Six heads in a little MG, like a circus act. I tied bandannas on the kids, tight as they could stand, to keep the road wind out of their ears. We were never once stopped by a cop or a tollbooth officer. We were fine.

And we were fine. Gavin had done everything, and rally racing was one of them. Gavin was an effortless speeder, never reckless, always in the moment. I never felt a shred of distress as we zipped up ugly I.S. 90, heads in the wind. Gavin cornered around the semis and slowed to an expert slow-roll through the tollbooths. After his 50-minute hour in New Haven, we headed for a beach. Later, we'd eat suppers at roadside lobster pots, and then drive back into the hot, bright, dirty city, sunburned and windblown, very late. Two or three times, we stopped in Westchester County for an overnight with Gavin's mother.

Jean Douglas and Uncle Eddie lived one stop further north on the New York Central line than my parents had when I was ten. It was thirty stops higher on the social and electric scale. Their house, a rambling white frame farmhouse of corners, nooks, and many outbuildings, had a large swimming pool and an exquisite rose garden. The huge red-tile floored kitchen was deep in the middle of the house, and while Jean "had people," she liked the work of cooking and presentation and did almost everything herself. Tiny, wired, magically efficient.

Baz, who did not have to have her as his mother, adored her, and she, in turn, appraised us and our children like the skillful art dealer she was. She pronounced our children interesting, even formidable. She bought them chocolate cigarettes and showed them how to act like ladies when they smoked. Eddie kept to the garden most of the time while we were there. Jean zoomed about tending him, so the presence of children, of whom she approved but he did not, wouldn't upset him. Her relationship to Gavin was not benign.

That was how Gavin had grown up. Some old man and some devious high-level dealing always commanded his mother's focus. He remembered his dad querulously demanding who'd let that little boy in the house and why didn't he go home. Meaning him. Even in good moods Gavin could occasionally project a perfect representation of invalid octogenarian full of whining self-pity. His bad moods, rarely seen that summer, could suck up all life energy nearby like a potboiler science-fiction alien.

In Mt. Kisco, depression seemed impossible. The cool tall rooms were filled with books to the ceiling. There were big leather sofas, beautiful old cabinets and sideboards, deep Persian rugs. There was a Bosch hanging in one of the living rooms and a Stubbs in another. Not bad free digs. Another summer of poverty.

Before Frank

Monster is not spelled the same in French as it is in English and it has a Frank meaning in French. Frank O'Hara, art critic, poet. O'Hara monster of prodigious talent, our urban dancer, man about our town, a wreck and a maker. A Fred Astaire. A Toulouse-Lautrec. Even casual acquaintances could feel his "our" about New York City. He lived in the glamorous swirl the gifted lonely can invent in a great city.

One story told says that when his loft was filled with enough people, he could leave the main area, close a door, and concentrate on writing. This could only work for someone who could shape his personal life into a work of art. All divisions. And none. Some painters have worked in a studio salon. Frank could write a poem in a subway car, and remember to hold the twenty-fifth line in his head until he reinvented it.

I never knew Frank as well as I wanted. Baz had known him since his first stays in New York. How could he not? Baz was everywhere then, and so was Frank. Frank knew everyone so Frank knew Baz.

Back when Baz first knew him Frank worked at the Museum of Modern Art as a sales clerk in the little bookstore right by the front entrance. The museum had an apprentice system then:

curators-in-waiting had to put in time doing scut work regardless of how fancy a school they'd attended. Harvard? Fine. You can sell postcards and catalogs. The museum store was a hole in the wall right by the front door and postcards and catalogs were about all they stocked, plus tickets for the movie theater which was down in the museum's bowels where subway rumbles went right through the soundtrack. Frank used to save movie tickets for Baz, for which you had to pay extra, and even better, he'd smuggle him in to save him the front door admission fee. This was relatively easy to do because MOMA was attached at the back to the Whitney, and the Whitney charged no admission. To go back and forth between the two, you passed though a guarded turnstile paying nothing on the way to the Whitney, but showing your MOMA ticket stub to re-enter MOMA's sanctuary. Frank kept extra ticket stubs in a drawer and all one had to do was take a walk around the block, enter the Whitney, and voila.

By the time I met Frank, we were living on 2nd Avenue and had two kids. Baz was no longer a teenager, and Frank was well beyond clerking in the store. He was a rising MOMA staff member who had curated exhibitions. He was a published poet with a growing coterie of followers. He was into everything going: painting, poetry, film, performance, theater, dance. He was buoyed by public attention and publicly driven mad by love rejections. He fell in love hard and often and everyone would hear tell about it. He bewailed his big nose and receding chin. He bewailed his appearance, which was certainly skinny, but clearly arresting, hawk-like and piercing. He bewailed but he preened wearing a jacket so it hung in an absolute fit from his shoulders. He was gaga for beauty, but not for dreamboats with empty heads. He might whine about his own life, but then he'd prod Baz to make intelligent calculations to protect his work and himself. I realized that meant he did so for himself too. What might seem like abandon, his willingness to give sway to his enthusiasms, was actually monitored. Frank wasn't self-destructive; he was ambitious in the best way. With no sentiment whatsoever he arranged for people to meet simply in pursuit of what might happen. He liked to see things happen. When Frank talked he drove right to the center, where the energy was. He was funny about art-world hangers on too; they were as acceptable as seaweed to him, while Baz was often driven into rages over faddish or uncommitted behavior.

In the early sixties, Frank visited Basil's studio, at first occasionally and as Baz's work picked up, more and more often. Now when Baz went up to MOMA, he would pay to get in and Frank would leave his curator's office upstairs so the two of them could eat lunch together. Two or three times, while I was still working at Random House, I'd take off from my office just over on Madison and come along too. Frank's favorite place for this was Larre's, a cheap white-tablecloth French restaurant serving mostly organ meat entrees for just a few dollars. I happen to love kidneys, sweetbreads, brains – legacy of my mother's cooking. I also liked Frank's smarts, his agile talk, and I loved his interest in Baz.

But Baz was cautious. We'd get a late-night phone call from Frank, an invitation to come over to his place, to meet these people, do that thing, and Baz would almost never go. Even before the presence of babies in our household meant I couldn't respond to impromptu invitations, he'd decline on behalf of us both. He was wary he said of "entanglements." I was ticked off by his reticence. Frank wasn't putting moves on him, it wasn't that at all. It was Baz, fearing exposure.

During Baz's breakdown, just after our second daughter, Hetty, was born, we saw almost no one. Even then Baz didn't back all the way away from Frank...he'd phone him. He'd initiate meetings. Then, in the pits of 1964, Max, our Second Avenue landlord, offered us another apartment. We were paying $84 a month for our 8th floor place, and we were two months behind in the rent. Our apartment windows cleared the rooftops of the surrounding six-floor walkups. Out back was a wide stretch of building tops punctuated by water towers, with open air all the way over to Broadway, a landscape that has been elegantly painted by Lois Dodd, who still lives two blocks over. Dramatic sunsets sent long angled shadows across the tarred tops and their water towers. You could watch clouds. The apartment Max offered was the exact duplicate of ours but on the 4th floor. There, every window looked onto brick wall airshafts, except the back ones, which had a view of another building's windows six or seven feet away. We could have this one for $41 a month. Or, as I saw it, horrified, for lack of $43 bucks a month we would live with no sun.

Because of rent control the empty apartment in the dark could fetch no more than $41 – it had been $38 – but Max stood to pull in $100 more each year if he could flip us. If we refused, well, we should expect to pay him the $168 we owed on Monday. In cash. Or we'd see the marshal's notice on our door on Tuesday.

Baz went over to Broadway to see Frank. Could someone float a loan? The next day, Frank called, met Baz downtown, and gave him cash. Not a loan. A gift.

Frank told Basil: "Larry Rivers wrote a check for me. He said you're not supposed to know where this came from. Larry knows you're a proud man. Of course I'm telling because I think you should know. But don't *ever* let on."

By 1966, Hetty was still too young to qualify for the free day care at Church of All Nations – and that made Mallory ineligible too as the program was intended to enable low-paid mothers to work. I'd found a small galaxy of oddballs who looked after little kids one way or another and I had gotten a job. I was working for Mrs. Burl Ives three days a week. Baz was picking up better temporary teaching assignments –a semester here, a six-week session there. The steadiest was a public service project for ghetto kids, a job he got on the recommendation of the sculptor Sylvia Stone (then married to Al Held). Before long, he was a part-time adjunct at Cooper Union and an Adult Ed art instructor for the Board of Education. Life was beginning to look up financially. Artistically too. In the old Anderson Theater Basil's painting had began expanding. From that weird beginning when he sat on our couch and inked circle after circle, he'd developed huge visceral shapes: soft abstracted body parts, vegetables, sea creatures. The paintings glowed with face-like forms that melded, dissipated, reshaped. They distorted dimensions and incorporated elements that normally would be separated. There came to be so much momentum in his evolving work that Frank would joke, "Another retrospective, King?"

By 1966 whenever Baz was excited about a new group of work, he'd call and Frank would be over. Baz was inventing a self that could exist in contradiction. That could marry romance and terror. The works were awkward and sometimes in-your-face aggressive. There was uneasy vigor below his beautiful painterly surfaces. In short, the paintings showed disturbance everywhere. Some gallery dealers Baz invited to look were unnerved, frankly uncomfortable. One woman who was not unnerved told Baz straight out she liked what she saw but since it wasn't American and it wasn't European she didn't know how it should be placed. She stayed to look for a long time and Baz has many times regretted not going to see her again and making her a friend. Her comment gave him his first solid external definition: "mid-

Atlantic." Decades later the poet Nathaniel Tarn would use exactly the same terms, neither American nor European. He would say about himself and Baz, "we Atlanteans."

For his part, Frank began telling Baz it was going to take him a long time to grow into this new work, and that a long time would also be needed to open a place for it in the art world. He shouldn't look for a gallery exhibition at this stage. His work needed to be in a back room, somewhere insiders meet. It might be five years – more! – before time would be right for an open show. Time invested in developing an audience as much as time for Baz to develop. Could Baz handle that? After all, this work was an expedition. It needed support, quiet conduction, ripening. Could Baz give himself the necessary patience? Over at the studio, Frank had given him a thorough grilling about that.

Baz and I both grinned as he reported the conversation to me. It had already been hard! Would waiting, with Frank's interested support, be *hard*? Frank was a glorious audience. Baz would come home from their encounters glowing.

Finally, one summer weekend we invited Frank for supper at our apartment. He and Joe LeSueur, no longer lovers but close friends, lounged together on our India print day bed. Joe said that I reminded him of Patsy Southgate, a loved and protected figure in their circle.

Then Frank said, "Baz, there are times when a person just needs money. You need to paint and not worry about Martha and the kids. When I get back from Fire Island, give me a call. We've got to do something to get you some money."

I was clearing the dishes away and heard this from Baz after they'd gone. I'd been rankled by the Patsy remark. Was I being asked to follow yet another impossible model? Don't take an interest in me in order to change me, I thought. But I probably didn't look as suspicious as I felt. In truth I was also wondering if Frank could help me learn how to write about art. And I had been pleased because I'd made cassoulet – home-cooked white beans, rosemary, chicken, Polish sausage bits. We had a cheap slightly vinegary white wine which set off the sweetness of the beans and I could tell Joe and Frank hadn't expected to be so well fed.

What Frank had said to Baz meant he saw what I saw. It meant this is not an illusion. Might actual money come from this promise? We held off saying too much. In truth, I had trouble imagining acceptance; I thought this was something that happened to other people. Baz, on the other hand, believed Frank could do exactly what he said. Turn up a patron, a grant, a much better teaching job. To interest people in seeing new work and talking about it was the normal road to becoming a well-known painter back in those days. Perhaps it still is.

We were back at 57 Second Avenue after one of our beach weekends in Connecticut with Gavin and Athena. Sated as usual. Toasted and sandy. Waiting in the oven-hot ground-floor hallway, hanging onto beach gear, holding a sleeping child apiece, and listening to that rum-pot elevator slowly clanking its way down the big shaft way. I was, as usual, bracing myself for our apartment – dingy walls, peeling woodwork, crumbly floors. One never knew what even a brief absence would do – would there be a wave of cockroaches? The elevator doors opened on three people. Frank O'Hara's friend Joe LeSueur, with our downstairs neighbors Frank Lima and tall beautiful Sheila Baikul – she was at the time a sought-after *Vogue* model. All three of them in tears.

"Frank is dying," Sheila said.

"Frank was run over on Fire Island." Was Joe saying that?

They were running somewhere.

What do you mean? There aren't any cars on Fire Island. Just little red wagons. Run over? Please, I have a job to get to Monday morning; we have kids to put to bed. This has to be all wrong.

Later that night Frank and Sheila came up to our apartment to tell us it was no mistake. O'Hara was now in a hospital in the city. It was a beach buggy that hit him. A beach buggy is a jeep, a lethally heavy vehicle, not a little red wagon. On Saturday the first hospital, the one in Patchogue, didn't believe it either. The medical staff there were habitually cynical about homosexual fights on Fire Island and confident of their assessment of queer life: fags lie and dramatize. So Frank hadn't been immediately treated for his deep internal injuries. Now he was in intensive care and complaining to Larry Rivers that the multiple tubes and drains in his body were "horribly unaesthetic."

The next day he was dead.

Frank was gone, dissolving as he vanished, dissolving the connections he had spun all through the downtown world, poetry, art, dance, theater – leaving many people beached, unmoored, disbelieving. Leaving Baz. Leaving me. Dissolving all the futures he didn't live to do.

Following Gene

Most people called art critic G.R. Swenson Gene. But he said he loved to be called G.R. Dear G.R. So I always called him G.R. to his face, though he was Gene when I talked about him with other people.

Two years after Frank O'Hara's death, G.R. wanted to organize a "counter-salon show." Right away, he said, with an edge of glittering mania. Other artists of Basil's generation were chaffing at the narrow choices acceptable uptown, G.R. said. How many others? G.R. who had blazed the way for pop art with his path breaking articles about Rosenquist and Wesselman wanted to see extended the permission for pop art that he'd identified. There were artists like Baz who stretched boundaries. G.R. proposed a search, conducted by a committee of one, himself, to find others. And one by one, he identified people and set up meetings with Baz.

One was a sculptor named Ivan Micho, who lived just three blocks from us in one of those tiny houses erected in tenement backyards in the late 19th century and built for the poorest of poor tenants. A century later, no longer housing six or seven people a room, they were cute house-like buildings of tiny rooms, hidden from the street. Ivan's had the semblance of a garden where a few squares of blue stone paving had been lifted and flowers planted. In Ivan's house he made small brightly painted wooden pieces, half toy, half sci-fi critter, half embodiments of cheerful sex and excrement (always playmates). They were antic and organic. The American surreal. Meantime, for money, he fabricated elegant minimalist sculpture for Sylvia Stone. His skill cutting and fitting her large translucent plastic panels produced the luminous seamless surfaces she acquired a reputation for. She paid him poorly but the pieces were selling so there was regular work.

Ivan was married to a sweet librarian, as bookish and modest as the cliché. Clara worked part time in a public library branch. Like us, the Michos had two daughters, but unlike ours, their daughters were exquisitely shy, pale, prone to allergy attacks, and frequently ill. I enjoyed Clara's company but the children didn't like each other. How could they? Mallory and Hetty exuded confidence and deviltry. Next to the Micho kids they looked like man-eaters.

Baz could pry ideas out of Ivan with great effort, but intellectual discourse wasn't his mode. He had the thoughtful demeanor of a European worker-craftsman, deferential to his betters, and happiest when handling materials. Just the same, Ivan became a member of the nascent G.R.-created group although our interchanges were always bounded by fundamental differences in attitude.

Next, G.R. found Carol Haerer and Philip Wofford. They were married to each other. They were not deferential. I was wowed by Carol's paintings: large abstract arrangements of rounded shapes, pebbles or eggs. She used a white on white palette, with shifting spaces conferred by very subtle color changes. They were painted with delicate open brushwork, never sticky. They were lyrical and she was often angry that her work wasn't seen as "tough." The boys' word, the boys' world. Her structure and space were exemplary, but to be called feminine was diminishing, even dismissive, in the late sixties, not withstanding all that the hippie culture loudly announced about bending/blending gender roles. Carol burned about this, struggling not to become shrill. Women are shrill. Q.E.D. That could sink her ambitions completely.

Philip's art was more problematic, and he was more problematic. Where Carol was a practical, disciplined planner, Philip was Mr. Romance. Skinny, rangy, craggy, with beetling dark eyebrows and unruly hair, he was used to admiration, and he got it. He was as nuts for Pollock and Charlie Parker as Baz had ever been. He too was wrestling with some of the same transitions Baz struggled with: how to imbue abstraction with new energy, or, more basically, how to go forward when the accomplishments of the great first generation abstract expressionists were so overwhelming. Like Baz, the conservative seductions of minimalism weren't his meat and pop art imagery offered no room for Philip's spiritual and philosophical aspirations. Like Baz he struggled for another way. He painted wild demon paintings sometimes marred by narcissistic showing off. But there *was* energy. Recently, he had devised a way to make expressionistic sculpture, very high-relief wall works, using some of the same techniques (soaking rags in liquid plastics) that would prove so dangerous to sculptors Eva Hesse and Robert Mallory at about the same time. Both of them suffered serious health effects from to exposures to the volatile chemicals in these liquids; indeed, Philip escaped barely. Within a few months of using these materials he developed nasty skin sores and chest infections. He had a crisis, part health, part domestic, and part aesthetic. He and Carol went to marriage therapy together and he went back to using traditional oils, applied by brush on canvas, canvases as large as their budget could afford.

Philip and Baz were soon thick with each other, on the phone, in and out of each other's studios, talking, drinking, hanging out. The Woffords had loft space two flights above a shoe store on West 34th Street, just down the block from Macy's. It was stringently commercial-only, but it was cheap. They lived in a tiny apartment in the old west Village, the part of town always called "The Village" then and now. Soon we were spending weekend times together, mostly at their place. Our Second Avenue building had several resident babysitters, some with kids who worked for trades and some who wanted cash but not that much.

So now there were four in the gang: Baz, Ivan, Carol, Philip. G.R. went on with his search. He recruited a graphic artist, Brent something, and more memorably Sondra (Beal) Freckelton, who at that time was making organic kinetic sculptures with ingenious moving parts: playful for sure but deeper and far more emotional than Ivan's.

Just like lifting up rocks in a drought, said Kansas Gene. I'm finding wet sand. He discovered some artists who had started new work and then stopped. Shelved or closeted it. He met painters who were working in new ways in private while still making and publicly showing only their older abstract or minimalist style. G.R. was not the only person plagued by dreams of glory twinned with nightmares of galactic conspiracy. The year was 1968. The political killings had been stacking up for five long years.

Martin Luther King was murdered that April. Robert Kennedy was killed in the middle of the summer. Malcolm X had been assassinated earlier, in 1965, and J.F.K. in 1963, when Mallory was an infant in a baby buggy. It seemed a march, a tide. It was impossible not to intuit some variety of conspiracy, or, I thought more likely and possibly more pernicious, the isolated vicious acts bolstered and were bolstered by a widespread, mostly unconscious resistance to change. All kinds of different people were goaded to group together and try different ways to strike down anything that threatened to bring in a new future. The Big Reaction had already started, right there in the middle of the golden sixties, even as bare breasted girls strutted through Golden Gate Park and poets we knew and loved believed they were affecting the direction of the world with songs, free-form fucking, and funny hats.

In New York, the art world was no longer a village of 200 people. Ascendant artists were no longer people weathered by Depression, war, and years of difficult poverty. No one was expecting years of struggle as an essential to establishing themselves in art. In prosperous 1968 America, art school education had become common. Art-smarts could be learned – and it was okay. Pop art demystified the product and toned down the dangerous qualities that had surrounded the earlier generation's art. New could be as easy as picking up an attractive comic book. Should be as easy, in fact. Get over it! In prosperous America there was money to be made. And why not? Ideas weren't dangerous. Drugs weren't dangerous. Sex wasn't dangerous. All the girls can take the pill; all the boys can grow their hair. Vietnam was visible but mostly it wasn't. For a great many, war protest was kind of party, the peace march first cousin to the rock concert and the shock level of being a political dissident matched the shock level of a Warhol Brillo box. The violent impact of the war was on that *other* America. Privileged kids didn't get drafted – they had deferments for graduate school or marriage or they joined the National Guard. Even when the war worsened and the draft-lottery system was installed to rein in the shirkers, *we* could go to live in Canada or Sweden or France. Fighting in Vietnam was for the rednecks who *wanted* to kill babies.

G.R. wanted to prove that wrong. For him, pop art was *not* a pacifying force reconciling us all to the joys of consuming. Pop art was a blow against irony, which he considered the succubus of passion. He clung to the belief that long hair expressed real meaning about the independent contents of the head on which it grew. Long hair had to be, he believed, a sign of commitment to free thinking. For him, intensity and honor were inseparable.

G.R. worked his contacts. Somehow he got permission to mount a group show of his gang's work in the main floor exhibition space at New York University's Loeb Student Center. Free. NYU was not the official sponsor; we were to pay all the promotion and publicity costs. But Loeb Center would supply security and respectable location.

Philip, Carol, and Baz were the exhibition ringleaders. The three of them came up with a mythopeic name: "Origins and Cycles," and wrote a mini-manifesto. Eventually five artists took part, Sandy dropped out for some reason, and well before most of the organizing was complete, G.R. had become too ill, too crazy to continue.

"Things," he said to us, "keep on happening."

The group soldiered on without him.

Opening night was crowded with friends and friends of friends. But nothing happened. The group waited for reviews, for calls from critics, for inquiries left at the Loeb Center information desk. Nothing.

Philip was irate, Carol wired, Baz sullen, Brent shrugged, Ivan appeared not to give a damn. Someone had hung a "don't touch it sign" on the show. Was it anti-Gene Swenson or anti-the work? Was it something else? From where we were positioned, how could we know? But I witnessed the "don't touch" for myself one afternoon as I waited for Baz on a leather-covered bench in the hallway just outside the exhibition room. Two men who strolled in had clearly come prepared to laugh – and laugh they did. Elegant conspiratorial snickers. I didn't recognize them but they carried themselves with that knowing, uptown look. It's one of those real-life clichés, the way those two men were groomed to look gay, whether they were or not. Expensive slightly arty designer suits. Expensive, slightly arty shoes. Very expensive very arty haircuts. They saw me look at them. They looked right through me.

One night a month or so after Origins & Cycles had ended, G.R. appeared in our apartment white-faced and shaking. The essay he had written for the catalog of a big MOMA exhibition of Jim Rosenquist spoke "off the party line," he said. He had been told to change his text or else. He'd declined.

Who were these editor/censors? I didn't ask. Did Baz know? I did ask "Why don't they hire another art critic?" G.R. just looked wild.

Baz explained: "G.R.'s their leading light on Rosenquist. He's the one who is expected to write something. And everyone already *knows* he was asked. His absence would be too big a message."

"They offered me the moon to make changes," G.R. raged. "All yesterday. Last night. Not just money offers. When Jim called me he was nearly in tears. I don't know what pressure was on him, but I got threats I don't want to tell you. I got a call from *Time* magazine. They'll give me a guest column to express my views. If I'd just adjust the catalog, that is. Take my ideas out. We always knew they were all connected, didn't we? Besides," he was suddenly cunning, "I don't believe *Time* would come through and actually give me the column if I did agree. Would *you* believe them?"

This wasn't nightmares of galactic conspiracy or messages inside a hollow tooth. This was the real investment of dollars and egos. An investment that could easily survive a crack-brained essay in a mainstream national weekly, but might be badly served if G.R.'s ideas were published in the catalog of a MOMA exhibition, a catalog that would grace art history libraries worldwide, enshrining value and position.

Baz asked to see G.R.'s text.

I have the copy G.R. gave him. The paper's yellow now. I've just re-read it to see if it's mad, to see if I can bracket the scandal so long after the fact. The essay is titled "James Rosenquist: The Figure a Man Makes." Three years later, in 1971, Baz and his editorial partners published the introductory section, "The Need for an American Criticism," in *Mulch*, their literary magazine. *Mulch* reached perhaps 1,200 people – poets and downtown art types. There was no huge response to G.R.'s essay in the magazine that I remember. In fact, I don't remember a ripple.

What's there? The writing is a bit flowery. G.R. was always rather flowery. His take on Rosenquist might have begun where mine did (that he is flat, and utterly what he seems to be). But listen to him, G.R. was advising. In Rosenquist's world an orange or a grapefruit aren't metaphors for the sun, they are the actual fruits you eat for breakfast in America. Swenson's essay makes a case for the brilliance of this. Jim's work is a blow against irony and irony as G.R. constantly proposed is used to mask a cynical dread of belief. An art that is exactly what you see is a blow against hermetic, self-referential cleverness. It offers a new – an essentially American! – way to look at the continuing tension between art (or urban life) and nature.

Flowery or not, the writing is personal, well reasoned, persuasive, making a case for an American, or specifically a Mid-Western, capacity for faith, a case poised against "imported" French and German principles of critical formalism. G.R. cites Pollock's tragedy, his self-destruction and early death, to support his thesis: "Pollock was still caught in the webs of reaction to American anti-art attitudes. He sacrificed himself on the altar of art, but he was kept from exploring deeper moral realms of our civilization because no one then was ready and certainly no one asked for it."

The essay goes on. Along with interview quotations and close readings of specific paintings, there's an attempt to link Rosenquist's pictures and the way they were painted to the terrible events unfolding in Vietnam and Detroit. Not the trite connection between a pile of canned spaghetti and the slaughter of Asians and civil rights martyrs, but what G.R. saw as a commitment to honor being mocked in America's ghettoes and in the art establishment.

Poor brilliant schizophrenic G.R. *was* bucking a galactic conspiracy – a conspiracy with the means to insist that anyone interested in un-ironic ideas about truth or morality is either uneducated or unhinged. G.R. was not uneducated. Ah, but he was unhinged. And soon became more so.

G.R.'s psychotic breaks were textbook-classic. When he was in a crisis he told us how messages from the cosmic computer streamed into his brain through the fillings in his teeth. He knew he was invaded because of the unceasing racket inside his skull. And he desperately wanted to shut down the din. He explained that hundreds of policemen were hiding in the street in plain clothes. They had one intention: to manage our thoughts. It was normal to feel observed, marked, alien, he said.

And it actually *was* normal. Every person who had gone in or out of Hettie and LeRoi Jones' apartment on East 14th Street knew their photographs were being taken from an apartment just across the street. Roi was a leading figure in the Fair Play for Cuba Committee. No Patriot Act was needed to put hundreds of us on FBI watch lists. Casual phone conversations by almost anyone involved in anti-war groups were routinely punctuated by the burps and squeaks of low-tech wire-tapping. We were reasonably sure the telltale static noise was delivered on purpose. They wanted us to feel marked, observed, or as G.R. put it, alien. There were so many double agents in some radical groups that one of our friends loved to show his statistics demonstrating that FBI support – in memberships and dues paid by the moles – was actually maintaining the Communist Party in America.

G.R. struggled to handle a real world craziness that painfully magnified his own. He was arrested one night on his roof, throwing raw eggs down on Fourth Street. He was wearing a white sash. He had a white plume. He had five dozen eggs to do battle for honor. The cops took him to Bellevue.

During one of his breakdowns Ann, his sometime lover and always protector, managed to get him transferred out of the Bellevue observation tank to the Payne Whitney Clinic, where he could be seen by some of the city's top shrinks.

Baz went to visit him there. He was sitting helplessly at G.R.'s bedside listening to a rant out of as crazed a face as Gericault ever painted, when G.R.'s features suddenly normalized. The mad face rolled itself up like a window shade and disappeared, Baz told me. And then he realized G.R. had seen the young doctor he liked entering the room behind Baz's shoulder.

"This is my friend Basil King. I mentioned him to you. I hope you two can talk," G.R. said graciously. The terrifying switch was seamless. Baz came home shaken.

Baz and the doctor did speak a few days later.

"Gene can take some control over his disorder," the doc had said. He went on to explain that schizophrenia is degenerative, and that each successive psychotic episode would do more damage to G.R.'s mental abilities. If G.R. would accept the truth that he was in the grip of an actual disease, as he seemed to be doing now, could he gather the strength to resist the delusions? Could he wait out the recurring demons? Could he learn to live with it?

"Most of the patients we see here, well, if we can get them sane, they can probably push a broom. Gene's brilliant. It's not that he doesn't have a real disease, but all we have for it is blockbuster tranquillizers. Just not a good answer for him."

Since we can't cure him, can he cure himself? the young doctor was pleading. Last refuge of a well-meaning healer?

The doctor didn't or couldn't recognize the helpless position of a lone crazy person. For example, every time the cops dragged G.R. to Bellevue's emergency room they would shoot him full of Thorazine. Then he'd develop jaundice, have liver damage, and be months recovering his strength. In the midst of his worst hallucinations, G.R. would always remember to shout out, "Don't give me Thorazine. I'm allergic to it!" But, well, he was crazy, so nothing he said ever stopped the standard emergency room routine.

G.R. did try to cure himself. He tried activism. His own, uniquely Midwestern individualistic activism. He carried a large blue plastic question mark and picketed artists he felt had betrayed his conception of art's mission. No one noticed much except perhaps the marked artists. Then he picketed the Museum of Modern Art, carrying the same symbol, that big blue plastic question mark. He was rewarded with some snickering man-bites-dog coverage on local TV news and in some tabloids.

Soon after, he took some small Basil King paintings under his arm, and walked them into the galleries. What a representative he was! Baz let him do it, too. G.R. would make the rounds of key uptown establishments and if he got into an office, which probably became rarer and rarer, he'd unwrap and lean the paintings against any convenient wall and talk and talk. He would never tell me or Baz what he said about the work, let alone what he was told in response.

Finally, he challenged Henry Geldzahler, who was by then a full curator at the Metropolitan Museum. He challenged Henry to a bloodless duel. A battle of wits, G.R. called it. He outlined elaborate rules in lengthy letters. He read these letters to us in our apartment on Second Avenue, and wasn't offended when we laughed. He meant the letters to be as loony as they sounded he claimed, "But serious!" He insisted the people who received the letters would know what was meant. I forget who were to be the judges. Leading formalist critics, minimalists, establishment stalwarts: Barbara Rose, Marcia Tucker, Michael Fried. This had to be fair, it had to be intellectually grounded, it was to be about wit in the most serious sense, he declared. It would puncture pomposity on multiple fronts! It would be "Saturday Night Live" meets Wittgenstein. The proposition actually was hilarious – in our living room over multiple cups of tea.

To our total non-surprise, Henry didn't respond.

After the barrage of letters, G.R. switched to telegrams. First one. Then another.

Henry didn't respond.

Then one morning, a Park Avenue florist arrived at the Metropolitan with a large black funeral wreath. The traditional purple ribbon was labeled simply "Henry." The deliveryman had instructions to lay it at the base of a particular Roman statue then on the Met's main floor. We had all remarked on how much that statue looked like Geldzahler. Of course the would-be delivery was stopped at the door by security officers.

This should have been funny too but Thomas Hoving, the Met director, was not amused. He said the wreath was a death threat. He said the perpetrator had to be apprehended, and jailed or hospitalized. I'm sure he knew exactly who had sent it.

A friend of Henry's phoned Baz.

It seems one of G.R.'s letters *had* contained a threat: "Meet me for this duel or I'll tell everything I know about your sex life." This was not just a threat, it was a death threat – political or career death. The term 'gay rights' had not yet been invented – and Met insiders knew exactly which parties G.R. had been to.

Henry just wanted a sane solution, the friend said over the phone. Could G.R. be calmed down? Whisked out of town maybe?

If money's a problem, just tell us. We'll fund what's needed. Henry also wanted to find out, not just for himself, the friend said, but on behalf of a segment of Met leadership, just how crazy is G.R.? Baz told Henry's friend that G.R. wasn't violent. Never that. But Baz was wrong. And the earnest Payne Whitney psychiatrist was wrong. Only Ann Wilson knew. She believed she was the only person in the world who knew how truly crazy G.R. was, but she was also wrong. G.R. knew.

G.R. came up to our apartment one afternoon when he was so out of control he frightened me and the children. I asked him to leave, which he did. Then I was so worried about the state he was in that I put Mallory and Hetty into the stroller and followed after him. We walked for hours. How crazy was that? I was as helpless as I felt, pushing my way along a half block behind him as he rushed, stopped, changed direction, rushed again. We went around and around the Lower East Side. The kids were wide-eyed and mum. I told them the truth. "I'm worried about G.R.," I said. I think they were too.

A few days later G.R. came over unannounced, and at night, when he said he knew the girls would be asleep. His long hair was gone, all cut off. He'd gotten himself a farm-boy buzz cut, shaved up the sides, flat on top. He'd shed the knotted string necklace Ann Wilson had given him. He was wearing a provincial necktie and a ten-year-old dark blue suit. He was carrying his cherished collection of 45 records in a box, a gift for Mallory and Hetty, he said. All his Beatles songs, all the Broadway show tunes he loved. I know now what it means when someone gives away important personal possessions. Then I was just baffled. "It's a part of my life that I'm through with," he explained He told me and Baz how sorry he was for scaring the girls and promised he'd never visit us in the daytime again. We both protested and I reminded him the kids adored him, would miss him and ask after him if he did that.

He said everything would be okay, and we weren't to worry. First of all, he was going to Topeka to see his mother for a few days. He was going to take care of a lot of things. In fact, he was leaving tomorrow. He already had his ticket. He was very composed and calmer than he'd been for half a year but he looked so completely wrong in that suit, with that haircut. The more he talked the more freaked we both felt.

Paul Yakovenko, a friend who didn't know G.R. at all but who happened to be at our house that evening, was freaked as well. He couldn't hold back: "Man, don't go home till your hair has grown back," Yako said. "This is a *bad* thing to do, man. Trust me!"

"Can't you stop him?" Yako said after G.R. left. "You shouldn't let him go."

So, in the late summer of 1969, Gene Swenson died just a few days after that evening, in a fiery crash on a Kansas highway, along with his mother and the driver of the oil truck into which he had ploughed his mother's car head-on. Our passionately idealistic friend was a stone cold multiple murderer. His illness made him able to kill his mother and reduce an uninvolved fellow human – a truck driver with a wife and some kids – to the role of tool for his lethal personal purpose. He took care of it all. They were all dead.

Was anything left of G.R.'s interest in Basil's art? Their friendship was intense. It has relics: some reels of tape, some manuscripts, copies of interviews, one of Gene's chapbooks. I have a very small collection of letters, now quite brittle in their file folders. There are no photographs that I can find. We didn't take pictures back then. I don't think we even owned a camera.

Eventually there was an exhibition at the University of Kansas Art Museum in Lawrence, called "Retrospective for a Critic" organized by Charles Eldredge. G.R.'s art collection, containing one Basil King, was given to the museum by Ann Wilson, G.R.'s executor. Baz added to it with a personal gift: the charcoal drawing of Carlos Blackburn that had been reproduced on the cover of the first issue of *Mulch* magazine.

Was there anything left after the loss of Frank? Down at the World Trade Center, the part never hit by the 9/11 attack, is a lovely fence along the waters of North Cove. Text from one of Frank O'Hara's poems is set in iron next to an excerpt from a Whitman text. You can read the words and see them side by side against the moving water. There are many books by and about Frank's work; his poems and poetics are taught in good schools. Some of his poems are even read to children. The love of his oldest friends still surrounds him. The admiration and attention of younger readers continues growing. He is in the American canon. There is a world of Frank that is not lost at all, that is public and ongoing. It's our part of his life which was never filled or equaled that is lost and gone.

G. R. Swenson is much further out. His small body of writing is known to insider art historians, mostly the earlier part when he focused on the pop artists. A collection of his essays was to have been published, but I can't find any indication it has ever appeared. What he might have meant to Baz, to me, to the kids, and to Baz's art was already gone before he himself went, swallowed up by his disease.

As for Gavin Douglas, he is gone to ground altogether, leaving only DNA behind in his multiple offspring. Sometime in the fall of 1966, Gavin Douglas's mother Jean made a deal with Norton Simon. She sold Duveen Brothers: the building, the name, the Old Master inventory, possibly even her address book. She did it without tipping her hand in the slightest, although Gavin knew Simon was visiting the gallery. In fact, it had been Gavin who had brought him in the previous year. Gavin had sold Simon two important Renaissance paintings – and his mother gave Gavin a 14-foot yacht as his commission. It had teak decks and pink sails. It slept four adults and was moored at a private dock in Oyster Bay, frontage owned by two elderly Russian ladies who had once been ballerinas. They were friends of his mother's. Another deal. Gavin was to "look in" on the ladies in return for the free docking. There was always a deal and a string; conditions were attached to everything Gavin's mother did. Jean Douglas was a true art dealer, every cell in her body.

By then Gavin and Athena had moved into a rambling flat on Madison Avenue in the 90s and their baby had been duly born. Gavin figured we could squeeze four adults, two children and an infant onto his beautiful yacht. He said we should plan a big sailing trip together the next summer. He had read Frank O'Hara's poetry, which he liked, but they had never met, and he had no idea of Basil's loss. Baz hadn't told him what Frank had meant to him or shared a word about what Frank had promised. After all, Gavin was a potential dealer, whom we pursued and were pursued by.

Jean told Gavin about the sale of Duveen's over the telephone. Norton Simon would use his purchase as the core collection for a new museum he was building in California. The deal had been in the works ever since the sale of those two paintings the year before. Gavin could go out to Los Angeles to work for Simon if he wanted to, his mother said. "He quite likes you," he was told.

By winter, the doors of the 79nd Street townhouse were padlocked. Gavin began to take a lot of Seconal, washed down with vodka.

"My mother wants me to show her I can make a million dollars," he told Baz. "Why should I make a million dollars when I'm going to inherit more than four?"

He took to yelling at Barry the dog. I think he hit him too; devoted Barry developed a habit of cringing if someone made a sudden movement. Athena's mouth looked like a cut line. Winter went by. Then Jean cut off Gavin's salary and told him he would have to get a job. He faked a working-class resume and got himself hired as a guard at the Metropolitan Museum.

Athena gathered herself and her baby and moved away. Soon so did Gavin. He went to Mexico. Baz said his mother paid to get him out of town. We heard he divorced, married again, had another child or possibly two in Mexico. We heard sporadic reports from Athena, who was living out on Long Island. One of her stories featured Gavin, monumentally drunk, goose-stepping out of a plane at LaGuardia for a visit with his son. We weren't shocked to hear of his death. We weren't shocked at the elaborate memorial mass his mother orchestrated for him, which we attended, in one of uptown's fanciest catholic churches. We were far too sad to giggle at what he would have said about it.

Triple losses to me and Baz: Gavin, Gene, Frank. Loss in public, loss in private, loss in connection, loss in what that essential cross-touch means for a person's art.

War

As the 60s ended there was war inside and war outside. It was
Allen Ginsberg going up to Cambridge to get gassed, not a dope
trip; it was anti-war demonstrations that began to mean cops with
tear gas and bludgeons. It was people we knew brewing half-cocked
plots. It was people we knew. Did they really believe they could
levitate the Pentagon? To stop the war, people bought roses and
handed them out to men in suits boarding the commuter trains for
Stamford and Greenwich. Then they gushed about how touched
the commuters were. Those guys have rose gardens to die for, Baz
fumed. Since when have tyrants not loved flowers?

I was just as much of a contrarian as he was. I made a
couple of enemies by pointing out that Hitler was a vegetarian and
a serious believer in astrology.

Some people went in for rage and some went in for free
fucking and it didn't seem to matter which. Except when it did. It
was people we knew. Like sweet Walter Bowe, one of LeRoi's
friends, swayed by a beautiful Québécoise radical and then busted
following her in a plan to blow up the Statue of Liberty. Symbol
destruction. What liberty? they said. Blow up that mockery! Even
when the plans for this were in the realm of late night brag-talk, it
was to be accomplished late at night when Liberty Island was

almost empty and done so expertly that nobody would get hurt. Mild, devoted, unworldly Walter. Musician. Jazz poet. It was hard for me to believe he ever sussed that this was anything more than an appealing fantasy. But perhaps it wasn't.

Walter had a patient wife and baby daughter he adored, living somewhere on the way Lower East Side. As far as I know brown Walter was sent to federal pen while the white Québécoise was let out and deported home to Canada.

"Miss Duclos, tall, blue eyed and nervous, pleaded guilty May 12 to smuggling 30 sticks of dynamite and three blasting caps into this country from Canada last winter for use in a bomb plot hatched by three American Negroes," according to the *St. Petersburg Times*, September 21, 1965. The talk around Roi's household was that Duclos was the hatcher, swinging her long blond hair and psyching up three others. Even at the time of the arrests, it was clear that it was *her* dynamite, *her* blasting caps. Just a little later one of three "American Negroes" turned out to be a cop. He too was psyching the gang to "take action" because busting this bomb plot would make his career.

It was war and it wasn't war, this sense of craziness careening around every corner. Vietnam was a process, a steam-roller; it mashed and subsumed what I felt was so much more pressing and more real: a focus on far away Vietnam instead of creating some path right here, in the U.S. not Asia, to end our very own ongoing civil war, our racial divisions, our exploitation, our class-driven ruination. The war, the war, the war.

Despair about the course of Vietnam seemed to merge with all our lives. At the end of 1963 J.F.K. had been assassinated. Mallory was a nine-month baby. In 1965, after Hetty joined her, it was the murder of Malcolm X. Baz and I were raising children. Baz was making art. The death toll continued. Watts burned. Detroit burned. Cleveland. Not by themselves. The people who lived there torched the stores where they went to shop, turned over the cars in their own neighborhoods. When Newark blew there were photos of LeRoi, bloodied by the police, splashed across the tabloids.

As the perfect metaphor, the never completed Second Avenue Subway was "in progress" right down the middle of our part of town. Large sections of Second Avenue were blockaded with huge timbers. Steel plates over the excavations rattled ominously with every passing vehicle. Yellow and green earth-moving equipment hulked behind orange plastic fences. Mountains of rocky red undersoil were piled along the gutters, and orange dust blew everywhere.

We had had a group of friends, more of whom were writers than painters, long before Baz or I wrote a single word. Our friends had been mostly heterosexual couples to an extraordinary degree. It was almost suburban. And the couples began to fray and split. White vs black? female vs male? Wars. By 1966, almost every couple we knew had fractured. LeRoi Jones left Hettie and moved to Harlem for life as Amiri Baraka. Gil Sorrentino broke with his wife Elsene after poisonous infidelities. Barbara left Fielding Dawson. A.B.

Spellman left Danielle. Bertha Harris detached herself from David Wyland in a grand burst of lesbian-feminist passion. A cluster of painters from the Wells Street Gallery in Chicago centering around Gerry van de Wiele from Black Mountain College played upset the fruit basket. They were all friends of ours. The splitting, like the war, seemed to take on its own life.

In the mix and the remix, the races had been crossed but in a tense way, bespeaking currents no one really wanted to think about. There were young white women from Long Island with sexy black boyfriends one after another, and there were other seemingly stable cross-racial marriages besides LeRoi and Hettie's but virtually all of them were black male, white female. Black women, near invisible, were where? And gay people? In San Francisco, gay men like Robert Duncan and Jess Collins had open domestic households but in New York with a few stalwart exceptions, say Edwin Denby and Rudy Burkhardt, it was rare to find gay people living openly as lovers let alone courting in public. Most were untethered and many were carefully closeted. Even downtown, gay people tended to be circumspect – they exposed themselves in gay ghettoes only.

Cubby Selby wasn't married. Not any more. His first wife had decamped to somewhere New Jersey, some time before *Last Exit to Brooklyn* was published. But he hadn't forgotten what it was like to be young parents with no money. He often volunteered to be our free babysitter. "Just go on out, take a walk or something. Have a beer." Wonderful Cubby. I remember us coming home one night to find him on the couch with both kids; wrestling on our TV as loud as it would go, and Cubby screaming "Kill the mothafucker, kick 'im in the nuts!" his blue eyes snapping and his wan wasted face a mask of murderous enthusiasm. There was a little girl on each side leaning up against him, watching half asleep, rosy and perfectly happy.

By the time Mallory and Hetty were bored with the sandpit and ready for more complicated play with friends, Tompkins Square, no, our whole Second Avenue neighborhood had filled up with feral suburban teenagers, street dogs, all-night bongo drummers, packs of shave-topped Hare Krishna's. Now that Johnson was president, the Vietnam War was on TV every night, and impotence heaved and boiled in all of us. Impotence roiled the crowds of voluntarily dirty young people who swarmed the streets. Many hadn't the first idea of how to protect themselves from boils, crabs, head lice or really bad drugs. Both pros and amateurs were turning tricks and selling dope in a swelling sea of hawkers, cons, and sharks.

No, Baz said to peace march invitations. He feared mobs of any stripe; he feared fantasies and over and over he predicted disaster from a left-wing program so unanchored and fundamentally fragmented. After a try or two I ducked out on consciousness-raising women's groups. In my world of fracturing relationships, I felt I was viewed with suspicion. I was with a man. I didn't want to be called on to defend that. And then there were the class-deaf pronouncements I heard from friends when I asked the big question: Who should do the world's boring, dirty, everyday work?

"There will always be someone who *wants* to empty the garbage," one woman assured me.

I could hear lurking what my Southern mother called "the servant problem." Like my mother, these women really wanted a hard-working and inexpensive maid. Everywhere quick angers were met by another quick fix, angrier than the last. There had to be other ways to live or love or fight – or were there?

On Second Avenue, Baz and I went on guarded. We went on half-shut down each of us in two very different ways; we went on for some long time only for the sake of going on, only because – don't stop me – because for Baz once he recovered from his breakdown, not to work would be not to breathe. And we went on because he and I both grew fierce to remember what our children need. To see our kids growing up to hate the world because of what we had chosen to do would be the most unbearable of losses.

At home, Hetty managed to catch up to Mallory until their 17-month age difference hardly mattered. By 1967 the two bonded as 'the girls.' They had learned charm and fearlessness, their four clear hazel eyes taking in the streets, the parks, their playground lives.

"Hello, goils," said toothless Mrs. Kalamanowitz every morning. She was one of the last of the tenants for whom living at 57 Second Avenue meant living in the heart of the Yiddish Theatre district and hobnobbing with its stars over thick bowls of potato-cabbage soup in Max Thau's Restaurant on the ground floor of our building. But now the Yiddish theaters and their denizens were ancient history. Thau's Restaurant was a filthy ghost of its own past, and on weekends, Mrs. Kalamanowitz's outraged suburban children visited. You could practically hear it through the walls: "Ma, how can you go on living in this dump! Will ya move to the Island!"

Mrs. Kalamanowitz hung on. She spent her daylight hours, except for the foulest winter days, sitting on a plastic webbed folding chair, right by the double front door. Nothing escaped her as the neighborhood grew more and more unsettled, drugged out, overwrought.

"Hello, goils."

"Hello, Mrs. Kalamanowitz," our children would reply, seeing charm and fearlessness in her wrinkled face.

Beginning Writing

Before Hetty was old enough to qualify for Church of All Nations full-day daycare, but after Baz began painting again in his studio at the back of the Anderson Theater, I signed up with a temp agency. My very first assignment was a hit. I was sent to an office called "Wayfarer Music." The address on West End Avenue turned out to be the home of Helen Ives, wife of Burl, and it wasn't an office at all. It was the whole top floor of a big old building, an apartment full of books and comfortable furniture, inhabited by a secretary, a maid, a cook, Helen herself, and Helen's – what was he, Horace something – Helen's male companion. Nervous work Horace had, being on the far side of forty. He had been something, a song or scriptwriter. He had a little den up a spiral staircase at the far end of the living room and he scurried the hell up it whenever I appeared. Helen watched everything.

I was hired to transcribe the alcohol-fueled rants that Helen spewed into her dictating machine late in the night: denunciations, imprecations, and impossible instructions to her teenage son now in his third or was it his fourth boarding school. Her regular secretary had refused to type them and that had prompted her call to the agency.

"She should leave the boy alone," the secretary told me,

looking pinched and stony. Her name was Elise. She was a proper unmarried woman of a certain age who lived with her mother in Queens. She came to work in a hat and gloves, shoes with heels, and carrying a pocketbook that matched her outfit, even though she had worked in Helen's house for years. Helen wore sweatpants and tee shirts unless someone like Jack Valenti, head of the Motion Picture Association, was coming over.

I offered no opinion about the assignment. This gig wasn't going to last long anyway. But I was wrong. Soon, I worked three days a week for Helen not the temp agency on a different project. She offered to pay me plus the cost of our babysitter directly. This was still a bit less that what she had had to pay the agency, she told me. I came to work in frayed sneakers and blue jeans. The maid brought me soup and sandwiches on a tray for my lunch, and I spent the next six months spread out on the living room floor in front of the big fireplace, organizing, cataloging, boxing, labeling, and writing up descriptions of Burl Ives memorabilia.

The material was a hodgepodge of junk: out-takes, drafts, test record pressings, bios of sidemen written by their agents. There were no original manuscripts, letters, or arrangements, which is probably why no one had wanted to buy the stuff. My job was to make it into a narrative, and thus increase its value, so Helen could give the lot to a library and claim a nice tax deduction for her donation.

Although Helen and Burl had long been living separately

she was still at work on the business end, promoting the Ives image. Endlessly. I listened with a voyeur's delight to her explosive phone calls. She sold her line even to me. I might have learned, had I been ready for the lesson, that true promoters never stop and let nothing slip. No one enters their orbit without whirling a little in the well-managed spin. In Helen's spiel, Burl was a fountain of spontaneous genius who had kept American folk music pure apolitical *volk art* and who had saved American culture and possibly democracy itself in the process.

I believe Mr. Ives had named names for the House Un-American Activities Committee. I learned soon enough one didn't mention Woody Guthrie or Pete Seeger in front of Helen. Let alone Dylan, Joan Baez, or Joni Mitchell. I sidestepped. I heard enough of her opinions on those tapes for her son.

Helen either took to mailing those midnight tapes directly to her kid or Elise relented and typed them fearing I might diminish her special position. At any rate, Helen very shortly left me to focus solely on the cataloging project. It was a nice puzzle and I didn't hurry it. We all settled into a fine habit together. Until I ruined it.

The search for narrative in the Ives hodge-podge alerted me to my bent for story. The proximity to Hollywood lit a small fuse, a little gleam of glory. I could write for money! I began a screen treatment of a wonderful Western I'd read in high school: Frederick Manfred's *Lord Grizzly*. The protagonist is based on an actual and famous Western mountain man, Hugh Glass, and also featured his young protégé, the actual and famous, Jim Bridger. I worked this over a number of times, copying the form from screenplay treatments in the Ives pile. And then I showed it to Helen.

She was enthusiastically patronizing when I explained it, grabbing a blue pencil and smiling as she took my manuscript off to her study. But it must have been more accomplished than she had expected. She returned it a week later, stony faced with no blue marking at all. My job for her had been completed to her satisfaction, she said.

About fifty years later, the film auteur Inarritu made *The Revenant* from some of the same material, though I believe his lens was another novel using the Glass and Bridger history, not Manfred's wonderful book. Back then, losing the job let the air out of my screen writing balloon.

Job loss or no, life was improving for all of us. Baz was at work in his studio, moving through startlingly different series: "biomorphic abstractions," "organic abstractions," portraits of "the Algate Brides," nudes of me and of Paul Blackburn's newborn son. Hetty finally reached her third birthday so both kids were eligible for Church of All Nations, just down Second Avenue from our building. The fee was pegged to household income and despite the school's name there was no religious expectation. It was "all nations" for sure, serving kids of every class and race, and it was a lovely solution. It opened at eight in the morning and closed at six, a true all-day service, rare at that time, and it offered nursery school stuff with no pretensions. All the kids had a cot for a nap, a cubby for clothing, a hot food lunch, and the regular drill: circle time, story time, and loose times to mess around playing with dolls or trucks. There was a play kitchen, a book corner, the blocks and Legos corner, the art area. Downstairs there was a large gym to run around in when the weather was bad and upstairs a playground on the roof when it wasn't.

Perhaps best of all it had Miss Burdick. Thelma Burdick, the redoubtable founder of the program, tireless protector and advocate for the urban poor, and for my purposes an enduring and curiously effective guardian of language and manners.

"Would you say that to Miss Burdick?"

Even three-year-old Hetty got it right away. So would anyone facing Miss Burdick. There were things one could do and say in certain places and not in others. It was that simple.

With child-care security, better jobs followed. Hettie Jones got me in for a stint at Mobilization for Youth, the big Robert Kennedy war-on-poverty potpourri down on Avenue C. Hettie and two of her friends were running tutoring programs for children who were failing second grade. Mobilization offered some other solid things – storefront lawyers and peer-provided health information. But without anything that would pass as education credentials, my options for program work were limited. I got an "editorial" job to convert social worker reports into clean manuscripts for publication. The pay was good but I deeply offended the social workers by converting socio-babble into straightforward English. I didn't last long. This wasn't the last time in my working life that I'd hear, "But this doesn't sound *professional*" after my careful translation. On the other hand, it was another brick in my writing foundation.

Soon I bagged a true editorial job with Praeger Publishers, then just up the street at Fourth Avenue and 11th Street. There I did more writing. Copy for book jackets, ad copy, and précises of books under consideration by senior editors. I was even allowed to ghostwrite introductions to scholarly books that needed to be toned down into more straight-forward English. That irony was delicious. I thought everything was great until I discovered a male editorial assistant, hired after me, was making $3,000 a year more than I was. It was a big difference: $15,000 instead of $12,000. The office climate was friendly enough for me to go straight to Fred Praeger, old socialist Praeger, founder of the house, and ask for a raise. It was also friendly enough for Fred to fire back at me, "Doesn't your husband make enough money?"

I was shocked wordless. Should I say my husband is a deadbeat? Should I threaten to quit? I did what so many other women did and do, I swallowed and shut up. I did feel justified about helping myself to some of the marvelous art books Praeger published. In the old South, this was called "toting" and was proof of the inferior morals of African Americans. I didn't feel the slightest pang.

In addition to writing chores, I was being trained to be a true copyeditor. I learned a great deal about the niceties of usage from Praeger's chief copyeditor, an old-school stickler who let nothing out for printing that hadn't been both fact checked and combed into grammar that conformed to his standards. He was so persnickety he insisted on use of *Second* Webster's Unabridged. The Third had committed egregious dilutions of form he would not tolerate. I actually loved him. So I stayed put.

Getting Paid

Money, money, money, it's the size of your plate, the last of your shoes, the measure of your measures. No story about an artist's life is true if money is never mentioned. The need for money is a refrain and getting paid a glorious chorus.

When Adolph Gottlieb was a cocky student he won a huge national art contest he told Baz once when Baz was his studio assistant. This was in the 1920s and the prize was an exhibition in a New York gallery. The contest was newspaper news, coast to coast. The new young American artist! he told Baz, "I thought I was made." A sale, a win, an opening door. It's a movie, a musical. See the young man in his first pair of spats. See integrity being introduced to decadence! But decadence didn't turn a hair. Gottlieb was paid but the serious art world paid no attention, and New York art critics made fun of the work. The prize money sluiced away, and soon no one in town even knew young Gottlieb's name.

Getting paid can also mean paid off. Mark Rothko negotiated a studio sale of a large painting for an eye-popping sum. His studio assistant (who was Dan Rice not Baz) was asked to wait in the utility room while the business was conducted. The buyer wrote a check on the spot. Rothko sat looking at it a minute before he handed it back. "You're too late," he said quietly, and led the flabbergasted millionaire to the door.

When the door was shut, he capered around the studio. This was why he hadn't sent Dan away. It was part of his plan; he knew he'd need to display his glee. This would-be buyer had completely forgotten that he contracted for a Rothko painting years before, when a Rothko went for twenty-two hundred dollars. The collector had taken it, and paid, and two months later sent the painting back. For a refund. Rothko and his wife had just had their first baby and the money was already spent.

Rothko paid it back, every dime. The buyer didn't connect that minor annoyance, those painfully made installments arriving in the mail month after month all those years ago. He only knew he wanted a world-famous Mark Rothko painting and was willing to pay top dollar for it.

"Too late," Mark sang, getting paid. "Too late, too late, he's too fucking late."

Pay, I was told yesterday, is a nautical term for caulking the hull. Sailors have to pay the seams, and the keel seams are the worst ones to do. So the keel's the devil, my informant said – he's the birdseed king of Brooklyn and has a lovely speedboat – and that's where the phrase comes from: you have the devil to pay.

Some payoffs are so indirect it's hard to recognize them. For example, it's 1968, it's summer at the Cape, and an artist and his family are guests of a patron who is taking his yearly two weeks at the family's summer house in Old Chatham. This story isn't about the week we spent with the patron and his wife – me and Baz, Mallory and Hetty, who were then four and going on six. We all had a holiday and it's enough to say that the kids were young enough to be happy with a pail and a tide pool; old enough to play with themselves, young enough to sleep all night, old enough not to wet the beds.

This story isn't about Robert Kennedy who was murdered in California that first weekend, although collective and individual hysteria welled through the neighborhood and gawkers clogged the turnoff to Hyannis Port making it ghastly hard to drive up the highway to get supplies.

This story concerns the weekend following Kennedy's death when the three young stockbrokers came up from New York on Friday night at the invitation of our host. Let's call him Tanner. You can figure their ages somewhere between George Herbert and George W. Bush. Just forget the media mythology version. It was the late 1960s but only a very few young men from elite Eastern families gave a moment's thought to leaving their sheltered workshops on the word of Timothy Leary or Herbert Marcuse. These young men would never have described their work-world as a sheltered workshop either. Anyone with gumption and good English could do what they do, they truly believed. These three house guests were sturdy proof that smoking marijuana doesn't shake the social order; it would never be that easy.

They were Tanner's mates, and with their arrival, Tanner hooded himself and blended in just as he did during his working hours on Wall Street. In the Old Chatham house, there weren't any jarring details, no watercolors by Basil King, no copies of Ed Sanders' *Fuck You: A Magazine of the Arts.* This could have been their grandmother's summerhouse.

The young men knocked the sand off their boat mocs before coming in, and offered to load the dishwasher. A weekend with Tanner meant poker, lobster, sailing – but no horsing around. Tanner was married, and they were not, to a proper New England girl, Susan was, with a few nutty passions, like the Democratic party. Could have been worse. She could have been gone on a screwy religion. Good old Tanner. They were here as buddies. They had not brought dates.

Can you consider any way to think of these three men as something more than their social adherences? This bothers me, but I can't solve it. Their souls belong to God, don't they? Well, they had effortless good manners.

Poker got started early, as soon as the kitchen was cleared of dishes and the checkered oil cloth on the long table sponged and dried.

Baz had been introduced as an artist. It was even explained that Tanner and Susan had purchased some of Basil's work because they thought it was so fine. Susan and I sat outside and watched the moonlight for a while. Her distress over Robert Kennedy had abated just a little but she didn't feel much like talking. Soon the sea breeze died and the bugs came up, so we headed off to our beds to read.

It was predawn blue when Baz woke me up.

"I'm in trouble," he said. He was pulling bills out of his pockets and throwing them on the bed. "I took all their money."

I sat up in a fog.

"They were so sure I was some delicate flower," he said. "The more I kept winning, the worse it got. Tanner kept saying 'I told you about him, I told you.'"

He was making a fat pile of money in the middle of the bed.

"Wow," I said.

"I've even got some I.O.U.s." He showed me. "Tanner had to stop the game." I was silent.

"This is going to be one long weekend," he said.

"Well, they can cash checks for themselves, don't you think?"

"That's not it. It was almost funny how easy it was. They just didn't get it. I'm an *artist*. They think that's other worldly. They just walked right in. It was as simple as stealing."

We talked about Baz just giving the money back, but we both knew better, just as we knew we needed to stifle our fits of giggles with the pillows. Hundreds of dollars on the blanket. After a while we decided to treat the house party to lobsters and champagne – Baz could buy out the town. He finally cooled out enough to get some sleep.

Next afternoon we bought a dozen lobsters, way too many for seven adults and two kids under six, and a case of champagne, and pounds of ice to chill it with. The lobsters were all banded so we let them out in the kitchen. Lobsters scuttling everywhere. Susan was actually cheerful for the first time since the previous weekend. Here was wicked cruel fun. We held an ugliest lobster contest. Susan scrounged every big pot in the pantry. We had kettles on all four burners and we fired up the kerosene hurricane stove for melting butter. We debated, while the critters struggled and turned rosy red under the pot lids, if lobsters really scream or is it just the steam venting through their shells? We ate for hours, washing down butter and lobster juice with cool bubbly. I think we had some fresh corn too. No one mentioned cards.

When it was over, the three young men and our host switched from champagne to scotch and began talking business to Baz. They were in on an upcoming coup, and could they put Baz on the tail end of the deal? He's cash short? Understood. One of them will buy, sight unseen, a large charcoal drawing that Tanner will pick out. That will hold Baz in the deal for $600. They had to work fast because the company was going public the next week. (Is the statue of limitations exhausted?)

It was a plastics processing method with a name like a Hollywood stripper. Somebody Bubbles. It meant one could manufacture plastic forms that were smooth and tough and extraordinarily lightweight. Huge forms from a few teaspoonsful of material. The process would be snapped up for everything from toys to advertising displays. Heaven sent for theme parks, then beginning to bud all over America.

The men talked into the night and once again Susan and I sat in the dark garden watching fireflies and stars. This time we did talk – about summer times when we were kids, about our parents.

Not quite six months later, just before some tax bite would kick in, the boys sold the lot, and our WASP surprise arrived as a check for almost eight times Baz's make-believe investment. Bubbles paid. See her shimmy. Tanner ended up with the charcoal drawing just as we had suspected he would, and we had bubbles to play. It was enough for us to live well for a year, maybe longer if we went to Portugal or Puerto Rico. We had bubbles coming up – not compensation exactly but surely a different kind of song.

Bubbles, I said, coming back to earth, will fund a permanent change of housing. I was the one who had to say: Forget Puerto Rico. We have to move to a part of town where public schools are possible. Mallory was about to start first grade and it was clear before she started – and even more clear once she had – that we had to live where public schools were different from what was then in our district on the Lower East Side.

In Mallory's first grade class, a hard-bitten veteran teacher, with one timid "paraprofessional," was in charge of 38 new first graders. When I went to the principal's office to protest I was informed, "It's an experiment in double staffing." "But there aren't two teachers," I said. That was only the first lie he blandly told. He denied everything Mallory reported. Most of the children were plainly terrified. I suspect they'd never been separated from family and most spoke only Spanish. "She gives us candy if we'll sit in our seats," Mallory told us. Even so, some kids cried all day while others couldn't be stopped from climbing on their desks or running about the room. Lunch time was worse. After eating, multiple classes were released all at once onto a large paved but toy-less and unsupervised school yard. When the bell rang to return there was a tsunami of kids racing for the doors. Mallory and a friend from Church of All Nations would cling to each other. They took to standing right by the door the entire recess period, "So we can get inside before they start pushing," Mallory said.

We thought first of moving to co-op apartments on the Upper West Side where some public schools had progressive or "open" classrooms. We got our children accepted into one of them (using the even-then magic words, "Black Mountain College") but our apartment searches in the area turned up nothing that would work. Then our friend Harry Lewis began promoting Brooklyn. In Brooklyn you could buy a whole house, he said, and dragged Baz out to Seventh Avenue in Park Slope where an old college buddy of his had purchased a shabby brownstone.

It was no big coup to buy a house in Brooklyn back then. Certainly Park Slope was not much of a deal. Especially if you bought on a block the real estate agents deemed "a war zone." While that was not actually true about Fourth Street, it was true of the park just across Fifth Avenue. On our block, the few remaining long-time Irish had made peace with the "new people," conservative home-loving blacks from the Caribbean. Most were in construction trades. Everyone on our block avoided that park as carefully as we did, for the park turf was hotly contested by rival Italian and Puerto Rican street gangs. This wasn't kid stuff: Behind the ten-foot tall handball wall that faced Fifth Avenue the Italians had a corner on needle drugs while the Puerto Ricans marketed young women. Or maybe it was the other way around. Either way, the metal, glass, and rubber detritus of their trades was everywhere in the patchy grass. Parking a car in the dead-end cul-de-sac that separated the park from a large dreary looking junior high school was profoundly unwise.

Never mind the bad park. We now owned a whole house. Never mind that dreary junior high. Our street was zoned for P.S. 321 on Seventh Avenue, a refreshingly ordinary grammar school serving a mix of middle and working class kids, a few of whose parents had old-Brooklyn political connections. Never mind our house had been chopped into SRO units who knows how long ago. Never mind the stink of cockroaches, anger, and poverty. It was a house. Never mind that as home-owners we had become capitalists. Certainly when he heard what we had done, Basil's father reminded us that property is theft. At the very least, he predicted, we were on way to supporting right-wing politicians. On the other hand, when the kids heard that a whole house was to be ours, their expectations escalated in a heartbeat: "Can we have a swimming pool?"

And when the painter Mike Goldberg heard Basil say, "We're moving to Brooklyn," he blurted out "Are things that bad?"

Maybe they were. But we now owned a house. It was four blocks from Prospect Park on top of the hill. It was a house with a back door to an actual strip of weedy yard, fenced in chain link. There were three full floors, and a sloped-ceilinged garret on the fourth, where the girls could each have a bedroom. I sit in it this moment, a brick townhouse with a South garden in the middle of Park Slope, Brooklyn – the envy of my oldest friends.

Money, old money, like blood, like chips, is blue, the filthy blue that measures the size of your plate, pinches your chest and whispers the news. Will you plant hyacinths, iris, or grapes? Will you die cyanotic and gasping? There's always a chance and a risk and an art when it comes to an artist getting paid.

Martha King at 22. Photo by Lynn St. John

Basil King at 24 in the Ferry Street studio. Photo by Lynn St. John

The family in 1964 at 57 Second Avenue, New York City. Photo by Lynn St. John

The family in 1973 in Grand Haven, Michigan. Photo by Earl Heuer

At the National Poetry Festival, 1973, Allendale, Michigan. Left to right: Robert Duncan, Basil King, Ted Enslin, Carl Rakosi. Photo by Allen DeLoach

The family in 2007, Mallory's house, Jersey City. (One more member will arrive in 2009). Photo by Andrew Perret

Filming "Basil King: MIRAGE" in the 4th Street, Brooklyn studio, 2012. From the left, Basil, Nicole Peyrafitte, Miles Joris-Peyrafitte. Photo by Martha King

Elinor Nauen and Martha King hosting their Prose Pros reading series at SideWalk Cafe, NYC. Photo by Basil King

Vitrine showing works of both Martha and Basil in "Between Painting and Writing," at Black Mountain College Museum & Arts Center, 2016. Photo by Sansana Sawasdikosol

PART TWO
BROOKLYN AND BEYOND

In Cars With Others

Our phone was ringing again. By the time we acquired our broken down Brooklyn house, we had friends who were willing to labor with us. A house was a novelty though no one else we knew decided to buy one for themselves. Still, many of our friends found it fun to help us tear down walls, patch floors, yank the overgrown hydrangeas out of the back yard. The sculptor Paul Yakovenko built us shelves, bookcases, and a kitchen counter with a butcher-block top. I think we paid him mostly in meals and company. He was dear.

Hello, hello.

Soon we were, all four of us, in cars with others.

Our kids were troopers, willing to sleep in weird beds and eat odd food. They talked easily to adults; they were funny and smart. One year we spent a string of winter weekends at a shared house in Sag Harbor with a gang of friends who had the use of it every third weekend.

We came along in cars with others to the annual picnic on The Land, a cooperative community out in Rockland County founded by and for former Black Mountain people. There a tribe lived in houses echoing the design of BMC's Minimum House. Once a year, through the late sixties and seventies the residents played host to fifty or sixty winter-bound escapees from the city's art-land. It was a ritual first outing of summer. There would be long tables in the meadow sagging under pounds of inventive and artistic food. There was skinny-dipping for those bold enough to use the trout stream. (Icy too mild a word.) There was dress-up stuff for the kids, pick-up bands for the grown-ups, intoxicants and screwing around galore. I felt Baz and I were there but not there. Baz was not exactly welcomed as a returned member of the Black Mountain fold. He had stood aloof when he was at school and The Land folks were aloof toward him. But we were there. We came along in cars, with others.

The summer of 1969, the first summer we lived in Brooklyn, one of the cars became our own. It was a light blue Volkswagen, and it was actually owned by Harry Lewis, Basil's partner in *Mulch* magazine. In Manhattan's West Village where Harry lived he had to change parking places every single day to comply with the street cleaning rules and a person could drive around for hours without finding a spot on the legal side. But on our block in Brooklyn, the rules applied just twice a week. Plus illegal double-parking on the morning of the change was totally accepted. Plus the number of car owners on our block was very low back then and there were almost always empty spaces. Baz could drive Harry's car anytime it was parked in Brooklyn, Harry said.

So first it was, "If I don't take the car back tonight would you move it for me on Wednesday?"

Then it was, "I'm not using it this weekend. Can you move it for me Monday?"

Finally it was, "Baz, uh, I need the car next weekend. Is that okay? Am I messing up your plans?"

Harry took to visiting his car like a divorced dad. It was an occasion; he'd bring presents. He and our girls would wash it together, toting sponges and buckets of water out to the curb. He bought car-waxing mitts, and pretty seat covers, and seemed quite pleased with the whole deal, especially the lower-priced insurance he could buy by using our address. Baz drove Harry's little VW until we moved to Grand Haven, Michigan, in 1972. For we were no sooner settled house-owners than we moved. We had the liberty to do so, because our shabby place on 4th Street was as firm an anchor to the city as could be devised.

A Grand Haven

Glittering sky to the grey blue horizon. An empty beach. Under a full sun. Under a blue sky. The white clapboard bathhouse is deserted. No one is sitting on any of the three white lifeguard towers. Far down the beach some young men are raking at the water line. Grey blue waves coming in. Curl. Crash. Sea gulls. I think this is odd because this is a great fresh water lake. Gulls like pigeons, I think idly, adapt anywhere. Our daughters race to the water edge, shrieking. Across the street behind us, the sand dunes are huge, and support pine trees and scrub bushes. High up on the cliffs are beachfront houses, with porches and huge picture windows. Baz and I sniff. No salt smell. Just glittering water and oh my god the waves are full of floating fish.

"Mommy, mommy!" The kids are circling us. "You can't believe how many dead fish!"

Then we see two mountains of fish near the beach house. Raked by patient Coast Guard boys. They're making a third one while we watch. There *is* a smell and it's not salt.

This is the beach of our Grand Haven. We've come early. It's June. We've come early because we have no income in New York. We have no income in Michigan either. Baz's teaching job begins with the second summer session and he won't be paid until four weeks after that. Meaning early September. Okay, I still have the unemployment insurance that followed the end of my job at Praeger. I had used up my allotted six months but the U.S. was in a slump and unemployed New Yorkers had been granted a six-week extension of benefits beginning mid- June. Whew.

"Mommy, mommy!"

We're wearing bathing suits. Absolutely no! No one is going into *that* water. Baz goes down the beach for gossip. Returns with: "They tell me it happens every year. It's the alewife die off. This year's a big one."

"How long does it last?" I ask.

"Well, they didn't really say."

Later that evening, Baz calls our realtor, the man who sold us the house we're in. He doesn't really say either. He's blasé. But then everyone out here is. They don't get excited. The world is okay. It's Fine or it's Just Fine. Your name becomes a nickname. Clichés melt like butter. Yeah, alewives. Some kind of Atlantic herring, maybe? Got in the lake in trawler ballast. Swam up from the ocean when the Seaway opened. Got in the lake from someone's aquarium. Don't really know how they got there. Smiles. They're salt-water fish. Never get big enough to eat, living in fresh water. In early summer the quick temperature changes kill a whole lot of 'em. The die-off'll stop in a while. It's just alewives.

Baz is told the state has seeded the lake with a special salmon, the Coho because Coho eat alewives morning, noon and night. Coho's a sport fish so it's good for the economy. Lots of folks come up here to fish for Coho salmon.

The townspeople snicker a bit about Thomas Jefferson College. TJC is the "experimental" school. It's for the pot smokers, long hairs, bad kids – but this is Western Michigan and the bad kids are probably just fine too. They are their own anyway. TJC is one division of the new Grand Valley State Colleges, in turn a part of the University of Michigan system, and it's theirs, serving prospering local families who are, for the first time, breaking with the past and sending their teenagers on to higher education.

Grand Valley isn't as far away or expensive or as full of dangerous ideas as, say, Ann Arbor. By Western Michigan standards, most of the school is sensible. There's a business college, a teachers' college. A college of "general studies" focused on psychology and management. TJC is sensible too. There should be a place for the kids who had wanted McGovern to be elected, who have a thing about "alternatives." McGovern fell a long way short of being elected, leaving area citizens relieved. Many do harbor deep unease about Vietnam, but they have no intention of saying so. Because, anyways, as the locals like to say, the draft is ending and Nixon is winding down the war.

What was Vietnam really about after all? They don't want to think too much about it. Anger over unpatriotic kids who won't cut their hair is now an unspoken embarrassment. After all, Nixon got re-elected. Everything's fine. Nothing scary happened after all.

We can see all this at Mr. Fables, the big diner out on the highway where Grand Haven's power elite eat breakfast every morning. We see the other side too. On a barn by the turnoff to the Grand Valley campus, the words "Be Here Now" and the giant yellow peace symbol painted on its side have faded to near illegiblity. These bad kids are going to reabsorb, just like the psychedelic paint. They'll become teachers and business managers. Everything is okay. It's just fine in fact.

Baz and I have bought a house here. We hadn't meant to. We wanted to rent. Grand Haven isn't going to be a permanent place for us. Here came another Midwest lesson: renters are transients, and single usually. Apartment buildings don't allow *children*. Nice houses for rent to regular people are rare, and very expensive. Rentals are dumps, broken down housing for the poor. Rent? Disapproving looks from more than one agent. Respectable people buy and sell. What's wrong with us?

Out in the country, many farm families have abandoned grandpa's house for a new one right next door: a one-story ranch house with picture windows and a huge TV antenna. Groups of TJC students often rent the old houses, with their antiquated plumbing, leaking windows, and rotting Queen Ann woodwork. With me yet to learn how to drive I make a stand: we have to live in town.

So we ask to look at the houses for sale. When we found

one we liked, a blue house, simple as a kid's drawing of a house, with three bedrooms, two big trees in front, and not much lawn, Baz ducked into the "other" bank –thankfully Grand Haven had two – and took out the max cash advance on our Master Card. That way we could plop down the "earnest money" and stall while we figured out how to get up the rest of the down payment.

We had left our house in Brooklyn with the top three floors rented as a unit, and Basil's parents living on the garden floor. We couldn't do what Paul Blackburn had done. We had to have a place in the city to come back to. The work we'd done on our place was not even a quarter of what it really needed. Windows, walls, ceilings, stairs – all bore the signs of age and grudging maintenance. We couldn't even afford to pay a plumber to remove the ancient sprinkler system, so the ceilings were crisscrossed by the water pipes that had serviced the sleeping cubes old lady Campbell had rented out when she ran the house under 'single-room occupancy' rules.

As we prepared to leave for Michigan I dreamed we'd get the kind of tenants who pour themselves into a rundown apartment. Those legendary couples who polish and paint, who ask permission to install ingenious improvements. Our Brooklyn house could be a dream, I dreamed. The tenants would love it and tend its needs. What we got was a comic-book writer, forgetting that success in that area profits from a three-year-old's mentality. But that's another story.

Right now, here in Grand Haven, we had to figure out how to get this pretty blue house. It was clear no one expected a large lump down because *everyone* lives in a house. Desperation serves: I was able to badger my parents into lending us the balance, a tiny sum by today's standards, but happily almost equal to the amount they had planned to pay for a fancy summer camp for the two girls.

So here we are in Grand Haven, with a house and two maxed out credit cards. Then my plan to collect unemployment crashes. After dutifully reporting every Friday for three weeks I'm told Michigan says no go to arrangements made in New York State. If *they* want to pay me, I should ask them. If I want to look for work here, fine, the state employment service will be glad to help. But no checks.

It's a very strange summer. We haven't got the few dollars in change to go to the laundromat. But all Grand Haven businesses offer charge accounts to professors. And their wives. We have our dirty clothes picked up by the snooty "we deliver" laundry – and returned ironed and packed in brown paper squares. It helps that our house turns out to be on one of the more respectable downtown streets, distinct from the streets a few blocks away, where families park their cars in the front yard and have large above-ground swimming pools out back. It turns out we can charge all our food at the town's fanciest grocery store, but not at the A&P. We can open charge accounts for shoes and clothes. When we discover that the Muskegon Sears feels the same way about us as

Grand Haven merchants we open a charge account there and buy a washing machine, a dryer, bicycles for the girls, and a good record player with speakers. Wow. Then we buy a car! A brand new car, on another credit line. It's blue like the house, a little Datsun station wagon. I do worry a bit about bill collectors. People lived this way in novels by Thackeray.

Mallory names the car Blue Buster. At ten, she's a committed feminist and tells Baz he is never to say, "Fill 'er up," at a gas station. "Or I'll jump right out. I mean it. Fill *him* up," she announces. "Or you can say fill Buster up," Hetty suggests breaking up giggling. For weeks, from the back seat she'll whisper, "Fill Buster up," whenever we stop for gas. Yeah, gas is on yet another credit card. We are so not used to America.

Best of all, friends from the East arrive like blessings, bringing actual money that we can borrow. Some even bring us food. Marc comes from Brooklyn and is strip-searched in the Detroit airport, where his bargain flight required him to change planes, because he has twelve cans of wonderful Italian tuna fish for us in his backpack. He nearly misses his connection to Muskegon while the cans are carefully x-rayed. The authorities don't apologize either. They blandly tell him he has "a high-risk profile." We laugh about that but we're angry too, since what that really meant is his dark complexion.

In mid-July the alewives do stop dying.

In August, thanks to the kind intervention of another TJC teacher, Baz is a member of the college credit union and we start to bail ourselves out.

In September, his paychecks start.

In Grand Haven, with a college professor's salary deposited automatically into a bank account, we catch up fast. We can pay all our bills at the end of the month. It's amazing. There's no painful agonizing over which ones to hold back, which ones Baz should call to "make arrangements." We buy real mattresses and good second-hand beds for the girls. (In Brooklyn they'd slept on homemade plywood platforms topped with foam rubber slabs.) We buy a nice old chest to put our new record player on, and a little tin desk, with a matching chair that I spray-paint dark green. We rent a freezer locker at a local market. Town folks use these lockers for deer meat and salmon, but we join the organic beef co-op at the college and end up with a locker basket crammed with pounds and pounds of ground meat.

Then we pretty much stop. Our house is still empty. The chairs around our old table from home are fold-up plastic lawn chairs we brought with us. Most furniture is so damn ugly, I think. I like the open space. When our front door is shut, the girls and I roll on the bilious yellow wall-to-wall shag carpet the house came with, and giggle. Yep. Haven.

Daily life in Michigan kicked in. I used to stand in one of our bedroom windows, which looked over the back fence, and watch Mrs. Cole leave her house, get into the car parked on the paved driveway by her front door, warm it up, back out carefully, and drive two houses over to see her friend, Mrs. Clemmons. She'd pull into the driveway right behind Mrs. Clemmons' station wagon and go in the kitchen door. Mrs. Cole was about twenty-five pounds overweight and she went to see her friend Mrs. Clemmons, who was too thin and having marriage troubles. I knew them both, but I avoided being friendly. Mrs. Clemmons' husband was on the faculty at Grand Valley. Mr. Clemmons had a lover, who was male. The two of them spent weekends in a motel on the road to Kalamazoo and everyone talked about it. Soon he moved out of his house and took an apartment with his lover at the edge of town and everyone talked about it. By then Mrs. Clemmons had a lover too, also male, another faculty member, and everyone talked about that too, especially because her lover had a wife and an infant of his own. The Clemmons children went a little wild, and every one talked about that, but not to their parents' faces. It wasn't tolerance as much as it was unwillingness to create upset.

In Grand Haven I soon discover there are three kinds of school: public, Christian, and private. Their social standing is not what I expected.

Public school is for normal kids, the center of the universe. Public schools focus on being normal in every way. Normal means play a lot of sports. Normal means don't get too smart on us. Rich and poor, college or town, "everyone" goes to public school, loves sports, and belongs to teams.

Private schools are for *abnormal* kids. Private school is virtually a code, not for wealth or ambition but difficult behavior problems. No one wants abnormal kids, least of all not the elite of Western Michigan.

The Christian schools are for the Calvinists and Evangelicals, of whom there are a substantial number. They live in Grand Haven among everyone else, not in a distinct neighborhood, but these reformationists clearly feel the Christian life is easy to corrupt and that it's best to maintain strict self-segregation. It would be twenty-five or thirty years before these groups took to public activism, demanding that the wider community fit itself to *their* standards. In all our time living in Grand Haven, self-segregation worked so well I was never to meet any of them. Their children never made friends with our kids, although they played on the same sidewalks and lived in our neighborhood. They went to Christian schools from kindergarten through high school. For college, they went to Calvin, not Grand Valley. They never used the public library, the town recreation programs, or the Y. They bought their books and toys in the Christian bookshop. They never went to the town's movie theater. Suitable movies are shown to them in their school or at church. They don't even come to our front door for trick or treat because, as one of their kids solemnly explained to me, "Halloween is Satanic."

But in the summertime they do attend performances of the World's Largest Musical Fountain. All the street signs in Grand Haven bear the legend, "Home of the World's Largest Musical Fountain." The Fountain has a modest amphitheater on the riverfront, and is close enough to our house for us to hear its sonorous male voice making cheerful program announcements every night about the kids' bedtime. The Fountain is a Christian entertainment and is one place where everyone goes.

It features large columns of water, siphoned out of the Grand River, and synchronized to squirt, pulse and bounce to recorded music –"Daisy, Daisy" is a favorite – while stage lights change the water from deep blue and emerald green, to fuchsia, orange, or gold. All four of us go on our first Fourth of July because we hear the Fountain's fireworks are spectacular.

The bleachers are packed as the water pricks perform a Technicolor porno roll. We're trying hard not to giggle too audibly. The display is accompanied by the Voice of the Fountain inviting us all to remember the good old days, our faith, and our freedoms. Then come rockets and Catherine Wheels and starburst fireworks that explode outward in ever-enlarging circles of glitter. The Fountain voice comments on the cost of these big bursts in admiring tones. Sixty-five to $80-thousand bucks a pop it seems, and the audience applauds. Comes the finale. Everyone stands up because they know what's coming. A twenty-five foot cross, picked out in red, blue and diamond sparklers, is raised on top of Dewey Hill directly across the river. As patriotic music swells, an enormous American flag is run right up the cross. It flaps languorously just below the cross bar. I can't help it. "That's sacrilegious!" I gasp.

People around us hear. They gape – and palpably draw back. Before anyone can say, "I never!" Baz hustles the four of us out of the bleachers and home.

This is where we are. We don't cut our grass much. We don't wash our car. But in Grand Haven, we're normal no matter what we do because it's unthinkable that we would not be. If there is no furniture in our house, and if, come fall, longhaired students are camped out on our yellow living room rug over the weekend, that only shows everyone how dedicated Baz is to his mission to educate. We're fine in Grand Haven. We're not pariahs. Except to Grand Haven's kids.

Several little girls are soon trailing into our house to play with Hetty and Mallory. They inspect our kitchen with solemn puzzlement.

Doreen comes out with it: "How do you wash the dishes?"

"Well, I use a dishpan."

Still mystified.

"Like when you go camping?" I offer.

No response.

"What does your mother do when you go camping?"

She's unable to believe anyone is quite so dumb.

"There's a dishwasher in the RV," she says.

And this is where I am. Once school starts the house is empty from 8:45 to 3:15 and I stare at my big electric typewriter on a work table at the end of our bedroom. It swirls and chugs. My brain rebels. The music flees, and returns but only sometimes. I pace. I smoke cigarettes and examine the view from every window. I start again.

There is no rhyme to my reason and just as I get into a flow, the kitchen door is slamming and the kids are home. Good god, how could they be HOME so damn soon. It's time for snacks, for making tomorrow's lunches, for figuring supper out. I can hardly be civil let alone be nice Miss Homework Helper.

And I can hardly justify my time being unpaid for. What do I think this is worth?

A Berth in the Haven

Our berth in Grand Haven had been dead Paul Blackburn's gift to us. A teaching position at Thomas Jefferson College of Grand Valley State Colleges, in Annandale, Michigan.

It was weirdly ironic. Baz and Paul had spent a long evening together when Paul was first offered a teaching job at SUNY Cortland. I heard the details: how it had been enormously difficult for Paul to think of leaving his haunts, his city, his pastorale. His apartment on East 7th Street was critically small, but babies and wives had squeezed into smaller places in the New York that we knew then. To take up the offer, Paul would have to give up the apartment, and giving up a place with location and rent control has never been an easy idea in New York City. Paul, natural teacher that he was, was racked with qualms about his ease or ability in a classroom. There would be, he said, a substantial chance that other faculty would loathe him. He would certainly arrive as an outsider, with unorthodox academic achievements. His publications and his connections, for example to Ezra Pound, could easily make him a target.

But, Baz argued, he was spending hours weekly scrambling for translation jobs and other ill paid literary scut work. Paul was savvy and could make it work at Cortland, Baz told him. In the end it would be worth it, a step into a more ordered way of living, with more time to think and write and be a family with Joan and the new baby.

So, in the summer of 1971, his last summer on earth, after little more than a year of teaching at Cortland, Paul orchestrated a return offer for Baz. Paul had flown out to Grand Haven to attend a national poetry festival hosted by TJC. The festival was underwritten by Paul's friend Dan Gerber, poet/publisher and heir to the Gerber Baby Food Corporation of Upper Michigan. The festival was organized by Robert vas Dias, who was also a beneficiary of Paul's recommendation, and had taken up the position of TJC's poet-in-residence a year earlier. Prompted by Paul, Gerber told the school administrators, who were eager to ingratiate their new college with a major North Michigan millionaire, to seek out Basil King as the lynch pin of a new art department for the school.

TJC held special promise for Dan Gerber. This is the Midwest, this is where normal is. If this new school was Western Michigan's answer to the social revolutions of the sixties, it might also be its answer to Eastern Ivy League dominance of high-brow culture. TJC was a school for self-directed education, a school inspired partly by Students for a Democratic Society and even more by ideals of other education experiments like Oregon's Evergreen and St. John's 'great books' school in Annapolis. By

Dewey, by Bauhaus. Could TJC become a place for art influenced by the ideals of Black Mountain?

Dan Gerber was a prince, the golden-boy son of parents who had lived the all-America story, building a business sprung from grandma grinding home-cooked apples in her kitchen into an international Fortune 500 corporation. After some fits and starts, including a few years as a professional racecar driver, Dan was inventing himself as a poet, a homegrown normal with straight-up maverick tastes. Along with the novelist Jim Harrison he'd started *Sumac* magazine and then Sumac Press – and he had designs on the new college down the road.

The first National Poetry Festival took place in 1971 and is vividly remembered by old friends for Paul Blackburn's appearance. He flew in from Cortland and let on that the throat cancer he'd developed was in remission. He was frighteningly thin, but recovering he implied. He gave splendid performances on stage and off. A poem by Jackson Mac Low recounts this vividly, for even as dear a friend as Jackson didn't penetrate Paul's defenses.

Paul knew he would be dead by summer's end, and he entertained with his usual wit. Robert Bly, Ted Berrigan, Gregory Corso, Robert Creeley, Robert Kelly, Al Young, James Wright, Diane Wakoski, Sonia Sanchez, Jerome Rothenberg, Joel Oppenheimer, Jackson Mac Low, Tom Weatherby, Anselm Hollo, Phil Whalen, John Logan, Armand Schwerner – the close and the more distant were all relieved to see him. Not to worry, said Paul's squint and his grin. I'm here where I should be, among the people who mean most to me.

He died in early September, 1971, a little over two months later and about three weeks after Baz drove me and Harry Lewis in Harry's VW up to Cortland to say goodbye to him.

Don't wait, he told Baz on the phone.

We had a weekend to spend together. Paul insisted on driving us around to see Cortland's countryside. Lush rolling bliss in a warm September, low blue hills, rich crops, farm roads with the kind of roadside junk shops that Paul found irresistible; dark forest patches; glittering meadows full of Queen Anne's Lace, goldenrod and Black Eyed Susans. Those broad sunny uplands that wait for us after a war.

Don't wait he told Baz, and got us all laughing as he mimicked Robert Kelly in nature: Open car door, look out at roadside weeds, shut door, rush home, write nature poetry.

"Don't wait," he said to Baz, and he was serious.

Paul's sister arrived. She knew how to administer morphine shots, a task Joan couldn't master. Joan was half locked down and half a vigilant attendant, urging Paul to drink tall glasses of unpasteurized organic milk and herbal porridges thinned to drinking consistency. Magic might sustain him. Sustenance might sustain him. Purity. Secrets in the grass. She was in her early twenties with a baby not two years old. Paul sipped for her sake as he was able, but refused prayers or spells. He was quite clear about what was happening.

Joan was bitterly angry that Sunday morning because Baz and Paul had grown heated and emotional in their final talk the night before. It seemed right to me; they had things to say; both of them lived with so many secrets. Joan saw only Basil leaching Paul's tiny store of energy. Anything misspent might prevent that possible miracle turn-around she was depending on. Late on Saturday night Paul had told Baz that he had a major poem to write and should get started.

"Don't wait," he said from the terrible perspective of numbered days. Paul was 46. Just coming into his own.

The next January, in the middle of a cold snap that drove the Midwest into wind chills of forty below, Baz flew out to Michigan for an interview at TJC and under the twinkly black sky of Allendale, Michigan, called me on a payphone to say he had secured Paul's gift, an academic time-out in Dutchman country, a piece of Dick and Jane Land for our daughters, who were now eight-and-a-half and ten; a loopy, as it turned out mercifully brief marriage to the great middle way so beloved of Dan Gerber and Jim Harrison.

A Place for Poetry

The Grand Valley college campus was midway between the town of Grand Haven and the city of Grand Rapids, laid out over a series of Ice Age ravines, in what must have been an enormous delta. The ravaging melt water and the scourging ice sheets left berms of ground rock and sand piled in dunes miles from the actual edge of the lake or the modern Grand River. It was poor real estate for agribusiness, which flourished elsewhere on the table-flat alluvial dirt. Thus it was cheap for the state to buy. The school built bridges over the ravines to create the campus and the steepest ones offered students important recesses for sex, dope, arguments, and alone-time. The ravines made some of the campus wild, riverine, geological, thought provoking. The rest of it definitely did not. The state of Michigan's architects vied with Howard Johnson motels and the Sunrise Mall for modern style, and where ravines were not, lawns and square buildings were. Grass was obsessively mowed, foundation edges planted with cemetery shrubbery. There were also acre-wide parking lots, with aluminum dinosaur necked pink sodium lighting fixtures far overhead.

In the 1970s, Grand Rapids was a city of antiquated factories where poor blacks, Mexicans and middle European left-behinds packed neighborhoods of big rundown frame houses.

There was the usual dead commercial downtown cordoned off by by-pass highways, and the usual miracle-mile octopus of chained franchises, shopping malls, corporate offices and suburban housing developments extending beyond. In the 1970s 'gentrification' had not yet discovered America. It was still the era of the car revolution, which had made "new" a synonym for "good" and "old" something that deserved to be stricken from recollection.

In little Grand Haven, the original Carnegie Library had been razed and replaced. The 1850 county court house ditto. Houses built in 1890 were considered extremely old and awful, and were certainly very rare, even though the town – first settled right after the French and Indian Wars – had risen to significant wealth well before the Civil War. The homes for those newly rich people were now long gone.

Once there had been an intra-city trolley network, linking Grand Haven to Grand Rapids and a dozen other towns up and down the shore of Lake Michigan. During the Civil War, farm-boy soldiers boarded trains at the Grand Haven station (also long since torn down) to arrive at Fort Dix, New Jersey, just 14 hours later. But in 1973, when Baz drove Blue Buster back to New York for essential trips home, it was a 16- or 17-hour drive. But of course, we had to stop as trains do not, so we might have been making, just barely, about the same miles per hour.

The Land of the Gerbers was some miles north. Dan Gerber lived on a private island, ringed by a rare strip of actual virgin forest in a vast area of orchards and Gerber Baby Food processing plants. The Land of Robert and Susan vas Dias was in Grand Haven. They lived near the golf course, in a well-appointed suburban house. Susan had her work cut out for her, to dominate a society she actually scorned. She made it very clear to us that Robert was big frog out here only because this was very tiny puddle. The fact that he was a published poet and the editor of an anthology that could be purchased in the college bookstore was apparently small consolation to her. In their tense household, she was swollen with scorn for him. Robert manfully kept his end up somehow. He didn't actually think of the faculty people as Susan did. He didn't think a lot of things she said and mostly hid out behind his mustache. He and Baz were both Gerber-connected, Blackburn connected, and of New York. Perhaps because of that Susan had not wanted Baz to come out to Michigan, as she told Baz explicitly when he stayed in their house for his interview at the college. And now their son and our daughters even went to same grammar school. We were linked.

The land of poetry. Empty Western Michigan. Where everything was just fine.

One very fine Big Frog thing that Robert was doing, with Dan Gerber's backing, was organizing national poetry festivals – big shindigs, sandwiched between the school's first and second summer school sessions when the campus was empty. They had the run of place, all the auditoriums and seminar rooms, all the grounds, dormitories for attendees, and the cafeteria running a full schedule.

The Second National Poetry Festival of 1973 had themes. I expect first one had them too but I wasn't there to see. 1973 featured a reunion of the Objectivists. They had not seen each other in years, and except for their elder, William Carlos Williams who'd died ten years before and Lorine Niedecker who died in 1970, all were living and in good health: Charles Reznikoff, Carl Rakosi, George Oppen, Louis Zukofsky. Zukofsky declined to attend and sent a film and some tapes of himself reading instead. All the others, and their wives, were there.

A second theme was the "long poem" – which was then for the children of Williams, Pound, and Olson, a major field of combat. Contending were Ed Dorn (*Slinger*), Ted Enslin (*Syntheses*), Diane Di Prima (*Loba*). And there was more: Robert also invited Allen Ginsberg, Robert Duncan, Kenneth Rexroth, Victor Hernandez Cruz, Rochelle Owens, George Quasha, David Meltzer, Chuck Stein, and George Economou to present workshops, give talks or be on panels. Jim Harrison, the novelist, Ken and Anne Mikolowski of Alternative Press, David Gitin, who founded the Poets Theatre in San Francisco, and many others attended. Acolytes, devotees, students, fans, and wannabees swarmed the bland campus, occupied a large dormitory, and loudly protested the college cafeteria's offerings of hot dogs, mac'n cheese, and waterlogged carrot sticks. It was a huge turnout.

Our status, mine and particularly Baz's, was bizarre.

Among the people *not* invited to participate in the festival was Basil King. Baz wasn't a writer then, but he was a founding editor of *Mulch*, an amazingly influential little magazine publishing poetry, fiction, translations, archival papers, art and art criticism, film scripts, anthropology, culture studies. It was and was meant to be glorious mulch! I'm pretty sure that *Mulch* was the first "little" literary magazine to take such a wide focus. I remember Ted Wilentz, of Corinth Press and the famous Eighth Street Bookshop telling Baz that you can't combine all that. It was the early seventies, and so many magazines have done so since that this no longer sounds startling.

I should also say that back then even our friends didn't get that Baz was an active editor. He was in fact the guiding brain for the magazine. The two other editors were Harry Lewis, of our adopted VW, and David Glotzer, a young poet with book layout and production skills. They were denizens of poetry bars like St. Adrian's on Broadway, they were publishing poems in the mimeo magazines of time, they were poets. Today, Harry is a leading practitioner of Reichian psychology, who lectures around the world and serves private patients in the West Village. David Glotzer moved away from poetry completely and works in private wealth management on the West Coast. Only Baz is what he was then and more, for now he's known to be active poet as well as a painter. But back then, even old BMC poet Joel Oppenheimer who should have been easy with cross-discipline ideas thought silent Baz was the art editor of the magazine. Vas Dias actually knew better. He also knew how unknown that fact was which may have increased his discomfort. It was very like the Baz of those days to let it all pass. He didn't, as he would today, get Robert to discuss his plans for the festival. He hadn't, as he would today, listed himself on the *Mulch* masthead as "founding editor" either. I also held my tongue. Perhaps I was doing the same thing he was – laying low.

The upshot was that Robert kept all the festival arrangements to himself; it wasn't until we picked up copies of the program on the festival's first day that it was clear a perfectly appropriate place for Baz existed. There was to be a half-day workshop on poetry editing and small press publishing. Di Prima, Economou, Meltzer, Oppen, Rexroth, and Robert himself were all scheduled to take part in it.

Robert's discomfort intensified as the festival got started. Why isn't Basil scheduled to do something? he was being asked. And worse, because people thought the reason was *Basil's* reluctance: Why can't you get Basil to do something?

When Robert Duncan realized Baz hadn't arrived from elsewhere but was on the campus as a full-time faculty member, he roared across the cafeteria, "The walls of academia have truly fallen if Basil King is on the faculty!"

Christ, Duncan, shut up! I thought, scarlet-faced. Deans and vice presidents had turned up for that first day. There was to be – there was – a hopelessly stilted faculty reception that afternoon, where cookies and a very faintly alcoholic sweet punch were served.

I'm not sure the editing/publishing workshop ever happened, or Rexroth's talk on the Japanese. They had had been scheduled for late the last Saturday afternoon and the festival was to close at noon on Sunday right after Rexroth's big solo reading. By the final days, the festival had acquired a powerful dynamic of its own. Impromptu sit-downs, campfires, spontaneous performances and readings had swept up all of us. Rexroth had arrived late, expecting to be a *deus ex machina*, perhaps, certainly expecting to be seen as the top celebrity, the Grand Father of the wild clan. He was way overweight and clearly not in good shape, whether from age, illness, marital tragedy, alcohol, or everything. All too soon he was clearly humiliated by the pervasive sense that his appearance was irrelevant. It was cruel and crueler still that no one really cared.

Rexroth was not the only poet in trouble. David Meltzer had a death in the family and left a day or two after the start. Ed Dorn stayed the course, and got through whatever he'd been charged to do, but he was in stark need of money, place, and some sense of possibility, some indication that he was loved and loving. The world was offering very little to him and he was deeply rattled. Duncan who loftily ignored both Rexroth and Ginsberg was clearly concerned about Ed's state and, as Duncan's position as the true kingpin of the festival solidified, he was more and more generous toward him.

Baz was simply Odd Man. My place was clearer and more conventional. I was Guest-Student. At least at first. I signed up for and attended a poetry workshop, my first and only experience with a writing class, except for those I would teach myself in a few years. The workshop I chose was with George Oppen, stooping, pensive, and glamorously haggard with his seamed face and thatch of white hair. The sonorous and the moral were married somewhere in his thorax and emerged as a resonating chest voice with a vibrato so emotional it swept everything before it. I had liked "Of Being Numerous" beforehand; hearing him speak and hearing him read from it I was hooked.

Baz listened to my rhapsodizing with thin enthusiasm. "His work is detached and disassociated," he observed to me. Baz has always had a healthy fear of crowd pleasers and their ability to stir emotions. He turned out to be quite right as far as Oppen and I were concerned.

"You're frightening us," Oppen told the workshop group after I read a poem. He had started out by telling the class he'd never taught writing and was totally flummoxed by the notion of "a workshop." "I'm not sure what I'm supposed to do here," he said. Understandable, I thought, but I was baffled and diminished by his response to my poem. Then, later that night, at the vas Dias's house in Grand Haven (how did everyone get there...cars must have been mustered somehow) Oppen told others standing near me, that his class had started out with "someone" reading a poem so good he suspected the reader wasn't a real student but a plant. Diane Di Prima stroked my arm and said I didn't look like a plant to her.

I settled it all in my head by deciding the classroom setting was as wrong for him as it seemed to be for me. Shortly after the Festival I sent him a poem and a letter asking for his critique. I've made up so much of my life by myself I wanted to find out what a teacher could do for me. I sent him "To my grandmother's garden" – a poem that attempts to get at some of my biographical contradictions and the crazed opposites always at hand in me when art is being forged. My hands were around my grandmother's throat, and hers mine in the poem, but it was also a rhapsody to the stuff that grows rampant in Virginia backyards, the plants that thrived on my grandmother's neglect and narcissism: roses, mimosa, bleeding heart. Was it a good poem? "Good" has a slippery side. Let's say just I really wanted it to be read. Much later I published it myself, in a chapbook called "Women and Children First" when Susan Sherman and I partnered as 2+2 Press. We published about eight little instant rare books, our own among titles by friends.

Oppen wrote me back. He had rewritten the poem on his own typewriter, removing two thirds of it. In the deletions he typed in ". . ." and inserted empty lines of space. He returned me a minimal shell, with all conflicts, and almost all the content, excised. The only line still holding substance was a politically correct assertion at the end: "allow, allow, what has become mine." He sent no explanation for this radical surgery. Just a piece of paper with his signature and something like "sincerely" or "very best" I don't remember. I took what he had done as arrant imperialism and tore it up in a fury, letter, envelope, poem, the works. I had trouble later on trying to tell one or two other people what had happened. I wasn't believed, except by Baz. Oppen was a saintly personage. And the evidence was gone.

At the Festival Duncan was on a roll. He was to give a solo reading at the end of the third full day, but he was already blowing minds. Much of the audience had streamed in intent on basking in Allen Ginsberg's presence. Allen was scheduled for two or three after-noon "Blues improvisation" sessions, plus a major solo reading. Duncan had started off Wednesday morning with the first of a three-part lecture called "Ideas of the Meaning of Form." He was in glory, with the time and opportunity to improvise, not as Ginsberg would have defined it, but as a Duncan-turn, connecting and disconnecting concepts. It was dizzying and fabulous.

His reading was a first for an audience most of whom had never been in the presence of a mage like Robert, with his hand beating rhythms, while his whiney voice soared through ideas, ideas, ideas. If he had notes, they were on tiny cards, something unobtrusive. It was words, words improv all the way. He was mesmerizing, and absolutely intent on competing with all the other poets. I took no notes. I wasn't attending the festival in the spirit of scholarship. In fact my most vivid memory of his lectures is the second morning when he was speaking about the unexpected in poetry and a white goat appeared in the lecture hall window. The window was a story and a half over the woods below; the goat calmly walked the wide ledge around the outside of the building and disappeared from view. Like me, it wasn't a plant. It was a goat.

Ahhhhs and giggles, Duncan with us, and then Duncan went on talking, of course.

I also remember:

A play about the creation of *Frankenstein*, set in the house party with Byron, Shelley, and Mary, the bet they made and their all night freak-out: In the middle of the performance, while Mary invented her story, Tara Marlowe, Diane Di Prima's eight-year-old daughter, with long light brown hair and a white nightgown, came out of her bed to ask the grownups to be quiet, or came out of her bed to lead them into spirit where imagination fosters. The program I have says "Whale Honey," script by Di Prima. It was so perfectly enacted it was impossible to tell how much was improvised and how much memorized from written text, which hardly mattered anyway.

Ginsberg's reading of anti-Vietnam poems with chants and harmonium: The biggest auditorium on campus was packed to the rafters. I was sitting next to Duncan who was sitting on the aisle. I had had no idea there was enmity between them, but when Allen came up the aisle by us Robert shook Allen's hand off his arm saying, "Get away from me!"

A lecture by Diane Di Prima and Ted Enslin: They spoke on homeopathy. Diane spoke at length on the 38 flowers to remedy moods discovered by Dr. Edward Bach, and afterwards gave me a tube of Dr. Bach's emergency combination rescue ointment.

I certainly remember how useful that ointment proved to be. In the midst of the festival Baz had gone down into his underground studio to work on his small sculptures, not noticing that he was sitting in a puddle of turpentine, which he'd somehow spilled on his chair. The result was grim: The skin on his balls was seared. It was so painful he had to walk bowlegged and thus had to say why. No one would laugh at a bad sprain or burned fingers, but burnt balls? "Baz, how yah balls," a faculty member bellowed across the quad. There was some variation of hilarity everywhere he hobbled – but the rescue ointment was almost miraculous. One application and Baz felt relaxation flowing down his body, almost literally pushing the pain out. Diane had said the ointment wouldn't cure anything but would remove impediments to healing. In two days of use new skin was forming.

The crisis over Duncan's stolen notebook: His notebook, his constant companion, had disappeared during a meal in the cafeteria. Someone was sent to find Baz. "Baz will know what to do," Duncan insisted, trying to contain his hysteria. As a matter of fact, Baz did. He knew the TJC students very well, knew that a wannabe poet was among the cafeteria crew, doing his work/study obligations. Baz went back to the kitchen. First he spoke about how much a notebook can mean to a poet and then suggested that if the notebook is put on a table in the hall, no one will question this any further. It worked.

An overdose at a late night bonfire: I only heard about this. About how understandably terrified vas Dias was and how calmly Enslin and Di Prima together had settled an unstable, freaked out festival-goer without having to call for help from emergency services or cops.

A quiet visit to our house: It was just Duncan if I'm remembering right. He was always a kid-lover. He talked easily and listened intently to Mallory and Hetty, but a car to drive him back to the campus came much too early for us adults. Talk had just begun among us. There were promises, which Baz and I followed up soon after by letters, to be in closer touch, to talk further. It never happened.

And a photograph: We have this on a wall in our kitchen. Baz, Ted Enslin, Carl Rakosi, and Robert Duncan are walking across one of the campus bridges. For years I thought the paper bag Baz is looking down at was lunch, and why had he not looked up at the photographer. "That was our stash," Baz finally told me.

Bourbon and beer. They were headed into one of the ever-handy ravines for a bit of respite.

And then they were gone, as completely as a revival tent show or a county circus, leaving behind scattered stories, lost underwear and rain hats, paper wrappers, mashed grass, dust. But really not as stark gone as all that. The Festival cemented two long friendships: Carl Rakosi and Ted Enslin. After that there were visits, letters, and Basil's art for some of their books. And many exchanges. We miss them both.

Poems for the Weather

In Grand Haven Mallory began studying classical guitar with
Bobby, the composer in residence at TJC. Bobby had been a
student of composer Meyer Kupferman – balding, slightly rotund,
self-pitying, almost absurdly talented Bobby. He hated danger. He
hated any hint of discomfort. Yet, at his previous post, he'd made a
mess of an excellent, eminently safe academic appointment by
having a risky romance with a star-struck freshman girl.

Bobby was not the only lost soul at the school. The faculty
roster was full of people beached on this western Michigan
lakeshore by mental illness, alcoholism, or the tangles pursuant to
hiding gay sexuality as required in those times. Bobby's problem
was what? I don't know what made him blow his good life, but his
affair with the student had produced predictable consequences and
then some. He was fired from his tenure-track Eastern university
job. He went through an ugly and public divorce. There were legal
threats from the angry parents of his 18-year-old lover. The
custody battle was the worst, for he ended up losing most of his
parental rights. He was allowed to see his eight-year-old daughter
in brief strictly supervised visits only.

Mallory wasn't a substitute daughter exactly, but she was a
child, an art child, and she loved his attention. She practiced her

scales obsessively every day, and wrote her own music, enchanting him with her innate feel for variation and repetition. She also made clay sculptures and charcoal drawings that were kid versions of Basil's work, and sometimes she sold them to our houseguests for twenty-five cents each, or, ever the deal-maker, "I'll give you five for a dollar!"

I was upset about that. Money in a WASP household is almost like shit...everyone knows we do it, but no one is supposed to say anything about it. Asking our guests for money! The guests laughed, paid up, showed us, and took Mallory's work away with them when they left. Baz said leave her alone. This was healthy, he felt.

In Grand Haven Hetty began studying ballet. "Real dancing," she called it pointedly. She had never forgiven me for taking her to a dance class in Park Slope – airy fairy theater games for kids, with a lot of romping around a big room "flying" or "swimming" or pretending to be vacuum cleaners. I thought it was fine for a six-year-old. Hetty objected bitterly: "She makes us jump around in garbage bags!" Baz backed her up.

What Hetty wanted was ballet. That puzzled us both. In a "real dance class" all the students would wear black leotards and pink tights and the teacher would have a stick and smack the back of your legs if they weren't in the right position, she explained with asperity. Wherever had she learned this? I was revolted. Classical ballet! Class-bound, restrictive, sexually repressive, smug. But what to do? Hetty had black leotards and pink tights and went every week to Mrs. Baum's, who while she didn't have a stick, did have orthodox principles and a schedule that included study every summer at Sadler's Wells in London, she let everyone know.

In Grand Haven I didn't have a money job. In the mornings, when the house emptied out, I went upstairs to the typewriter on a big wooden table at the end of the bedroom. Most of the poems in my New Rivers book *Weather* were hammered out at that table, while I sweated and swore and smoked cigarettes. I wanted to use the personal for more than a personal story. I wanted to use Olson's conception that the resonance of a place is revelatory and that out of a jumble of information – personal stories, devices, connections, extensions – could come *form*. I tried to take on the place I was in: the filthy Grand River that tailed a brown plume of industrial wastewater miles out into Lake Michigan. The madcap ice floes in winter. The town dump on an arm of land that was a dump itself from the most recent Ice Age. The citizens' continual obliteration of the past, and the past's continual cryptic intrusion.

It was wicked hard going.

If adults asked me what I was doing, I'd mumble, "writing." The interrogator was usually a woman recruiting new members for a group, as women do in transitory communities like academic towns or military bases.

The next question would almost always be admiring: "A novel?"

"No," I'd say, "poems, poetry," The face would fall.

"You mean you just sit down and write a poem!" one woman blurted. It was clear to everyone who heard my answer that poems are supposed to come unbidden, in states similar to seizure or orgasm. Disbelief would wash over their faces.

It got worse from there. I didn't drive a car, I didn't play golf, I didn't play tennis, squash, croquet, bridge; I didn't sew. I didn't like tag sales. I hated shopping. I didn't even read the best sellers. I was no damn fun. So I was easy to drop, an option not open to Mallory and Hetty. If that writing of mine had just been a PhD dissertation, I would have been respected and left alone. At the very least, I would have been believed.

Baz *was* believed. He was believed by his hungry students: they wanted something to trust – and there he was, a believer in art. He threw himself into teaching. He was believed by Grand Haven townspeople, too, and soon he was believed by the TJC administration. Sooner than I would have expected, the Grand Valley bosses cheerfully ignored anything about Baz that they didn't understand because they did understand what he was doing for the school. He invented a stream of ways to energize the place: critique classes for the visual arts based on the Black Mountain model, a visiting expert program bringing artists and performers in to do demos, studio visits, and one-on-one's with students. (Baz schemed that some students would then have door-opening letters of recommendation for their postgraduate life to supplement their credentials from an unknown college). He organized bus trips to Chicago museums, to Kalamazoo (because Cage was performing there), to Ann Arbor for the library. He started an outdoor sculpture competition, he collaborated with Bobby Schectman on cross-discipline classes on music and visual art, and even offered a half-credit course on how to cook cheap food after hearing awful stories about food from students ganged together for communal living. (The final exam for that course was to invite the two of us for dinner. We ate some *very* strange meals in the name of the future.)

In the limited time that was left to him for his own painting, Baz pushed on.

The minimalists of the 1970s were serious artists upholding serious values. Conservatives of the original stripe. Large bands of others rolled giggling on the great shaggy carpet that Andy Warhol had provided. They had talent, they were art-smart and they wanted to have fun, set trends, and enjoy the very best dope. Both sides were in the art business; with loops that included audiences and sales. Baz was not. His art had to carry his personal freight or he wouldn't survive as a human. He had to subvert the formalism supporting abstraction, he had to allow dislocation. He was unmoved by the rediscovery of found objects or the lure of the computer. He was not avant-garde at all.

In Grand Haven, he painted in a high-ceilinged utility

tunnel underneath the campus lawn. The administration hadn't supplied anything for his working space – and barely enough for student use either – but he discovered a network of hallways that formed a subterranean shadow campus, connecting all the college buildings. The tunnels were punctuated by a number of large high ceilinged rooms, completely underground. A few were in use for storing furniture or supplies. The others were simply vacant. The whole network was referred to as "ventilation tunnels" by campus maintenance, and indeed there were aluminum heat and air ducts attached to the ceilings. But why the space? Were they shelter for a nuclear Armageddon? For cyclones? To defend against urban rioters? Whatever the intended purpose, Baz seized a good large room for his own. Now and then strange drafts would blow, but Baz had doors on both ends of his room that he could shut. Once in a great long while a maintenance worker would knock respectfully and walk through. Otherwise, he was, once again, a painter in a beautifully lighted cave, just as he had been in the storage loft of the Anderson Theater. There he worked. He was painting beach friezes with clouds and body forms, full of awkward sexuality.

Could the forms of Guston or Kline be his means? Should he raid the Byzantine or the Middle Ages for his compositions? His paintings remembered narrative, insisted on illusion, refused to make themselves easier or more accessible by removing contradictions.

Your work is literary, he once told me. Your poems are

good. They move in expected directions and have a lot to offer but, he said, I should be prepared for problems having my work accepted because he and I were connected.

"I trouble people," he said. "And that will keep them away from you. You'd do so much better without me."

Relief

"What are you doing here?" The voice was sculptor Ronnie Bladen's coming over the balcony railing at the Detroit Institute of Fine Arts. We'd driven all the way across Michigan for some big-city respite.

Baz stumbled for an answer. What indeed?

"I never thought I'd see you of all people involved in a tenure fight! " The voice was my academic sister Charlotte. Her visit to Grand Haven was punctured by multiple phone calls, ring, talk, ring, talk, more ring, more talk.

Baz tried to explain that he had engineered the fight because TJC's dean had tried to fire Robert vas Dias. The dean was doing a power grab conveniently aimed at a faculty member who was not very popular. After the big poetry festival Robert wasn't very popular with me either, but Baz could see an ugly future for everyone connected to the school if the dean weren't stopped. And stopped he was. Vas Dias left the next year, wisely understanding the situation and escaping the onus of being kicked out. It was harsh for him even so and he never acknowledged Baz's effort on his behalf.

"If you don't get out of here, they'll carry you out on stretcher." Ted Enslin's voice was wry and gravelly but he wasn't kidding. He'd come out to TJC the year after the festival to do a reading and workshop and had been waiting outside Baz's office for an hour while a stream of students went in carrying their problems.

Baz tried to explain. Needy kids! But Ted just shook his head. It wasn't a good enough reason.

And so at the end of our second year we did get out. Goodbye security, middleclass salary, pension fund, health insurance. Goodbye all of it. Two flares went up warning of rocks in the water, of disaster lurking. The first was a performance of *Sleeping Beauty* by the Grand Rapids Ballet. Our huge anti-ballet prejudice notwithstanding, we took the girls. Their anticipation had been building for weeks, as the "star" of Mrs. Baum's older class had a small featured part. All Mrs. Baum's students were agog. This was the city of Grand Rapids' very own professional ballet company! Watching our innocent daughters glowing and ecstatic at what we saw on that stage that night crushed us both. "We gotta get out of here," I said soon as the kids had gone to bed. "We can't let them grow up thinking that was good!"

The second flare was even clearer. It erupted at a dinner party at the dean's fancy home in Grand Rapids. After the meal, the men repaired to a large sun porch for drinks. The women were meant to stay with the dean's wife and chat in the kitchen. It really was that way. A recipe for making a super-moist cake using Campbell's Tomato Soup was the topic of the kitchen conversation. An offer of a vice presidency for Baz was the topic out on the sun porch. So Baz told me as we drove home.

"They want me to start an arts school. They want me to hit up the legislators in Lansing and the donors in Grand Rapids. I can raise the funds, they say. They want me to design the programs. They want this to become the Yale Art School of the Midwest. They want us to move to a bigger house in Grand Rapids so we can give parties. Oh yeah, a raise. We didn't discuss numbers. They said the school will underwrite a mortgage for a new house. The dean even promised they'd get me a motorcycle as a bonus."

Baz squinted into the darkness following the white line west. I was speechless, trying to take this in.

"You gotta write me a resignation letter. You gotta do it tonight, as soon as we get home," he said.

Baz wasn't drunk. Not a bit. He'd been empting his glass into a potted plant on the porch for last hour of this encounter. Out we were going to get, he insisted, and out we got. I wasn't sorry at all.

We hit Canal Street at three a.m. in an overloaded car, with two sleeping children and two intoxicated cats. The vet had prescribed tranks for Zeke and Persephone. What a mistake. For nearly all of the long drive east they'd kept up unearthly high-pitched keening.

The Brooklyn neighborhood that greeted them the following morning was pure shock for those clean Midwestern felines. The two of them took off the second the front door was opened unguarded, skedaddling down Fourth Street in a flash, and defying all our attempts to find them. I was terrified of finding a squashed corpse. But when there was no sign of them anywhere I was heartsick for the kids.

We never saw Persephone again, unless that *was* her, months later, sitting in a top floor window on the street opposite. Zeke was another story. Dawn of our third morning back big white Zeke was calmly perched on one of the backyard fence posts, majestic and dignified. How he'd found his way there since he'd exited the front of the house and all backyards of our block are encircled by row houses, I never knew, but he knew and he knew how to do it from then on. He had his turf. So did we.

We reclaimed the top part of the house and decided Baz should paint on our second floor – the "parlor floor" – the floor with the highest ceilings and the best light. It could and did do for a while.

Strauss and Other Stories from Vienna

In Grand Haven back when Hetty was eight-and-a-half and
Mallory ten we all watched a TV bio-drama on the Strauss family.
A lavish public television costume saga, with scores of extras
playing the waltzing haute bourgeois. The girls found it so exciting
we had to buy albums of Strauss music, mostly Johann the
Younger's but also nephew Richard's. The five or six installments
over as many weeks were the first adult entertainment we shared
with them. The records were played and played. Strauss was
actually a welcome break. David Cassidy, Glen Campbell, and Joni
Mitchell were their staples and we had only one family record
player.

Before this, we'd chosen harmless kid movies for family
outings: *Chitty-Chitty Bang-Bang, Yellow Submarine.* When we
watched TV with them, we accommodated to their choices: "The
Partridge Family," "The Brady Bunch," "Little House on the
Prairie," and kept, or tried to keep, our savage comments about
idiot morality to ourselves.

The Strauss drama told stories of social intrigue and
maneuvering for advantaged positions. Competition for power,
favor, fashion. I don't think the storyline was all that sophisticated
but it captured something about artists' lives. Is that what kept our

children so absorbed? had them talking to us between episodes or while the records played?

Baz and I were in Vienna in 1997. I was 60 by then. We knew no one. We came as tourists, with maps and guidebooks, to look at paintings, buildings, tropical butterflies. The Venus of Willendorf is in Vienna, and seemingly more Brueghels than anywhere else on earth. We had a five-day break between visits with a writer friend who had set up readings for us in Slovenia and more of the same through other friends in Prague, where we were scheduled to perform in the center of the Prague ex-pat world, the Terminal Bar.

We'd taken an early morning train from Ljubljana, over the Julian Alps, passing through a landscape of weird dolomite formations, jagged pillars of pale karst darkened by crazy pine trees. The scene framed by our train window had looked like Chinese scroll paintings. But as we neared Vienna, it changed to something much more familiar. Hills covered with hemlock forest, small fast mountain streams, and little holiday towns with wooden chalets. In between them, now and then, we caught glimpses of the splendid originals of big Adirondack mountain lodges in America.

In Vienna we found ourselves among buildings that embodied real and urgent battles for artistic power, more far-reaching than the skirmishes fought by rival 19th-century orchestra leaders in Strauss's day. The Secession building – to which modern architecture everywhere owes acknowledgment of ancestry – squats on a rise in fabulous white. Secession, with its use of industrial materials, its space and balance and possibility, its freedom to bring together aesthetics of East and West with neither subsuming the other or claiming orthodox certainty – Secession was built in 1896. That was before Strauss the Younger's death, and just a few years after the final ersatz-Baroque public palaces of the Hofburg were completed. We goggled at the dates. Secession 1896; the Hofburg's Museum of Natural History, 1895; the Metropolitan Museum in New York, 1880, is older. Hofburg wasn't ancient regime at all: it was a 19th-century middle-European Disneyland created to lull the middle classes. The contemporaneous Secession was thus a promise and a threat. All of them were built a bare quarter century before the Chrysler Building went up in New York City.

Competition. Contradictions. From 1884 to 1898, Otto Wagner was building a dazzlingly efficient flood-control canal, with a white and blue tiled pump house that could have sat comfortably with the austere architecture of Black Mountain College. But this was Vienna: Otto Wagner also set screaming imperial lions created by a court sculptor at the canal mouth, just beyond the locks. They stand there now, still shrieking refusal to admit Turks, Jews, Africans, Gypsies, or Hungarians. Get back down river! Never welcome here!

We took a boat ride on the canal in 1997. That season, the public greens that line the canal were decorated with large banners celebrating Vienna's culture heroes. There were portraits of all three Strausses, and Brahms, and there too were the refusés in all their cosmopolite intensity: Mahler, Freud, Schnitzler, Schoenberg, flapping away together all along the waterway.

Our daughters had been four, five, six years old when Basil's painting, the six-panel corner piece "Aldgate Narcissus," was exhibited at Judson Church and panned in *ArtNews*. When "Origins and Cycles," the five-person show Baz planned with critic G.R. Swenson, opened at NYU's Loeb Center and was not reviewed by anyone, the kids had been seven, eight, nine.

When Mallory was ten she and her sister Hetty listened while Baz and I talked. They were kids. It was natural for them to think that lack of control on our part was our fault. In Brooklyn and Manhattan they had school friends whose parents' art was shown in galleries, reviewed in glossy magazines, photographed in the *Village Voice*. They had already felt the sting of superior sympathy from these children, whose mothers or fathers won fellowships and arts council money. Their parents didn't know Basil's name. But they generally knew of each other.

One little girl's father made sealed Plexiglas boxes in which old bits of bread slowly decomposed and grew spectacular molds. Baz told Hetty this work was just as creepy as her instinct told her it was. Still, Freya's father was "famous" and Freya's mother didn't have to have a job.

Anna's dad installed strings in huge Soho loft spaces. The

photographs in art magazines were austere and glamorous, accompanied by long articles. Baz looked at the pictures and told his daughters curtly that the idea was basically boring. How could he tell them to respect conceptions so antithetical to his own? The minimalists were the winners, conserving and clarifying a glorious idealism, while Baz was alone, working dirty, struggling to permit violence, ambiguous sex, and contradictory devotions to coexist.

He had enough on his plate.

The kids were on their own to sort out what to think.

The four of us watched the Strauss story from the safety of our bourgeois house in Grand Haven. In that grand harbor on the eastern shore of great Lake Michigan, our daughters were protected by their daddy's status for the first time in their lives. He was a college professor, a position with moral authority just slightly under a minister's and far above a cop's. His bushy hair and the big beard he soon grew didn't blemish that. Nor the fact that he taught at the "experimental" college. Nor the fact that we lived in a house with no sofa, no matching dining room suite, no dishwasher, no color TV, no RV in the driveway. We were from "New York" and that was enough. The children's friends weren't the only ones who were a little awed.

Family discussions about Strauss were slantwise but intense. Money buys social advantage. That part was easy to understand. Popular art becomes appealing through fashion – and fashion influences what is popular. Why? It's a loop as seamless as a

Mobius strip. Is there an Oversoul? A temper of the time? How much is simply personal? Simply high school politics at its plainest? How much is a cultural contract, an unconscious agreement? Does art become appealing through fashion or need? Which of the two influences what is popular? "Who" or "what" tells "them" or "us" what to think?

Our daughters have eyes of almost the same color, a clear hazel, fringed with thick eyelashes, light brown on Mallory, black on Hetty. They were not guileless. They were good at deception as smart children always are, but their motives, like their gazes, were direct and without sentiment.

"Like why everyone thinks something is pretty and then they don't," one of them said.

"But it's silly to say that if something is serious then people won't like it," I inserted. "It's rarely that simple," I promised, trying to keep it simple for them.

In Vienna, we stayed in a hotel on the Graben, which turned out to be the hub of downtown nightlife. The street was blocked to traffic and every day before noon huge tents and umbrellas were opened over tables and chairs set out cheek by jowl. I figured this goes on all winter because it was already October, and patrons in hats, scarves, and overcoats, hundreds of them – teenagers, old people, middleclass professionals, art types, suburb families, nightclub groupies, all crammed under the tents. There was raucous conversation and food and drink that ranged from giant steins of beer and huge German meals, to bright little snacks and gilded desserts – a saucer with a tiny almond biscuit and a thimble glass of brandy. The Graben cafes rocked to the small hours every night we were there. Then folded like a biblical army and emptied out. At dawn only freshly scrubbed-down paving stones were left behind.

Crazy luck. I'd picked our pension from a guidebook; it turned out to be two blocks above the epicenter of the action. For the first two days it was perfect. We had a luxurious room, paneled in honey-colored wood, with a huge mirrored wardrobe, amber shaded bedside lamps, and a tiny anteroom, where one could stash wet coats and packages. The French windows overlooking the Graben faced the top of a white palace-like bank building, its lintel embellished with a large golden beehive in bas-relief. Ah self-congratulatory capitalism, where thrift and industry produce good times for the lucky.

Suddenly, on the third morning, we were evicted. Mumbo-jumbo about prior reservations from the icy-faced proprietor. We could leave now or accept what she offered us instead. The new room did have a double bed and private bath, but it was downstairs at the back, with sour plaster walls, discouraged carpets, a window on a dark interior court. There was mildew on the plastic shower curtain (upstairs the shower had a glass door) and the remains of clandestine cooking (spoiling sausages and onions) in paper bags out on the windowsill. The room smelled passingly better after I threw those out, but onus was everywhere. We only had three more days. It wasn't worth wasting a whole morning looking for another place. Oh but it rankled.

I said it was our refusal to purchase extra breakfast: the complimentary breakfast was a Spartan bowl of rolls, coffee and hot milk, while a menu for expensive breakfast goodies, waffles, omelets, hot spiced ham, was presented every morning. Baz said no: they don't like Jews.

For certain, xenophobia seemed to seep out of Viennese sidewalks. The Turks in a stall on Wienzeile, a double street with a center strip packed with food and flea-market stalls, sold us hot meatballs with reluctant suspicion. People stared at us as we rummaged the bins. Among the poor folks and students, we were wrong. Too adult? Too foreign? Too rich looking?

In St. Stephen's Cathedral a 15th century pulpit shows St. Francis stomping on the belly of a screaming Turk. This is not "our Sister Moon," this St. Francis. He's squashing his victim like a bug. In the Secession basement is Klimt's racist masterpiece "The Beethoven Frieze" which miraculously survived the bombing in 1945. War is a huge brown gorilla, thirsting for white girls. Rachel Whiteread's Holocaust memorial was under construction when we were there: it appeared to be a solid block of white stone – a book that won't open, deliberately too high to see over, too big for the public square it occupies. When finished, will it be a totally appropriate metaphor? Or will it simply fuel an underground blaze, a hateful hidden force like the fires in old coal mines that smolder deep inside mountains, year after year?

Smolder. I grew up in the 20th century in a family where people hashed over grievance and loss from the U.S. Civil War. It was a very present past. Almost half of Vienna was destroyed in World War II. It was the most bombed city in Europe. The Secession building, the Opera House, St. Stephen's Cathedral, and I don't know how many more great landmarks, are actually later 20th century reproductions, painstakingly reconstructed in the decades after 1945.

The day we walked through Secession, wigging over how much Frank Lloyd Wright learned here about space and light, a late 20th century artwork was on view in the main hall: scattered heaps of dirty rags and other garbage-dump detritus lay on the softly shining waxed concrete floor. Art like this could be found everywhere from SoHo to Tokyo. We're shit, this installation said to me, we make shit, and we leave shit around. The motto over the Secession front door translates as "The Time Our Art. The Art Our Freedom." The late 20th century taught us all something very sadly else.

In Grand Haven, father Strauss invented waltzes and the whole family went into the music business. Nineteenth century Vienna was to be modern but not new: Franz-Joseph had the medieval fortifications taken down, creating the space for the wide

Ringstrasse which was soon filled with giant backward-looking buildings. Strauss the Younger wrote "The Demolition Polka" to celebrate the knockdown and floated into history along the Blue Danube. He died younger, died before his father's younger brother who was also a composer. That Strauss died as the century ended. The wars of the 20th weren't in his life or in the TV presentation we watched in our Grand Haven.

We saw the older Strauss give way and give over, fighting and then losing first to his rival band leader, Joseph Lanner, and then, with Freudian aptness, to his own son, the younger Strauss, who attained the big fame dad had always hoped for. We watched the younger Strauss grow more frivolous and stressed; he was laboring like a TV sitcom writer to churn out the next sensation and the next. To support all that he had won. To keep from losing. He was running on coffee – running on nerve – running on cocaine. The TV program didn't actually say this last, but it didn't need to. It clearly showed that it's always easy for the Toast of the Town to burn.

The program showed nothing of angry workers, the rise of socialism, the rebellion of the Secessionists, the Vienna of Freud, Otto Wagner, Arthur Schnitzler, young Arnold Schoenberg. The program gave no hint that the Strauss family might have been, secretly, Jews. The Viennese professional classes, with ample money, education, and time, were the unquestioned center of its universe.

Yet even bleached of these issues there it was: competition for dominance, for the authority to be a maker of manners. Winners. Losers. We watched our children running difficult calculations in their heads, because the program reflected things that they had already observed and pondered.

In Grand Haven Baz and I laughed as we talked over what Poppa Strauss would need to do *now*. Baz sat in his poppa chair, one of the few pieces of furniture we'd brought from Brooklyn. The girls and I rolled on the rug and propped ourselves up on cushions, in a milieu that was by turns hilarious and repulsive, suffocating, and stabilizing.

I think that I can't keep doing this: the factors compelling response of audience to artwork are too slippery and ephemeral and, for Baz and me, sore. Competition for power, favor, fashion. How much is simply personal, and how much is basically high school politics? How much is a cultural contract, an unconscious agreement? Is there a temper of the time? Who or what tells them what to think? Art becomes appealing through fashion or need. Maybe. But only when someone says. A loop as perverse as a Mobius strip.

Studio on Hudson

Basil's studio on Hudson Avenue was a bar until Maggie decided to
sell. It had been marginal for years. Most of the neighborhood was
gone. There were empty lots of concrete chunks, automobile pieces,
broken bricks. A few lots were sketchily fenced and farmed in a rag-
bag way by long-time residents. They were Ukrainians and Serbs,
and from a distance, picking beans or tomatoes behind their
impromptu pickets, they looked like 1910 Szeged or Olgopol –
certainly not Brooklyn, 1976.

Famous Hudson Avenue. Infamous Hudson Avenue. It
runs only six blocks, from the river around the Brooklyn Navy Yard
to Myrtle Avenue, but it ran 24/7 while World War II was on,
serving anything money-flush shipyard workers might want who
were away from home and working every shift they could handle.
The street housed a Chinese-menu of whorehouses, bars, and flops
for many inclinations. W.H. Auden once called it paradise. The
old-time residents remembered. Like Maggie, the older people in
the neighborhood were remnants, holdouts.

In the 1950s Con Edison had moved in, building a huge red
brick generating plant with two tower-like smokestacks. Con Ed
had five or six city blocks enclosed in chain-link and filled to the
edge with humming energy-storage installations. In the blocks

beyond, the odd remaining houses stood in between vacant spaces like the odd teeth surviving in the mouth of one of Maggie's old boarders.

Had she waited too long? She had to sell now. There was desperation in her white-blue eyes, but she was unaware of her tell. There was peasant smugness in her manner as she offered Baz vodka, confident that drink or guile would bamboozle him. She filled his glass and confided her assessments of the reasons for ruin in the world. "Joos and niggahs, dey got everything. Dey work togetah," she said. She included Baz in the safe haven her knowledge could provide, sure that this would convince him that her interests were his.

"$40,000, for you," she said with a sly smile.

"Too much," Baz said, sipping thoughtfully and letting his glance stray away, out the smeary window. He needed a long hot shower after these meetings.

Still he'd decide to go back. One more try. We had a partner in this enterprise, so the financial burden of buying a building was shared. And we were no longer housing Basil's parents in the garden apartment of 4th Street. We'd managed to move them to an old-age residence in Long Beach, where we hoped the services would be better for them. They'd become ingrown and frail during our Grand Haven time. Despite some household help, they weren't keeping up and Esther in particular almost never left the apartment. A more feasible, more reasonable solution was for us to take over Baz's studio floor plus his parents' ground floor for our living, create a rental on the top two floors, and find Baz studio space elsewhere. Added income would float music and dance lessons for the girls as well as cover monthly studio rent.

In the late 1970s, much of Brooklyn waterfront was a ruin, a mix of ancient manufacturing lofts, small commercial buildings, and very plain working-class row houses with ground floor storefronts. Many were long deserted. The property should be cheap, and from Baz's point of view it was suitable being right at the East River edge of Brooklyn. It should be relatively easy to persuade Manhattanites to come over for a studio visit. No long trip into what was then Brooklyn's terra incognita would be involved. It was also a quick drive from our house on 4th Street. So Maggie's building had advantages it was hard to give up on. But it was hard for Maggie to give up too. Her dream of riches made her lips moist and her eyes tiny.

It was Maggie's daughter who intervened.

Baz heard her yelling as he came up the stairs: "F'crissakes, ma. The guy's offerin you twenny-two grand for this fallin' down dump. You count yer blessings!"

The ground floor bar had long been shuttered and the space that would be Basil's studio waited for us to cart out the splintered bar stools, rusted mirrors, cabinets, shelves. We had to kill the roaches, trap the mice. With the bar gone there were great holes in the floor and cutouts along two walls.

Baz called Greg and Greg called Richard. Both of them were recent graduates of TJC, now living in New York. Greg was a good carpenter and Richard knew classic cabinetmaking from his dad. Together, they fitted in new floor planks. They built free-standing rolling easels big enough for twelve-foot canvases and rolling walls for drawings, and rows of storage racks squeezed into the back hall by the bathroom. Neighbors who came by to watch leaked Maggie's story out in increments.

Maggie hadn't run the bar, not Maggie. She was much too dumb, her neighbors said. She closed it up the week her husband died. It was the husband who did business, ran the cribs upstairs, and the after-hours crap games. Nostalgia for crimes that no longer paid colored their rosy recollections. Under Maggie the place was a nothing. She should have sold years ago. Instead she boarded pensioners. Baz had seen them in the building, furtive men, who hunched defensively when Baz passed them on the stairs. Maggie told Baz they wouldn't be left behind and they wouldn't be out on the street.

"Dey come with me," she grinned. "I take care of dem."

We learned indeed she did. They had to endorse their pension checks to her every month. She used to hit them. She took their extra boots and overcoats and sold them. She dosed them with etherated wine and rotgut vodka. They were desperate.

There had been a fourth boarder who had died, and after that the surviving three began to talk. The neighbors said they planned to run away together, hoping they could make it if they stuck together.

The truth was Maggie needed to sell so she could buy a building with just one front door, not a common hallway with exits back and front like this one. Everyone in the neighborhood knew that. The back exit that had been an advantage in the days of police raids was now a terrible detriment. She wasn't as fast on her feet as she had been. Her meal tickets were trying to run away so she needed a bedroom and kitchen on the ground floor – and a gate. She needed to hold the only key to it.

We already owned the building by this time we heard all this and Baz and I only half-wanted to know more. Even so, news came in drips over the months. Maggie had taken her sale money and bought another house three blocks away, but the move had upset everything. Maggie was sick. Sick with worry. Sick with illness. The men did run away. They were drunk down by the base of the Brooklyn Bridge. Maggie said the men had stolen money from her and called the police. The priest came. Maggie was furious. The social worker came wanting to know what was happening to the men's checks. Maggie was sick. A neighbor who had owned the house that Maggie bought got angry about payments he claimed Maggie owed. People took sides on who was telling the truth. Maggie went to the hospital. The priest paid visits all around. We heard that Maggie blamed Baz saying he had tricked her and she should never have sold. One of the men was sent to a shelter. He came back in a few days and wanted to go home to Maggie's house, but Maggie was just back from the hospital and wouldn't let him in. He cried on her front steps and wet his pants, and banged the door, and this went on all night until more cops and social workers came in the morning. Then we heard that Maggie died. Baz and I shivered.

Remember the faces in the Shoah documentary screaming "Goodbye Jews"? That was Maggie.

The work to make 50 Hudson Avenue usable was grim. And expensive. We had to rent a dumpster, and pay to have the dumpster hauled away. Con Ed first demanded a huge commercial-rate deposit for utilities. We had to get the building "unzoned" as a bar. Fees. Then there was neighborhood talk about "insurance" for the plate-glass windows. It was that kind of area. Baz managed to get it across that he was not re-opening the bar. The space would be a simple workshop. He didn't use the words artist or studio even though there were a few other artists nearby, because, he told me, the neighbors would come over to see his models and he'd never hear the end of it.

The building needed new stairs, new plaster ceilings, new framing for the windows. Our results, like our finances, were timid and raw, even though the space heater worked. Riverdamp seeped up from the basement, and harbor wind shook the windows, easily defeating the insulating felt I'd stapled along the edges of all the windows and doors.

We could paint it. We bought lots of paint. Paint abolished the roach and dead-mouse smell, and light that had been sucked up to nothing by the tobacco colored walls and blackened ceilings poured into the space. Two big windows were clear again, after hot water and vinegar scrubbings. Baz sprayed them with white paint to diffuse the sun and keep the neighbors from staring in. When the result proved to be too transparent he fastened paper across them, photographer's transparent backdrop paper, like tracing paper but stiffer. Baz got a huge roll of it from a photographer friend. The light was turned pearly-gray, even the slanting afternoon light from the west side windows.

The plate-glass panels were flush to the outside of the building. Inside there were deep cutaways, paneled with tongue-in-groove board. They formed wide windowsills ample enough to sit on all along the north and west sides. In time, these sills filled with studio life. They were stage sets for the things artists keep and play with. Rocks. Tools. Odd bits of wood. Toy figures, little cars, postcards, art books with paper markers stuck in them. Jars, lots of jars. In some jars there were wood screws or stretcher keys. In others black or white pebbles we collected visiting friends on Shelter Island and the Hamptons.

In one long row of jars, there were sticks from Basil's walks in Prospect Park. He was drawing and painting leafless winter trees, trees with limbs chopped back, and young trees, and tree trunks. He walked in the park a lot, and took some photographs. Then he painted "The HA in Prospect Park" – almost as big as his rolling wall – and showed me a place in the park where a grove of trees really did make huge letters, H,V, N, A. (The HA he reminded me, Jane Austen's *Mansefield Park*? I hadn't got it. Nor had any of his friends.)

He did more than a hundred drawings for "The HA," in colored pencils, ballpoint pen, red ink, pastels, oil crayons. When he finished the big "HA" painting our friend Louise, George Ault's widow, came over to see them and said, "Baz, you're free."

Up the street, another bar had survived. It didn't need a neighbor-hood of drinkers to sustain it. Pimpmobiles made regular stops there, late morning, usually. Once, while I waited with Baz for our lunchtime beer and sandwiches, I saw a guy in the back pull an enormous ball of bills from his pocket. It was so large it was hard to imagine how he held onto it with just one hand. But he did, using the other hand to peel away a few leaves for the person standing in front of him. Baz gave me a nudge to stop me staring.

Men from this bar did begin visiting the studio. Not to ogle models but to offer Baz deals. New radial tires, $40 each? Alpaca topcoat, $75? Baz made them stop with a beautiful coup. He'd sold a painting to a woman whose boyfriend was a big Long Island potato dealer. The boyfriend liked the painting and liked Baz and me and when the painting was being delivered, he drove over and unceremoniously dumped a hundred-pound sack of prime Long Island baking potatoes in the back of our little station wagon. Back in Brooklyn Baz got the bag up on his shoulder, walked up the block to the mob bar, and just as unceremoniously laid the sack on the bar. "Thought you guys could use these."

Was it ever a good studio? Yes, very, and no, not really. It was never fixed; it was always damp, always cold in winter; always a bit small. It grew smaller as new paintings filled the racks and took up space along the walls. The distance between this studio and the world at large was just as huge as it appeared to be.

Was it ever a good studio? Baz worked there for more than eight years. And moved his vocabulary, extended his form. He painted his loving farewell to Paul Blackburn in "Paul and Joan" placing the two of them in the unicorn's scarlet circle. He began his work on baseball players, relying on an old friend who had become a photo editor for *Newsweek* to send him outtakes of marvelous baseball photos. He did a magnificently fucked up portrait of Edward Hopper, with grass and pigeons, called "The Painter in the Park" – and he did many trees. He tentatively began on the playing cards again. He had first drawn playing cards in San Francisco when he was friendly with Jack Spicer and had just met me.

On Hudson Avenue, we also produced studio shows of Basil's work. Together we put up paintings, printed invitations, and hosted openings. The shows were "Winter Trees," "The HA in Prospect Park" which featured a huge wall of his many studies and variations, and "Paul and Joan." And when my first book of poems, *Weather,* came out, and New Rivers Press, the publisher, had in the meantime moved itself to Minneapolis, we hosted the book launch there, with Basil's work on the walls and piles of books for me to sign and sell. We were delighted that so many friends made the trek out to what was still, in 1978, the strange and faraway borough of Brooklyn.

Was it ever a good studio? There was a partner in the building as ownership on our own was out of our financial range, a partner who shared half the contract, the down payment, the plans for maintenance and repairs. The building had two floors above the former bar, and the partner tore out the walls and ceiling of his space on the top floor but only fitfully began the work of creating a useable place up there. The plan had been to renovate the floor in between and rent it for building maintenance money. But the partners' basic intentions were at odds. Baz needed a studio for work. The partner wanted – what? At that time, his conflicts kept him in limbo. He always had dream projects. The stream of dreams flowed on and on. He was going to open an after-hours jazz club. Have a bookbindery. Do photography. Make space for his enormous collections of books and records. Later, in the cruel light of hindsight, Baz recognized that the partner had wanted Baz to help him have a purpose. One night the partner stared angrily across a barroom table and said, "The day you hammered your last nail and started painting, you forgot about me."

Eventually the partner locked his top floor, leaving a broken window. He refused Baz's request to let him go up there and board it up. A pipe froze and split and water streamed down through the floors above, staining 38 of Basil's oils. Several stacks of works on paper were reduced to mush. We couldn't even count them. The dirty water also dissolved the already broken partnership. The building was sold; we paid back money we'd borrowed to buy our share, and Baz made a deal with the new owner so he could stay on as a tenant until he could find new studio space.

Our panic about the flooding never subsided. For almost a year, until Baz moved out, we got in the car and drove by Hudson Avenue every single night. Stop. Listen. Any running water sound? Anything odd? Then we'd go home to bed.

Was it ever a good studio? Pearl-grey light flooded the two sides, and the hum of the city across the river was very far away. There are many things people can do in a quiet place, if there are books, and paper. If they can take their time. If they can move an arm across the body and out, so that what is in the chest extends itself out through the fingernail tips. If there are sticks held upright in glass bottles or in dabs of clay, springing along the windowsills, with grey-blue shadows crisscrossing on the white boards. Thus *17 Walking Sticks,* a book of 17 poems by Martha King facing 17 drawings by Basil King. It was published in 1997 by Basil's cousin Malcolm Wiseman in London; his daughter Eva named his venture Stop Press.

The Man Who Wasn't There

As I was going down the stair
I met a man who wasn't there
He wasn't there again today
I wish to God he'd go away

If you look for Basil King in the 1950s, 60s, even the 70s, you won't find him. Records of Black Mountain College, San Francisco Renaissance, Cedar Bar, the Beat world? No Baz. Though he was there and contributed to and was formed by it. You could encounter him in print in 1971, when he and David Glotzer and Harry Lewis began publishing *Mulch* magazine but even then you might not have noticed what his role was.

The cover of *Mulch* number one (1971) was his charcoal portrait of William Carlos Blackburn, age 18 months, son of Paul and Joan. That first issue also has Basil's essay on the common pigeon, and a group of pigeon photographs which he took in Central Park and – on one extremely cold day – lying belly down on the pigeon-shitted paving stones of the small triangle just behind the Cooper Union Founder's Hall. Hettie Jones thawed him out in her Cooper Square apartment with many cups of hot tea. This was the beginning of his interest in those city birds. To formulate that first little piece, he'd made an appointment at the Museum of

Natural History and spoken to an ornithologist. He wanted to find out why his research had turned up so little about the European rock dove once it became the whole world's city pigeon.

Politics, the ornithologist told him. Politics had squashed research. Pigeons have powerful partisans. He told Baz some fascinating stories about thwarted municipal efforts at pigeon removal. It seems those birds can home like nobody's business.

In the photographs and the essay for *Mulch* #1 lay the seed for many bird-themed art works to come. The sturdy, adaptable, filthy, beautiful, ugly, ubiquitous city pigeon became a kind of guardian for Baz, a totem perhaps, a continually unfolding image, right up to today.

In later issues of *Mulch* Baz wrote brief takes on George Jackson, author of *Soul on Ice*; Spam (the food); Fred Astaire; deChirico's self forgeries. "Spam" was one of his favorite pieces. "I love Spam" it starts. He really *does* love Spam. Fried and on toast with mustard, just as it was served when he was a small boy and Spam arrived in wartime England in magic packages from his American relatives in Detroit.

The first issue of *Mulch* came out in 1971 just before we moved to Michigan and the last, number 8/9, was completed in 1976 well after we'd returned to Brooklyn.

At the magazine's editorial meetings, at our house on 4th Street, in Grand Haven, or up in Northampton, Massachusetts, where Harry and David moved after we left for Michigan, Harry and David would argue for hours, outdoing each other with outrageous positions. Baz would let them. After hours and hours, the two would think they had discovered what to do, and Baz would let them. Even editorially he was often the man who wasn't there.

Despite his camouflage, a few people knew better. When Allen Ginsberg visited Thomas Jefferson and stayed with us in Grand Haven he had a bead on it. "Let the kids do the work," he advised Baz, immediately spotting the socialist-egalitarian conflicts that were part of Baz's reticence. He gave Baz quite a lecture on the importance of self-promotion. Lack of a record will lead to lack of a record! Allen warned prophetically.

While we were in Grand Haven Baz made a foray into poetry. "The Ballad of Henry Moore" was a long, loopy, intensely uneven poem, chock full of Baz's early Shakespeare education, his surrealism, love of juxtapositions, and uncanny talent for propulsive lyric narrative. He pecked it out on a beautiful old Underwood office standard manual, old even at that time. This typewriter sat on the dark green tin desk we got in a Michigan junk store on the sun porch of our Grand Haven house. Electric typewriters responded way too quickly. His spastic right hand would inadvertently hit a key and a dozen letters would machinegun across the page. Suburban pleasures ours for the first time in Grand Haven: sun porch, play room, station wagon, washing machine! I was upstairs, with the fancy electric typewriter on a big wooden table. I had no trouble controlling the keyboard, but I struggled to write far less ambitious poems.

Baz worked on "Henry Moore" for months. Then he sent copies out to writers we knew who were just coming into reputations, writers who edited magazines or anthologies and many of whom knew each other. He got a massive response. I understood their enthusiasm all too well because I felt it too: "Henry Moore" made me wildly eager to give Baz editorial directions.

This was Baz back then: instead of relishing the attention, he fumed. "They all want to edit me!" He must have been deeply terrified. He might be eaten, demolished, turned into something he wasn't – or excoriated for resisting. As he saw it in those days, there was no middle way. There was no steady floor. It was better to be in the rowboat all alone, on an unpredictable sea, where he wouldn't have to answer to anything but those things he knew to be essential. He told this to nobody, not even me. He left all the Moore letters unanswered, and the poem unfinished. None of it was ever published. He wasn't there.

Harry and David published their poetry in some of the transient small press magazines and chapbooks of the day. I began publishing my poems too. Harry made sure I was included in *The Pioneer Valley Advocate* – an alternative newspaper still distributed around Northampton. And *Mulch* published me: book reviews of Doris Lessing and of Kenneth Koch, and a long Olson-esque piece I wrote in Michigan called "Batchawana Bay –

Michilimackinac." But except for his brief prefatory essays, cover art on three issues, and drawings or photographs here and there, there was not much obvious Baz in *Mulch* magazine although the concept was his, the direction was his, the mix of subjects and disciplines all encouraged by him.

There is even less about Baz in earlier records. Not a single photograph by Fred McDarrah, the tireless chronicler of the Cedar Bar, shows Baz in the middle 1950s. "I ran into the bathroom whenever he came in with that camera."

Baz isn't in the annals of The Club if there are any annals though certain meetings of those sometime riotous artists meetings in downtown New York in the early 50s, are vivid in his mind.

As for the Olson archives at the University of Connecticut at Storrs, there's not much on Baz we've been told. Apparently Black Mountain faculty reports on him are cryptic and incon-clusive. To a person, they responded to the puzzle he presented by refraining from saying too much. He had been a mercurial, sometimes self-destructive unclassifiable boy – 16 when he arrived, and just over 21 when the college closed.

And it goes on.

Baz wasn't in a big 2005 exhibition in San Francisco celebrating the San Francisco Renaissance 1956-1976 which fostered so many extensive collaborations between painters and poets. He had been there for part of that time but the drawing of a Hebrew letter Baz gave to David Meltzer, vividly remembered by them both, could not be found. David had packed many possessions away when he sold his house and the Hebrew letter drawing never resurfaced. And the sexy red-ball tomatoes, oil paint on paper, whatever happened to them? Baz did them soon after he moved in with me on Fillmore Street in San Francisco. Were they as good as I remember? I remember how Michael Rumaker laughed, scandalized, when he came over one night – and Baz thinks Mike took one or two of them home with him but Mike doesn't remember.

Baz's first use of playing card images, which he has continued through a lifetime, was sparked by conversations with Jack Spicer. He did a series of face card drawings in black ink for John Wieners' magazine *Measure.* He gave them to John but the issue was never published. We all left California soon thereafter, John to Boston and later Buffalo, us to New York City. The drawings ended up in the keeping of Joe Dunn (then publisher of White Rabbit Press) who preserved them "for a long time" he told us, until, well, they were lost in the course of Joe's travails.

Shortly before I met Baz in San Francisco, Leo Krikorian put up an exhibition of Basil's drawings at The Place, the art bar that was a center of North Beach life. About twenty of them, Baz recalls, pinned to the walls. Did anyone take a photograph?

Baz isn't mentioned in Mary Emma Harris's book, *The Arts at Black Mountain College,* (1987, reissued in 2002), although after he protested a fine small oil of his was included in the exhibition she curated at Bard College in 1987. It was also hung at the Grey Gallery at New York University in 1988 when the show was mounted there.

Baz's name appears just two or three times in Fielding Dawson's autobiographical *The Black Mountain Book* (1970, revised 1991) but there's not enough supporting detail to give a sense of him. For example, Fee writes about the fire at the school that burned down Joe Fiore's house and almost killed Joe when he ran into the burning house trying to save some of his paintings. Fee notes that Baz "had been in the London Blitz" to explain the rescue Baz accomplished. He soaked a blanket, put it over his head, ran into the fire, and dragged Joe down the stairs to safety. You'd never know from Fee's book that Baz was four years old during the London Blitz.

You certainly don't get that Baz and Fee were roommates during Baz's first year at BMC either, although it was there that the two began a lifelong relationship of great complexity. Fielding wrote *The Black Mountain Book* to address his fathers, not phantom sibs, rivals, or boy loves. More recently, Baz makes only the briefest appearance in Michael Rumaker's *Black Mountain Days* (2003). Michael's book is about Michael, just as Fee's Black Mountain books are about Fee.

Some major museum exhibitions on the arts at Black Mountain College since the new century started have not included him, sometimes despite a big push from people who expected to be influential. In England, the poet and critic Andrew Crozier, known for his deep interest in things Black Mountain and their relation to poetry in England, nearly stood on his head to have Baz's work included in a Black Mountain show organized in Bristol that ended its run at the Kettle Yard in Cambridge. That experience made Andrew call Baz "The man who wasn't there." He planned to write a major essay on Baz and his work and, loving irony as he did, told us he would use that very title. It was not to be, horribly. Andrew was overcome by the brain tumor that took his life in 2008.

"Untranslatable. Missing section," as Armand Schwerner liked to put it.

Vincent Katz's 2002 exhibition of Black Mountain arts in Madrid is one brilliant exception. Baz's works were on the walls of the Reina Sophia in Spain and two of his paintings are finely reproduced in Katz's catalog, *Black Mountain College: Experiment in Art*. But even there, Baz was a late inclusion. His name had not been on Vincent's initial lists. Given the history that was available to Vincent as he prepared the exhibition in 2001 it's not surprising.

History belongs, as I like to insist, to the person who writes it down. Whether the writer takes Herodotus' or Thucydides' approach hardly matters. Though I'm still on Olson's side there, preferring the old gossip's take to the objective scientist's.

The Man Who Wasn't There, Part Two
The Martin Duberman Interviews

In 2000, we packed up all our belongings so we could renovate our Brooklyn house. I consigned a large number of materials to cardboard file boxes marked "Archives," which I stuffed and sealed up. Correspondence between us Kings and the historian Martin Duberman is in there, along with audiotapes of two interviews we had with him. When I began to write these memoirs, I did not open them.

Here's what I remember: It was late summer or early fall 1970 when Fielding Dawson told Baz that an historian named Martin Duberman was interviewing former Black Mountain students for a history of the school. Fee had had several long sessions with him and he was upset to learn that Duberman had not contacted Baz. He'd given Duberman our phone number the year before. Further, Fee felt Baz should be "on the record." So much so that he gave Baz Duberman's phone number and insisted that Baz contact *him*. Which Baz did.

Two interviews took place in our house in Brooklyn, the second of which included me. That one might have been on a Saturday, as I think our kids were at home, upstairs. I remember it was afternoon, and rainy. It was definitely fall, because it got dark in the living room as we talked on and on. I remember Duberman got a hard-on. I thought that meant he'd fallen in love with us, and perhaps it did. I remember watching from a third floor window, in what was then our living room, as he walked away down 4th Street in the failing light using his umbrella as a walking stick and lugging a case, heavy with tape recorder and reels.

He was small, wiry, somewhat intense, a predictable enough academic intellectual, properly dressed in suit trousers and a jacket, with glasses, but without a necktie and with longish hair curling down his collar. The hair and the tieless-ness were major gestures of bohemian sympathy in those days.

We were novice interviewees and we were flattered by fairly standard interview techniques such as claiming ignorance about events: "Oh, I haven't heard anything about that. Tell me more." We are also assured by his repeated offers of editorial control: "It's all confidential. If there's anything you don't like about it, we'll just take it out."

Duberman promised both of us so persuasively that we forgot the first rule of testimony, of any interrogation, however benign: There is no unsaying of anything. Nothing can be erased from memory by the promise of the questioner or the stern request of a judge. We also ignored the second rule of testimony: an interviewer may use any technique (even shaving the truth) to get corroboration of material. The interviewer's debt is to the record not to the individual informant.

"This has been a truly gratifying interview," Duberman gushed after the first session, saying that Baz had been clearer than anyone he'd spoken too. He was very frank about how writing the concluding chapter had been troubling him. Then he spilled the beans about his experiences with other former students: "You can't believe how difficult some of this has been." Fielding had cried. Victor Kalos had cried. Joel Oppenheimer had cried. Eric Weinberger had seemed close to breakdown. Dan Rice had been angry. Gerry van de Wiele, had he cried too? Was all this true or was Duberman milking? At the time, Baz believed it totally. Fee had already confirmed his part. "I cried like a baby," he told the two of us. I thought Fee sounded as if he wanted Baz "on record" the way a priest urges confession on a wavering sinner. He, Fee, had gone through it. Baz would find it liberating.

A second interview to include me was arranged.

It wasn't as much liberating as it was exciting, at least for me. I found myself formulating words for what I thought – and recognizing what I knew at the moment of saying it. It was almost like writing. I was being questioned about myself, but in a gentle haze of total acceptance, not inquisition. I didn't sense an axe being ground. I felt Duberman actually wanted to know what *I* had to say, which was something that almost never happened to me back then.

But afterwards, thinking about what we had told, we were both more than uncomfortable. How much we had said about other people's behavior! We had discussed events that compromised others. Baz realized too late that it wasn't up to him to go on record speculating about other people's motives or allowing his own emotions, his talent for ecstasy, to paint such dramatic pictures.

It's now many years later, many people have died, and the history of Black Mountain is still sorting itself out, as histories do. I think it's always better not to think in absolutes like "truth" but Baz and I have always had queasy feelings about comments in those interviews that we never should have made. Back in 1971, we nervously awaited the promised typed transcripts when we could trim the comments and black out what we shouldn't have discussed.

The transcripts didn't come. Months went by. Then something else did. Duberman sent Baz several short stories. They were submissions for publication in *Mulch* magazine. The first *Mulch* was published in April, 1971. We were interviewed by Duberman in late fall, 1970. So the interval was already over four months.

There they were, a group of short stories in a yellow clasp envelope, and Baz, with his co-editors Harry Lewis and David Glotzer unanimously decided not to accept them. I remember reading them too, though I wasn't part of the editorial trio. The decision to reject wasn't made on the basis of the homosexual subject material. The stories were stiff, self-conscious, and despite the authorial assumption, neither exotic nor actually illuminating. We'd all read Trocchi, Burroughs, Selby. Banal, said David or Harry. Like I'm going to be bowled over in shock by gay sex, said

Harry or David. Agreed! said Baz. Don't publish, said all three. I thought the stories read as if their main reason for being was to expose Duberman's sex life. Perhaps I was right.

Homosexuality seemed a non-issue to people like us – though not to respectable American college professors with public reputations to protect. The matter was fraught. See any cultural history of the 1970s that discusses public attitudes toward homosexuality. See also our casual use of the term "fag" in our interviews. We were all wrong to assume we knew what this meant to Duberman. But we were right about the stories.

Without access to the *Mulch* archives, which are gone altogether or split up between Harry and David, I can't be sure who actually wrote the rejection letter but I doubt that it was Baz. If he'd written it, I probably would have typed it, and I think I'd remember. Was the letter signed on behalf of all three of them? Probably. Whoever signed, the letter certainly wasn't drenched in diplomacy. Immediately upon receipt Duberman telephoned Baz in a roaring rage to say how angry he was that his stories had been returned – and with such a disrespectful letter. "You will regret it," he promised.

You don't want to put Baz up against the wall. You especially don't want to accuse him of doing something he didn't do. This man is the seven-year-old boy who had let himself stay locked in a dark closet for a day and a half rather than give his grown-up tormenters the false confession they demanded. He kicked back at Duberman, I'm sure of that. If Duberman expected conciliation, either then or later, he miscalculated. Would Duberman be as angry and vindictive as he threatened to be?

More time passed. Now we weren't surprised that the promised transcripts didn't show up. Now, we worried even more about our indiscretions being in Duberman's hands. Finally, Baz telephoned him, not about the stories or the letter but about the interview transcripts. He told Baz that transcripts had never been made. It was too expensive. He'd run out of funds. We'd simply have to trust him. It wasn't a very pleasant conversation, Baz told me, and I had the feeling he softened what he said about the conversation for my benefit.

So we were hostage – or our interviews were. The book would be published and Baz and I would be shamed. We were frantic. Couldn't we do something to protect ourselves? Together he and I composed a formal but hostile letter in which we asked him to give us the tapes themselves since there were no transcripts for us to edit. Our letter told Duberman that he did not have our permission to quote from or use any information we had given him in our interviews. Period. A short time later he sent us tapes (we didn't destroy them; I have them in that box) with a brief formal note assuring us that our names would not be mentioned.

And, indeed, our names don't appear anywhere in *Black Mountain: A Exploration in Community*, New York: E. P. Dutton &Co., 1972. It was as if both of us were never there.

But when we read the book in 1972, we found a number of things we'd said in the text. "A resident said." "The tale is told about." "One student mentioned." And so on. We knew we were burnt. Beyond the specific stories, we found *our* interpretations of what that small gang of life-raft passengers had been doing, going through, and thinking in the final trying period of Black Mountain. The poison and the poetry of it. Some of it was even recast in Duberman's voice. We were betrayers and we had been betrayed.

Does this matter today? Duberman remains the most distinguished historian who has taken on the story of Black Mountain College to date. What does our absence in his text mean? What is he inclined to say or imply if he is asked about either of us?

Re-reading it, I think the final section of the book is not nearly as unsavory or intrusive as I thought in 1972. Compared to earlier sections where Duberman takes crazy liberties with history (inserting what *he* would have said had he been present at a critical student/faculty meeting, for example) the final section is mostly poignant.

When the book was published, there was general annoyance among Black Mountain people that the history of the school had been used as Duberman's vehicle for coming out – Baz remembers Robert Duncan telling him in a fury, in Michigan, in 1973, "If we were different people, we'd sue!" But that too has softened with time and the easing of popular anti-gay prejudice.

It now seems both more trivial and a great deal sadder than it did to me in the 1970s. Until very recently what struck me most about the Duberman debacle is that one more time Basil King is the man who wasn't there. Never mind that he's absent from this particular text by our choice. Baz might well have been absent in any event. It's fair to restate that Baz had to make the contact to initiate Duberman's interviews. If he hadn't done so, Baz (and I) might have been absent anyway. Duberman had been talking to people for two or three years before he showed up at our house on 4th Street with that tape recorder. Apparently no one, except belatedly, Fielding, had even suggested that Duberman speak to Baz. My absence is actually normal: I had been at the school only three summer months.

We both remember Duberman saying that he'd already written almost all of the book but was having trouble pulling the final section together – the period when Black Mountain fell apart forever. Our interviews would never have happened if Duberman hadn't been having these problems. He told us he was way past his deadline. He said the front of the book was already in galleys and his editor was becoming angry.

There is a kicker. Two kickers in fact. The first came many years later, in October 2001. We received a package containing two copies each of two typed transcripts, the transcripts that Duberman told us didn't exist. One is marked: *with Basil King (October 25,*

1970) and the other *with Basil and Martha King (November 15, 1970).* The pages are covered with working notes and underlining in handwriting. The copies were sent to us by a North Carolina State archivist. The official asked us to verify the transcripts, and to sign two different releases. The first would make the material available to researchers. The second would assign copyright to North Carolina's official archive. I never answered. Everything felt tainted. I stuck the package in a closet, stuck as to what to do.

The second kicker came much more recently. Our old friend and fellow Black Mountain student Gerry van de Wiele was invited to the opening of the big Black Mountain show, "Leap Before You Look" at the Institute of Contemporary Art in Boston in the fall of 2015. He'd been asked to lend a few drawings to the show. While there, he looked throughout, expecting to see Baz's work. Although Baz had been recommended for inclusion, especially by the Black Mountain College Museum in Asheville, he had been passed over. Gerry was incensed – rare for him – and he cornered one of the curators to protest. After all, he said, Baz has been working steadily for six decades and is continuing to do amazing new art. The curator did some hemming and hawing, and finally offered, "Basil King is not documented." He explained that Basil King is not mentioned in Martin Duberman's 1972 history.

It had never occurred to either of us that this omission might mean so much. Gerry's story spurred us to retrieve and finally review those transcripts. We saw we had been correct all those years ago. There *were* passages of inappropriate comment and speculation. And we saw again the many promises by Duberman: "I'll have it all typed up. I always do. And I'll send you the typescript – and the tape too, if you want it. So it's all confidential. If there's anything you don't like about it, we'll just take it out. And I won't – even if you send the typescript back and say it's okay, I'll still check with you. Before I use [two voices overlapping on the tape]."

Eerily, a few sections we would have redacted had we been able to do so, are X'd out in what we guess is Duberman's hand. But others, that we also would have removed, turn up in his narrative. And now, reading back and forth between our interviews and Duberman's text, I've come to suspect that rejecting the short stories, however ugly that incident was, might not be the real reason for his reluctance to keep his promises. Our two interviews gave him the substance, the approach, and many rich supporting details for writing up what I've called the poison and the poetry of Black Mountain's last days.

Where else could Duberman have learned about how Baz and Joe Dunn – longing for city streets and sick of the rampant green – spent a long night painting trees, leaves, and grass white? Or about Robert Creeley's attempt to grow marijuana that left two circles of burnt earth in the grasses just uphill from the Studies Building? And all the specifics of how impoverished students shoplifted at the Black Mountain A&P? This surely comes from comments we both made. We admired the anti-establishment attitudes of the local mountain women who clerked at the store and never blew the whistle on us.

More serious, and more deserving of excision, were comments about Robert Creeley and Dan Rice. In the transcript, Baz calls them "lovers," citing their "intense mixing of emotions and intelligence." The description of Creeley's problems teaching a writing class could have been directly damaging to him in the 1970s. We would certainly have X'd that out. The discussion of the respect the Black Mountain ethic placed on volatility (Duberman's word) or madness (mine and Baz's) and its role in creating art might have been developed without our comments, but we did not want to be named making those judgments. My point is if we had reviewed the transcripts at the time, we might have redacted material Duberman needed. Everyone who has ever used interviews as source material knows why he was tempted.

Over the years, "the man who wasn't there" anonymity has acquired a life of its own not simply supported by Basil's need to protect himself. In the intervening decades, how many other curators, critics, historians, gallery dealers have been as influenced as the ICA curators were so recently?

What happens now when the subject of Basil and Martha King comes up? Suppose Duberman opens a magazine and sees an article about us? This happened in the fall 2015 issue of *A Public Space* magazine though nothing about Duberman was included in that excerpt from my memoir. But suppose it is this book? Suppose, on the other hand, I open the *New York Times* tomorrow to read his obituary? It can be damned hard to distinguish what matters a little from what matters a great deal.

Money Again

Artists don't need money. Artists are true believers; they starve in garrets. Didn't they? Don't they? Artists die young of drugs, alcohol, AIDS. Or plague. Or TB. Or sphyllis. Artists, if they are any good, become so easily and quickly rich, they wallow in money, and laugh at it. They forget to cash their checks, but they don't forget to be easy with their buyers.

Here is the brilliant daughter of working poor Brooklyn. She's a criminal lawyer. She was sent all the way through law school gratis by the neighborhood mob and now she's repaying the debt with a wicked record of court-room wins that free big-time drug suspects in New York and Miami. She's skinny and detail crazy. She's also warm, direct, a dynamo of energy. Even when she uses her most Harvard voice there's always a trace of Bensonhurst in it, the drive and throb of someone who never forgets her past, who can use it to wring your heart. She thrives on strategy. She tells Baz how she retains a clinical psychologist to help her frame her court appearances. Everything, the clothes she and her client wear, their body language, the buzz words she'll employ, is prepared, trimmed and cooked to get her to her goal. Baz loves talking to her.

So she comes to the studio and buys a painting he did when we lived in Michigan. It's a beach scene painted as a long horizontal frieze of bathing figures merging in and out of blue clouds. It'll look wonderful in her big condo in Florida, where she lives much of the time she says. She wants it; she's buying it. Italians don't need to explain their taste in art, whether it's bathtub madonnas or Georgiones.

"So how do you want to get paid," she asks Baz. "Is cash okay?"

Cash is always fine.

She hands over five one hundred dollar bills and tells Baz a messenger will bring bring the balance Thursday, Thursday afternoon. It might be a little late. Better deliver to the house on Fourth Street they agree.

It's after four when the bell rings and Baz lets in an elderly woman in a not very clean cloth coat and ramshackle black shoes, popping at the lasts. She's carrying a wrinkled black plastic garbage bag, which appears half full and rather heavy. She clambers awkwardly up the stairs to our third floor kitchen, where she accepts a chair but not anything else, not water, juice, coffee, or tea. This is business. She opens the bag, pulls out packs of five dollar bills held together with rubber bands, and lines up ten of them on our big table. The bag is filled with many more.

"That right?" she asked.

"Would you count it," Baz says after a moment.

She snaps the band from the first pack onto her wrist where it dangles like bracelet, licks the broad base of her thumb, and begins, whispering numbers to herself, and looking up at Baz when she stops to catch a breath.

"One-ninety-nine, two," she finishes each time, banging the pack against the table and snapping the band back around the notes. She's counted out the whole $5,000 in less than two minutes, Baz says later. He had to shake himself.

"Laundromats" she said slyly, as she neared the end of the last stack. "S'why they're all old."

Baz never asked why they were old. He never said one word. But Irene, the teller at our corner bank, gave a horrified look when Baz piled the packets in front of her.

"What have you been *doing*, Mr. King?" she said. "Are you okay?"

A Little Tale of Family and War

Bernadine Loden, thin and smart, left the Midwest in the 1940s, insisted on having a college education, sought serious work in New York City, and wanted the world of news. She did all that. She did more. Bernadine broke with the sexual mores of her middleclass American childhood. She was "plain" so she would sleep with whomever she pleased; and she was not going further herself by working to marry up. She would marry, if she married at all, to have a partner for *her* brains.

Eventually she had married – and married up. Thus, Tubby. "News man," he called himself, not "journalist." He'd been dashing smart and for fifteen years they'd been everywhere, her juggling a brace of children and following him to his ever more interesting assignments.

We met him far later than that. In 1977 what was important about Tubby? That he was a wreck, a waste to himself and others. His well of grief was expressed in asthma and the elaborate rituals he used to accommodate it. He spent much of his time in his old armchair, belly bulging comfortably across the top of his soft wash pants, with a high pile of clean bandannas in a host of colors on each arm of the chair. His coughing and clearing of bronchial tubes and his folding and stroking of bandannas were as constant as his conversation. Tubby was a liberal intellectual of the old school: well read, informed, cynical, idealistic, and somehow certain that opinions even those expressed in a shabby living room in upstate New York had import and influence.

But of course he also knew that he was only going through the motions. His journalism career was long since gone to illness and disabilities; his influence which might (or might not) have been extant when he was a contributing writer to this or that national publication, was totally gone.

What was important about Tubby?

That because of Tubby, Bernadine Loden would be moved to sponsor an exhibition of Basil King's art.

Tubby and Bernadine were marooned in Utica, where they lived on pensions, disability social security, and whatever was left of his once substantial family funds. They certainly could not live on what Bernadine was making as director of The Foundry – an artists' space funded by the modest 1970s federal largess in support of diversified, disseminated art activities.

Baz and I saw The Foundry first in a movie made by Dave Gearey who was back then a friend of a friend. The film was riveting. It showed what was left of a massive dark industrial structure, populated here and there by the intense activity of abstract sculptors. In their sunlit pockets, where old windows had been opened and new skylights dropped light down twenty feet or more, new materials were being forged by old techniques, rusted chains and pulleys pressed into service to move chunks of fiberglass, painted plywoods, CorTen eye beams. Dark spaces where there were pools of water, where the roof was failing, lazed between the active areas. The film picked up the glint of fresh solder drippings underfoot, the shadowy presence of massive machinery. For what? Civil War cannon? For sure to produce mechanicals for railroads after that war was over. Gung Ho West over the decades as Utica filled with middle European factory workers. Then the Foundry worked all night, and worker-families packed the new wood-frame triple-deckers.

By end of the Second World War the Foundry was hopelessly out of date. Work had gone elsewhere and the triple-deckers, rotting for lack of maintenance, filled up with jobless welfare clients. The Foundry grew streaks of green moss on its massive stone walls, housed small animals in the soft dirt of the big rooms. Now it was haphazardly sheltering sculptors who'd won state arts council stipends. All this lovingly filmed by Dave Gearey.

In Utica, Bernadine showed us Dave's film.

In New York City, Del introduced us to Dave, and we've been friends since.

Back then, Dave wasn't sure what he thought of Basil's art, but even when the work baffled or confused him he trusted the intentions he saw and believed both man and work were authentic.

Bernadine was also convinced. She gave Baz a solo exhibition in Utica in 1977, one of his rare one-man shows. It was not at the Foundry, which was for sculpture exclusively; it was at the Kirkland Art Center of Clinton, which she also ran, and where she had recently shown a collection of male nudes by Sylvia Sleigh, much praised by her lover, the critic Lawrence Alloway. From that Bernadine had begun to believe she might have a chink, maybe even a ramp, that could move her into the New York City art scene. She had begun to believe there were going to be ways for her not to be marooned in Utica, not left behind by her two grown children who had already launched themselves, not left stuck with Tubby's wheezing rages about the endless betrayals of his smothering family.

In the house he patted his two stacks of bandannas while he talked. Bernadine ran the washing machine every day. And worked her smarts about what one might do aslant, as Emily Dickinson puts it. A female solution. An old American ploy. She had nerve and she could see.

The Kirkland Art Center in Clinton was housed in a plain white clapboard American protestant church. You've seen its steep roof and modest bell tower, the pleasing balance agreed on by its anonymous builders. The arched church windows with their austere woodwork were visible from the outside. Inside, large white panels had been put up to cover without destroying them so interior walls ran unbroken up to the rafters. Excellent lighting had been installed.

In this glowing space Bernadine hung: *Aggie and Bill* (1971-2), *Celo Compound #1* (1975), *Celo Compound #2* (1975), *Celo Compound #3 – Sunset* (1976), *Nightlife* (1975), *Female Torso, Back* (1971), *Female Torso, Front* (1971), and *Mallory and Hetty* (1976). She may also have shown *Martha in a Yellow Hat* (1973) – one of the scant dozen paintings Baz had been able to complete in Grand Haven.

Most of these paintings are large – six by eight, nine by seven – and they soared in the open space. It was 30 feet to the ceiling peak.

What happened?

What did we feel?

What did it mean?

In the end, Bernadine's personal rescue devolved from an ordinary divorce. There was a nursing home with therapists for Tubby. Bernadine sold her house and was gone. She reconstituted something, I hope, but it was not in the New York art world. She paid dearly for her leap of faith as far as Basil King's art was concerned. No New York critic took the train upstate to see this exhibition. No local art reporter knew what to say at all. Her employers were not at all pleased. The Kirkland Art Center board did not renew her contract.

The exhibition still hangs on in my mind's eye to be savored. A collection of well hung, well spaced, well lit paintings in a neutral public area – away from the personal ambience of a studio and in the company of only other Basil Kings – it was a rare experience and deserving of far better art writing than I could ever do. But I can review one of them:

"Aggie and Bill" Oil on canvas. 9' x 7' (1971-1972)
This large painting was reproduced at 6"x 9" on the cover of my *Little Tales of Family and War* (New York: Spuyten Duvyil, 2000), a collection of stories. It was also reproduced even smaller on a postcard which Spuyten Duvyil printed to promote my book. In both reproductions, the picture is framed, not unpleasantly, with a black border carrying my name and the title of the book in drop-out white. Except for the show Bernadine put on, the actual painting has not been shown anywhere else. Not in the flesh.

And flesh it is, this piece of canvas covered in oil paint. Looming on the left, sits a large naked woman, with exquisitely tender pendulous breasts, huge sexy nipples, one full moon and one erect, and a glowing belly on which a navel floats – see up close: is it a tiny little man in a curved fishing boat on golden sea? The woman, Aggie, sits with her feet in the water. More properly, her feet disappear into a white hole descending into the foreground's graphic gray waves. They may not be water. Behind her, a motionless blue sea extends to an horizon that crosses behind her head and neck and the shoulders of her little boy.

That's Bill on the right. He too is naked, but his body is not flesh. He wears many colors as his shield. The colors section off his body parts, legs, arms, chest, neck: white, gray, lavender, red, pink, blue, brown. A section of belly is explicitly a shield: it is painted in military olive brown and banded in dark gray stripes. His spindly legs disappear into his mother's huge left leg so his feet, like hers, cannot be seen. His little penis is naked and he is peeing on his mother's leg.

The faces of these two repeat the story: Aggie's face is rendered in shades of dead dark gray, her eyes are shut, her mouth curved in disapproval, her expression remote and stony. Bill's face is also gray, but anxiously alive, a very pale bluish white-gray. He eyes are alert, wide open and turned away from his mother toward the far off right. He is that ancient/infant combination common to children who have seen too much and been protected too little. He is already old, though small enough to be completely helpless.

It's a classic Madonna and Child.

There are many from Europe in which the Christ attends his business and Mary is utterly removed, in which the Christ is preternaturally mature, ready for crucifixion, but in those paintings he is calm, not anxious, and he is often holding out gifts or warnings. Whether baby or manikin, he is rarely shown without the presence of a mother's arm or hand presenting him or resting on his body. Mary may be disengaged, but not as here, openly disdainful. This painting is a more modern classic; the sexual activity between mother and son as he deliberately leaks hot piss on her knee is assiduously ignored by both of them.

It's classic in its execution. The paint is luminous, thin and sensuous. The layered forms glow as if the underpainting were an actual source of light, cool blue-white dawn sky.

It's a classic nightmare, a murderous drama known to many of us, a devastating personal battle presented as calmly as some sensuous nude lounging beside a bowl of fruit.

At the Kirkland Art Center, Tubby looking at it stopped wheezing. Stopped in his tracks, as the cliché would have it. I think he wasn't sure he wanted to talk to Baz afterward. But then, as he was Tubby, he couldn't not talk. So he wanted to tell Baz more, to extend his long sad story of mother bites and overlove, from which he'd been, just barely, able to flee. All his life he was able to keep six steps ahead of her until illness took his running legs, he said.

Several visitors wrote comments about this particular painting in the gallery guest book: "Emotionally devastating," "Frightening," and "This is obscene."

The Aggie depicted is a portrait of my grandmother Agnes, and Bill is the name of her youngest child, my Uncle Billy. When my sister Charlotte saw the promotional postcard she asked Baz if he had seen our grandmother in her coffin. She died in 1965. No he had not. The likeness was uncanny, Charlotte said. Had he worked from a photograph? He had not. He had seen Aggie alive, not dead. The little boy has the face of Basil's father, Mark, not my Uncle Billy. He is shown with the grim clenched mouth Mark carried to his death way after this show in Utica was dismantled and trucked home. If it did not already have a title of its own, this painting could be called "A little tale of family and war."

It Starts to Drizzle

Maybe Baz had a point about his persona making it hard for me to get my writing published. It was hard and I never quite understood why. But the reasons were just as likely me, not him. People couldn't place me. I had no public identity; I was not from a school or a group so I had no allies or supporters. And I was so easily discouraged. One turn-down was usually enough to persuade me to let an effort lie. I failed to persist, failed to send my work out, failed to reach out to other writers and cultivate friends. I didn't play well with others. Instead I played on my own. I created *Giants Play Well in the Drizzle.* It was a six-page mini magazine, a zine if you will, and I simply mailed it to a list of people I liked. I made the list up. It started with people I knew, of course, but from the start it also included people I didn't know personally but whom I wanted as readers.

The *Drizzle,* the little *Giant,* was three pieces of paper, printed on both sides, folded into thirds. It was exactly what could be mailed for the price of one first-class stamp. As for contributors, I wrote to people I wanted to publish asking if they'd send me something (all copyrights back to authors upon publication). More rarely I simply reprinted things I'd found (fair use, maybe). And in many issues, but not all, I included poetry by me and by Baz, and some of his black & white line drawings.

After I started, I discovered there was a large scene for casually produced publications like this. I knew the classic models: *Floating Bear* and *Migrant* from nearly twenty years earlier. In the 1980s, they got the name "zines" and thanks to ubiquitous photocopiers in shops and offices nationwide there were hundreds of them though most weren't literary. Many were devoted to the work of a small group where science fiction fantasies and apocalyptic conspiracy beliefs met and mingled. Others were the precursors to graphic novels and comix. I found a number of writer/publishers whose anarchistic sensibilities could mesh with mine. There was even a tireless reviewer named Mike Guderloy who wrote hundreds of critiques, challenging and connecting the amorphous scene. He published these and reviews by other people along with addresses and prices of zines from all over the U.S. in a magazine he published called *Fact Sheet Five*.

In every issue of my *Drizzle* I offered to add new names to my list, and slowly unsolicited requests came in. I also asked for stamps or money. And occasionally people sent one or the other. By 1990, I had an eclectic mailing list of over 800 souls, a backlog of work I wanted to publish but hadn't got to yet, and had switched from a typewriter to what could be produced on a word-processing computer. My print run had grown far too large to print on my office's copy machines on the quiet so I paid a modest sum for reproduction at a neighborhood copy shop. I learned much later the proprietor, a sweet familiarly scruffy looking guy named Allen, was my friend poet Barbara Henning's love. He was already enduring the liver ailment that would kill him.

I loved my *Giant*, my autonomous playpen – and the connections it brought me to *Tray of Laboratory Mice*, Blaster Al Ackerman, *Fell Swoop*, Arnold Fallender, *Luna Bisonte* and other non-cooperators. My personal demesne of willfulness was housed in the corporate back offices of Memorial Sloan-Kettering Cancer Center. I was employed there.

In Dagwood Bumstead's day, a boss, always a fat male in a dark three-piece, usually with a hat and a large cigar, simply screamed "You're FIRED!" and the target character was upended and blown out of the frame. "Reality" TV notwithstanding, corporations changed all that. Starting in the 1970s, corp-speaking people were pouring out of Madison Avenue into professions and callings almost everywhere.

Mainstream artists were thinking strategy, and learning to morph their obsessions into a "brand." By the 1980s even small nonprofit employers were using corp-speak language and tech-niques to instill fear and obedience under the guise of building office esprit de corps. High among the corporate tricks were the ways to make a person leave a job without exposing the organi-zation to legal, financial, or public relations hazards.

By the 1980s people were actually fired only if caught in the act – say stealing, fornicating, smoking or injecting something illegal, vandalizing company property, or selling corporate secrets. Of course people could be laid off, a job could be eliminated, indeed an entire department could be merged or morphed out of existence. But generally, like water worming around the edges of a dam, corporations managed to flush out unwanted personnel by moving sideways. Slowly. The steps were relentless: Remove responsibilities. Limit exchanges with others. Erode status. Enforce idleness. So suddenly there's the planning meeting to which she isn't invited. Or his annual nightmare assignment is inexplicably assigned elsewhere or blandly dispensed with altogether. Soon there are whole days when the desk phone doesn't ring. When the person has nothing at all to do. Finally, the demoralized employee slinks away, sans benefits or good referrals, leaving behind a terrifying example for the remaining staff. The technique is devastatingly effective and though it takes a bit of time it's almost universally successful.

Who figured this out? Was it Bernays, Freud's cousin, the founder of "public relations"?

Here is Sloan-Kettering Cancer Center's PR department, chastely called the Office of Public Affairs – and here is Amanda, long-time senior editor, in her lovely big windowed office, with her 18 years of service. She's red-faced. She's unable to control her tears. The department director who had been Amanda's friend, co-conspirator, and protector has gone, induced to retire by an extravagant payout. He's been replaced by a patent leather bitch who makes no bones about her superior social connections and expertise. She's Elsbeth and she makes it clear to all of us that she's been empowered to clean out the mess left by the old boss.

Are you frightened yet? Or just vaguely guilty for the common liberties you've taken? We all keep our eyes to ourselves as she addresses her new staff.

She has been hired *personally*, she makes clear, by the new top doc who heads the entire institution. Sloan-Kettering is a small city on its own with employees in the hundreds and a substantial array of workshops, labs and onsite services. I'd already gotten to know it well, from the cedar-shingled water towers on the rooftop to the cyclotron five levels below ground. Elsbeth knows where her bread is buttered. She is the new top doc's ally and agent, there to ensure that everything will be remade in his image. No change too small. No level of control too petty. The hospital logo. The cafeteria hours. All aspects of her department and whatever else top doc wants her to take under her wing.

Amanda has to know her days are numbered. Amanda, the person who taught me to check institutional announcements against the most recent telephone number listings for an index of actual goings on. Amanda who cheerfully shared after-hours gossip about the transgressions of others. Now, the magazine she had edited and I made ready for publication has simply been eliminated. (See first item on list above.) Suddenly I'm given a raise and a title identical to hers. I'm called a senior editor too. Though of what is unclear. The injustice stuns her. She seeks shoulders to cry on. Shoulders comply. They've little to lose. A Kleenex, a glass of wine, some telephone time. They can't help her. When Amanda lashes out, she's not blaming her friend the former boss who'd taken the money and run, spoiling her Eden, and not the new boss either, she with the prissy-perfect fashion and carefully controlled enunciation. No. It's me, her odd-ball underling. I should have been loyal to her. I should have broken down too. Wasn't I being meted out the identical treatment?

Truth is I was. Despite the "senior" in my new title and a salary finally delivering our family into a New York City middle class, a new position was created above me. Everything I did was now to be monitored by Gerri, Elsbeth's hatchet-woman, usually with condescending demands for do-overs. Not that there was much actual work. I too was being given less and less to do. I no longer have to research facts, polish press releases, manicure the Annual Report, take part in work groups designing initiatives to support new research programs (aka fund raising) or new buildings (aka fund raising) or manage special events designed to quell neighborhood uneasiness about the Center's endless appetite for land and buildings. Instead I'm asked to prepare a weekly news sheet for the Center staff – requests for return of trays and

silverware to the cafeteria, announcements of concerts at
Rockefeller, public lectures at Cornell, blood donation drives, safety
reminders. Even with Gerri's mandatory do-overs to handle, the
chore takes a very few hours to assemble and maybe two more for
layout and proofing.

It really wasn't fair. Amada loved her job, loved the
importance she felt it gave her, her membership in a mission. Who
doesn't approve of the search for cancer cures? And the early 1980s
was a dramatic time. Insights had begun pouring out of cell biology.
With the unraveling of genetics a flood of new cancer hypotheses
was in progress – and ever-more provocative puzzles. Moreover,
the cancer world had just been upended by the appearance of a
strange illness.

For the first time in medical history immune system failures
could be clearly connected to the onset of a cancer. The clinicians
were calling it GRID – Gay Related Immune Deficiency. The
research immunologists, for so long scorned and ignored by Sloan
Kettering's grand gurus of chemotherapy and radiation, were now
being romanced by funders. As the ill population increased from a
rare few to dozens of mostly young men every week, white-bread
clinicians out of Choate and Yale began seeking information about
vectors. Could Roger McFarlane help? (Roger was the rare out
senior staff person and also the top respiratory therapist at the
Center before leaving to build the Gay Men's Health Crisis.) Gay
men do what? Do where?? The activities they learned about were

way beyond the Boy Scout circle jerks they understood. Could these practices be clues to how this infection traveled?

Notwithstanding the Center's increasing corporate fascism, medical detective work of all sorts was heating up. The city's millionaires were noticing. Act Up was on the move. Politicians and their backers were hunting for havens and for scapegoats. And all of this to happen without Amanda being in on it? Her ire for me increased. I was staying on and getting away with it because I'd thrown in with Elsbeth was her conclusion. I was worse than Judas.

More weeks pass. Then Amanda leaves one Friday afternoon, hardly packing up her office things. She's just gone. She has done exactly what was wanted. She leaves as if she'd never been. She never speaks to me again.

I wasn't exactly "getting away with it" as she thought. But for me, Sloan-Kettering was a practical paycheck, not a calling, and it was clear to me the Public Affairs Department staff were voyeurs, not on the front lines of anything. Still I wasn't dead to what was going on, both the excitement and the hollow feeling of dread. It was soon clear that the odd cancer, Kaposi's sarcoma, was just the tip of this insidious thing. AIDS got its new less pejorative name, but without being fully understood, and without effective treatments. It was a medieval nightmare. New horrors were revealed weekly. A friend of ours doing her medical residence in the ER of Bellevue was exposed daily to every effluvia human bodies can produce. Was she going to be okay? And what about many other people we knew? What about our friends with acey-deucy love lives? What about the wider scene, the dancers Hetty studied with, the musicians Mallory admired, the filmmakers and photographers and theater people who make New York tick?

It was a while before Tom and Peter and Jack were sick, a while before plague raced through the dance world like something out of *The Seventh Seal,* it was a while before the parade of unthinkable funerals for people who should have had years to live and produce. It even took a while for the paranoia to come to full boil. Was it toothbrushes? Toilet seats? Our friends began making nervous cracks on the order of 'thank god Frank O'Hara's already dead or he'd be down with this' or 'Shows god loves us lesbians; none of *us* get it.'

Was it good to be where research gossip circulated? Where reports from the CDC were posted weekly? It was definitely hard to be newly aware of how slow and inconsistent research always is when talk downtown flowed as if researchers only needed to try harder or the government only needed to open a no-limits funding tab. Not that there weren't some old-line impediments to research and development that did need to be dismantled.

Amanda's suspicions notwithstanding, all I did was just stay in place. Beyond the withdrawal of workload and office status, Elsbeth had few options she was ready to use against me. And I was happy on the job. Honest Amanda had had no concept of living underground, of any form of white-collar crime, nor had she any need. But I did. In my smaller, but still very pleasant office, I could close the door. I could take my time. I could be Brer Rabbit in the briar patch. In addition to privacy, the department abounded all sorts of lovely things: electric typewriters (and soon, word processing desktop computers), high-speed Xerox machines, automatic staplers, endless supplies of quality white paper. I could fold a blank "This Week at the Center" into thirds, put a stamp on the bottom back third – and voila – a five-and-a-half page mini-magazine awaiting my pleasure to fill. In fact, the stamp was my only cash outlay. I held back from pinching postage as that would have involved the central mailroom.

Every collection of five poems is a sixth poem. Robert Frost said this, I think. Or not. The statement is true whoever said it first and links elegantly to my faith in the use of existing materials. This aesthetic formed the heart of how I learned to put my publication together.

As for the name, I had a small collection of titles for unwritten poetry books. The best was a headline from a tabloid sports page, deciphered from my upside down view as I hung on a swinging metal subway handle on my way to the early morning office. Giants. Play. Well. In the. Drizzle. YES!

Decade 39

Studio space, studio space – the theme runs like a relentless river or puddles up like a foot-sucking swamp for almost every artist. Even today I can't stop myself from eye-balling empty buildings – derelict gas stations, abandoned factories – almost any unused space anywhere can start me dreaming. Baz could paint here; we could live there. Suppose we put in skylights? A fence here, a bamboo thicket there, a plausible way to subdivide – and the dream propels itself.

I don't remember now how Baz found his 39th Street studio. But I do remember my first view of it: A wall of windows 75 feet long, through which one could see over the elevated Gowanus Expressway down the hill, taking all the Route 278 traffic to and from the Verrazano-Narrows Bridge. Just beyond the expressway, the Bush Terminal buildings sprawled, then the open harbor, the Statue of Liberty a little doll figure way to the right, distant cranes in Jersey, freighters and tankers on the water in between. Sky and light, light and sky. The loft was all concrete and huge by our standards with a hard concrete floor and enormous round support columns big as trees. Typical construction for turn of the twentieth-century manufacturing.

The building entrance was anything but fancy: a wide loading dock that was closed with a rolling steel shutter but otherwise open to the weather, steps on the side and inside a miniscule hole in the wall an enterprising Puerto Rican family made great hot food. How they managed the quantities they cooked in that tiny space was a mystery. Nearly everyone in the building bought their food. The family taught Baz that pork *hates* wine and should be cooked slowly in beer and they regularly touted island real estate to him. "Let us know when you go there…we'll fix you up great." The food stand was just by the ancient freight elevator. The whole ten stories above hummed with industry.

Baz was the only artist in the building. He had about a third of the third floor in the back which was quite high up because the building was on a steep hill. In 1983, when Baz moved in, all the other tenants had high-class garment businesses.

Baz met a guy who made leather gloves for Bergdorf's, "exclusive contract"; others were doing rainwear, jackets, business suits or elegant women's clothing for places like Bendel and Sak's. The shop owners were old hands, in their late fifties and sixties, a familiar type of New Yorker now passed into history. They were hard-bitten men, proud of their achievements, prejudiced about outsiders but generally gracious to the skilled cutters and sewers who actually made their products. After Baz got to know various owners he'd get calls when there were samples to sell off. Courtesy sales, way below wholesale. I found myself going to work in Hervé

Benard and Liz Claiborne. At my uptown office Elsbeth and Gerri would try not to look surprised.

This time moving into a new space meant building, not tearing down. Soon there were rows of new storage racks across the back, 12-foot wide rolling walls for paintings, and our old round table from Delancey Street set up near the window wall. There was space for doing little sculptures and for graphics, room to have two or three paintings going at one time, and Baz put his green tin desk, chair and typewriter from Grand Haven all the way at the opposite end of his main painting area so he could look up at his works-in-progress if he was writing. Beginning in 1985, he was writing every day.

Room to swing a cat, just what I'd dreamed for him. The only factor I bewailed was the ceiling. It was a little over ten feet high, and in that huge space looked lower. Two or three more feet and I'd have called it total heaven. The only other factor we both bewailed was the need for Baz to drive home after work. Parking places under the expressway were always available and the route to our house was a straight shot down Fourth Avenue but Baz can be tolerably out of it after a day of work. His head may be anywhere, or he may be simply used up. We both worried about the drive — and sometimes he even took the subway that stops at 36th Street as a compromise.

A heavenly time, a quiet time, a dreadful time, a liberating time. This was the decade our daughters endured the storms of adolescence, their first loves, their first bouts of broken promises. We broke promises too. The girls went off to college, and we have long family stories as to how.

Mallory was admitted to Bard thanks to Leon Botstein, the president, and his belief that test scores aren't everything; Hetty went to NYU's School of the Arts because she concluded it was foolish to go away from New York to study when modern dance was so clearly right here. Both of them went into debt for their schooling and despite our intentions, we were never able to pay them back. They managed the debts for themselves. They managed. They grew psychological muscles in the effort. Not a bad thing – nor at that time a total impossibility. In those distant days tuition costs for schools like Bard or NYU hovered around fifteen thousand a year. It seemed, it *was*, gigantic but both girls were awarded scholarships and applied for government loans and every year a financial aid formula was applied to our household, leaving a sum for us to pay that was a squeeze but not impossible to meet.

Ominously the interest charged for student loans inched upward every year, and we had to put up with it. Money aside, the school choices were good fits despite Hetty's disappointment that NYU's dance program provided conservatory training, not the liberal arts education she wanted. The schools brought them both into wider worlds and helped them make friends and connections that wouldn't have happened somewhere else.

Almost miraculously in the fall of 1985 they were through. Hetty had sailed through NYU in three years, catching up with Mallory, and the deal was done. Degreed and graduated. We had no tuition payments to make! Both kids had jobs. They no longer lived at home. We could make that squeeze for tuition money one more time and spend the money on ourselves.

We took a trip to England. A whole month. It was Basil's first visit since he and his parents left in 1947 when he was eleven. It was my first travel abroad ever.

We couldn't have needed the escape more urgently. A huge betrayal by an art world powerbroker brought Baz face to face with the realization that his hope of showing his work publically was dead in the water and might well be dead for many years. He'd been promised the lot: a mainstream gallery, a critical article in a mainstream art magazine, a teaching job, possibly at Bard, introductions, "the works" in short. And then a freeze and a thud. Nothing dramatic, just sudden inexplicable ice cold.

Virgin Airlines was the party plane back then, the booze flowed, the sound track was classic rock 'n' roll, and our fellow passengers seemed wonderfully mellow. I think we drank all night. A steward sported a Rod Stewart hair cut and a smart gold earring. Hey, this was 1985 and it wasn't so common to see that if you weren't in a club or living on the Lower East Side. It felt as if we'd just dozed off a few minutes before strong breakfast tea was served and we hit the ground.

Almost immediately we were in the din of Heathrow and then off the connecting train into one of London's cavernous train stations, looking for the "left luggage" room to park our bags, and wrestling with money as unfamiliar to Baz as it was to me. No ha'pence, no farthings, no crowns.

"Mate, help me do this," he asked a grizzled luggage room attendant. "I've been gone since 47."

Everything we saw was in the loud and brilliant-bright colors well known to the hung-over and the sleep deprived. There were masses of fresh fruits and flowers stacked for sale, gaudy stalls of hats and socks, buildings of clear yellow, tan, and fresh brick red where all had been austerity, rubble, and black soot stained in Baz's images from the late 1940s. Loud cars. Booming busses. The taxis were all black as memory had them for Baz, but teeming crowds of people in clean new clothes? Piles of oranges and ripe cherries? He was stunned. In time we found ourselves on the Embankment and grabbed the chance to take a tour boat so we could sit and be taken up the rocking rushing Thames all the way to Kew Gardens. There things settled a bit. That is, Baz took off at a run on the pathway from the boat landing. He went straight to the red pagoda. He knew the way. And it was exactly there, exactly as he remembered.

We spent the whole month of October wandering: London, of course, meeting and staying with some of Basil's remaining family. And there was The Tate. The National. The Courtauld. St. Martin-in-the-Fields. The British Museum and the bookstores behind it. We also spent one long day searching for Basil House in the East End where Baz had lived his first five years. There what had once been storefront Huguenot churches and had been storefront synagogues in the1940s were storefront Pakistani mosques. They broadcast heart-stopping calls to prayer from their roof-mounted audio systems. But where in the world was Basil House?

We asked in restaurants and shops. Nothing, just head shaking. Alongside the crowded Moslem neighborhoods were the telltale signs of gentrification starting up. We roamed from Petticoat Lane, crammed with shops but with no Pearlies, down to Stepney Green and back all the way to the Whitechapel Gallery on Commercial Street. "I know we're near it," Baz said. "My dad used to walk me over to Toynbee Hall for the socialist meetings."

We stopped asking in shops and began just stopping people walking in the street. No one anywhere had ever heard of Varner Street or Basil House. Had the whole street been blasted out of existence in the war? Finally we asked an older Jewish-looking woman if she knew about the Oxford and St. Georges Boys Club, this time trying the name of one of the settlement's biggest youth organizations instead of saying "Basil House."

"And girls," she said tartly. "I was a member!" Bingo! She was full of stories and even wanted us to attend an old members' meeting scheduled for the end of the week, but we demurred. Turned out the street name had been changed from Varner to Henriques Street, in honor of Sir Basil, for whom Baz is named. And Baz was right. We weren't far from Whitechapel. Basil House had survived the Blitz but lost its name. It was now a condo and looked expensive. As was the Bernard Baron House next door, the building that had housed the center where Baz's dad Mark had worked until war changed everything. The neighborhood had been "discovered" all right. Plus, as Baz noted, the Blitz had eliminated some incredibly nasty slums.

There were more roots to search. We took a car trip to Cambridge with Basil's cousin Malcolm and another jaunt with him out to Alpha Road, Chingford, the suburb where Baz had lived just before the family's move to America. Then the two of us took a train trip to Cornwall. A day's long walk in the hot sun from Penzance through Newland (marvelous smoked fish), to Mousehole (with its deep bowl of a harbor and welcoming pub,) and up the hill to Paul (past the churchyard where a plaque claimed the last native speaker of Cornish is buried). Then a day trip by bus to St. Ives and Barbara Hepworth's house. Finally, a slow drive in a rented car, up the Devon coast. Yes, we stopped at Stonehenge. Yes, we stopped at Windsor. We did all. And all that month glorious early fall weather held.

We did so much England that on our last day in London, I begged Baz to take me to an American movie. Clint Eastwood on a horse under the high blue sky of the West. American space. We had been thinking seriously about moving to the U.K. as there was so little left for us in New York. Baz has U.K. citizenship. But no. Though we made friends and have made many more in the intervening years, though a trip to England is always rewarding in some deeply complicated way, no. For all the bliss of that trip, and despite all the reasons we wanted to leave New York, we agreed that England was too tight, too measured, too class infected. The faint stink of anti-Semitism was still too detectable. No.

We decided as we've decided so many times since to stay here, here in New York, here in Brooklyn. The U.S., despite despair, despite the seemingly never fading thrum of fascism and racism, despite the never-ending wars. We keep reminding ourselves that the U.S. has slipped, just barely, through its dance with evil many times; we keep our knowledge that every nation's flag is drenched in blood; we keep counting on the drive of New York's people; we keep deciding yes we'll hang in here.

Our trip to England was a diversion. This quick account of our trip is a diversion. Amazingly the trip was more than a diversion for Baz. It brought on what he has called, "a season of digestion" as recounted in his book *mirage: a poem in 22 sections*. When he returned to Brooklyn in November he could not stop writing.

Baz often cites this trip to England in 1985 as the beginning of his writing life. And in many ways that is true. In terms of a public career in the art world, his choice was stark: start over or give up. For him, starting over meant writing, with the hope of coming in from a different direction. Using his imagery differently might bring people into what he was doing in his art. Soon he was writing a place for himself between writing and painting, bringing together disparate things which has always been his gift and his burden.

Jack Spicer and Paul Blackburn had been right. Baz always was a writer. Kline, Vicente and his high school teacher Blossom Coho had also been right. Baz always was a painter. Without the crushing defeats that left his art sidelined, he might never have opened himself to the writing. Or put another way, if he had had a career as an exhibiting artist, he would have been too busy to ever manage the time required to develop it.

For me writing took second place to editing the *Drizzle*, at least for a time, in part because keeping my place at Sloan Kettering absorbed my weekday energies. I could no long drift in a day job as I'd done. I had to be observant, attentive, weigh my moves. I had to be a little invisible and yet just visible enough. It was work.

In 1988 we were sitting at the counter of a local sandwich shop waiting for Anthony to do our fried eggs when I saw the *New York Times* announcement of Robert Duncan's death. A loss of something that never was. In 1988, the *Drizzle* was five years old. Baz and I decided we'd throw a party for it. Make an event. We had the huge space of his 39th Street studio for our venue and I invited all the writers I'd published over those five years for a marathon reading. We decided to include a showing of portraits Baz had painted of various writer friends.

We hung up two of Baz's large David Rattray portraits including my favorite showing David pulling back stage curtains on cavorting playing card figures. In the large space of 39th Street, Baz had plunged full bore into playing card iconography, completing four huge Aces, and sequences of "The Two's," "The Three's," "Four of a Kind," and "The Fives" all on big canvasses. He had painted a series showing Meredith Monk as Queen of Diamonds with her then partner Ping Chong as Jack of Hearts. We showed one of those. We pulled out "Cubby and His Friends," a portrait of Hubert Selby, Jr. with a crowd of the people who'd inhabited Red Hook when Selby was a boy.

While Baz was working on that one he had been visited by a delegation of workers in the building. They rang the bell and stood together in a group. "We hear you're painting Puerto Ricans," the ringleader said. Baz let them in. The men in his painting were wearing porkpie caps and short 1940's neckties. His visitors were very satisfied.

At the Drizzle party, Nancy Metcalf was very satisfied with the large charcoal of Paul Metcalf: "Baz, you really got his knees," she said. But Robert Bertholf, who was then Rare Books Curator at SUNY Buffalo and much involved with the Black Mountain circle of poets, was sour. The two portraits of Rattray showed him in a dark green top with a small circle of white around the neck. Apparently Bertholf read that as a clerical collar. His remarks were sneering. "So now you're anti-clerical?"

It was a false question but Baz didn't pursue it. Perhaps he should have. That day, too much was going on. Twenty-eight poets were reading! Our turnout was huge. I'd had five white tee shirts printed with the typeface and double line that I used on the Drizzle masthead and the shirts said "Drizzle Crew." They were gifts for the dancers our Hetty had recruited to help with coats, chairs, coffee, beer, and cleanup. Hetty later said we'd have made a fortune selling them but it hadn't occurred to me to do that. We spent our money instead on beer kegs, ice, a coffee machine, and rented chairs. I paid the sound guy from the St. Marks Poetry Project to set up a mike and make tapes so the readings were properly recorded. But the world wasn't photo-obsessed as it is now and no one took pictures.

The event mixed up people as nicely as the *Drizzle* itself did. Rich Blevins came from Pennsylvania, Laura Kennelly from Ohio, Maureen Owen from Connecticut, Paul and Nancy Metcalf from Massachusetts and Gerald Burns all the way from Texas. He decorated the door, hallway and downstairs entrance way, not with the simple signs I asked him to make – "Ring bell for elevator" and "King studio, Third Floor left" but used huge sheets of brown paper for jaunty line drawings of baseball players (all Giants of course) giving the directions. And downtown folks showed up too. Greg Masters, Lorna Smedman, Hettie Jones, Simon Pettet and many more all braving the subway out to 36th Street, Brooklyn. The nastiness of Bertholf easily sank in the cheerful din. But something was surely up his craw, for he later torpedoed an effort by Bob Creeley to get Baz an exhibition at the Albright-Knox Museum. He was an odd bird, Mr. Bertholf.

Worms Turning in the Mud

I'd been doing the *Drizzle* for at least seven years when Baz and I went to a reading in the great hall of Cooper Union in celebration of the Finnish poet Paavo Haavikko. Anselm Hollo had done English translations of his work and as was typical of his wide generosity for a community of poets, he was reaching out to everyone he could think of in the downtown literary world to garner more readers of Haavikko's work. We said hello in the hallway; he was glad to see us. I introduced myself to Anselm's wife, Jane Dalrymple. "Oh," she said in her deeply charming Southern accent, "aren't you the woman who sends us that newsletter, 'Worms Turning in the Mud'?"

T'was a sure sign the *Drizzle* had made me known and unknown. But I didn't reform. I was having too much fun.

Elsbeth did have one more trick.

Poor Gerri, Elsbeth's finally impotent hatchet-person. She could not figure out why she kept hearing typing coming from my office. Or why I was clearly engaged and alert, so unlike the undone Amanda. It was easy for me to be patient and compliant when Gerri blue-lined my weekly newssheet with insanely petty requests. Just a few more t's to cross and i's to dot before I could get back to doing all that went into getting the *Drizzle* contents selected, the whole assembled, and ready to send out. I was also writing poetry. My situation was more thrilling than having a grant; my work had the frisson of illegality, requiring tricks for disguising what I was working on if someone came into my office.

The department was enlarged and new projects were begun without me. Fine! After a year or perhaps more, Elsbeth tried another tack: she gave me an assignment she was certain would drive me crazy or garner powerful external complaints about me – hopefully both. I was made Public Affairs Coordinator for The Society of MSKCC. The Society was – still is – New York society. It was the organization for what would have been called in earlier times, the ladies' auxiliary. These were the wives of some of New York's richest and most powerful men, A-list socialites, the women Truman Capote portrayed and betrayed, the boldface names in Bill Cunningham's photographs in *The New York Times*.

Elsbeth assumed the snobbery, cliquishness, obsession with appearance, and the sheer exercise of Money by these women would disgust me. She thought I was a downtown radical snob. But my mother had been a New York socialite before she opted for a life with a middleclass intellectual, a Southerner with ambitions for New York's literary world. I knew what I was getting into.

There was even more to connect me: many of these women seemed parallel to women I'd met and worked among during my short stint at Mobilization for Youth. For both the upper crust and those who lived in deep poverty, the inferiority of women was a deeply embedded belief. For both, keeping a man meant providing ego-enhancing services to him at every turn. Having a man promised position and safety, but the union was unbalanced and constantly contingent on the woman's performance and appearance, as well as sheer dumb luck. The man might lose his money, crash and burn and turn. The man might arrive with a younger more glittering trophy woman. Both wealthy and very poor women were acutely exposed to changes of fortune. Their shared beliefs were all exactly like my mother's.

Abuse, overt or implied, was often possible. Not surprising that the women took comfort in alcohol and drugs; the wealthy for fine booze, prescription meds, and luxury rehab. The poor might have to steal or turn tricks for coke, speed, or horse. To live like this, alliances with other women are indispensible, and on the Upper East Side and in the city's red-lined neighborhoods, alliances were constantly made and unmade.

I'd watched my mother sink herself with her belief of being inferior so how could I not be empathetic? I also struggled with internalized beliefs. It was impossible not to notice. How could I not be fascinated?

"She's just not oh kay oh pee," says Mills. The kiss of death to be called "not our kind of people." It wasn't simply that Ennie was Brazilian, although it might have been. Her English was English English, upper class. Okay, fine. Her husband was extremely rich; theirs were too. But the eager way she greeted the others, her hair just a hair too brassy, her perfume a bit too husky. One didn't have to have gone to Miss Porter's, but one did need to know the rules.

Frankie gently strokes the curly head, muzzle and ears of her little white dog. "So lovely. Such a sweetie," she purrs. Her friends ooze approval. Frankie is menopausal plump and completely comfortable with it. She's still young enough to have her hair colored yellow not champagne but she doesn't diet. Her loose princess-cut blue dress is undoubtedly very expensive but it's at least size 14 and she's so not worried. Her childless much older husband has died and left her *everything*. I am told in private by one of her friends that I should never worry about Frankie's life. She's free. She has her lovely apartment, her work at Sloan Kettering, at the Hospital for Animals, at the Metropolitan; she has her house in the Hamptons where the dogs can romp all summer. She'd be more than hurt if I ever said, "she needs a man like a fish needs a bicycle," but her demeanor to all her friends announces this as firmly as if she were wearing one of those T-shirts. She's never going husband hunting again and her girlfriends can love her. In fact she's the first of the clique to include me in the gossipy conversations.

Old Mrs. Grinable had also lost her husband and "got it all" but not before reaching her seventies. Widows who make it safely through the deaths of their mates without encountering long-buried scandals or unexpected ruinous debts are the golden grail for these women. Mrs. Grinable, had a barbed tongue; her assessments were much more vivid than anything Frankie would ever come up with. She could tell a bawdy story with perfect elegance, sending everyone who heard into laughing fits. I came to suspect she had managed a third way and served her husband as a co-conspirator, partner, and strategist as he built his law firm into Wall Street's stratosphere. I could see her sharing cigars and brandy with him of a late night. She was the top – and, yes, we liked each other.

I listen and smile. I never act as if I were one of them but I'm not awed. My mother always had rich girlfriends visiting her in Chapel Hill now and again. I needed to churn out a few puff pieces about Society doings for internal publication. But not much else. External coverage handled itself: these women were naturally news to *Vogue, W, Vanity Fair, The New York Times*; their dresses and their husbands attracted society photographs. No one in the Sloan-Kettering PR department had to put a thumb on the scales.

    The Center's ladies organized huge fashion shows, auctions, dinner dances – events that required the wearing of spectacularly expensive outfits. They not only recruited big gift-givers for these parties, some of them worked hard on the productions, selecting and supervising the artisans who did the food, flowers, decorations, music and so on. Others selected art for the hospital walls or did flower arrangements for patient rooms.

They helped stock the pediatric playroom, recruited free hospital concerts by noted nightclub musicians and on and on. I didn't mind attending these splashy benefits as a "reporter." Sometimes I'd take along a seedy old former newspaper photographer I'd befriended. (He was quite marvelous as he had only one working eye and did weird contortions to get the shots he wanted. The results were often soft focus, but intelligently composed and what the heck.) I didn't mind a bit being taken to lunch at Maxwell's Plum, the Colony Club, the Sherry-Netherland. And I relished Elsbeth's pursed lips even more than I enjoyed Gerri's puzzlement. I still had plenty of time for my editing and publishing. For a nice long time my position was totally safe.

Thus there were 31 irregularly spaced issues of the *Drizzle*. And an eventual, but very casual, connection with 132 writers. A lovely cacophony.

Then as now my editorial acumen lived in the pit of my stomach. I never harbored principles of poetics, a strength and a weakness. In part because of my hostility to authority and in part because I harbor such huge doubts. That made it simple for me to mix it up – the delicately etched with the angry stripes, the rude with the carefully constructed. I placed poems by members of vastly different cliques and communities in, amongst, and across from each other. I was looking for an essential energy, the jazz of conversation, and was buoyed by my conviction that many people who write will write a real poem then and now, even if the bulk of their work is dross.

Only one person ever explicitly objected to my lack of policy. Hilda Morley, the composer Stefan Wolpe's widow, was a writer of elegant and sensitive verse, fully supported by her formidable classical education. I'd met her at Black Mountain. She came out with it: "I can't see why you want to publish my work when you publish these other things." I suppose this meant I didn't know what she was really doing, or she felt her work would be compromised by unseemly company. I'm not sure. At any rate, she would not send me anything, she wrote. I didn't answer her. Just as I did with the Society ladies, I kept my own counsel and never acted as if I were one of them. Not with the poets, any more than with the ultra-rich. Thereby continuing my odd course.

Baz would say, "You never asked."

He was right. It was a holdover from my childhood indoctrination in inferiority. I never asked for readings or to be published elsewhere; I never asked for membership in any group. I never asked for him either, never imagining that this omission would puzzle or confuse people who might otherwise have been his readers or buyers. Or mine. A terrible gaffe.

When I bragged that my age gave me job protection, that I could counter any attempt to fire me on grounds of age discrimination, a lawyer friend of ours told me I was dead wrong. "When that boss of yours *really* needs to get rid of you she will." And she did.

Baz knew before I did. The entire department along with mates and partners had been invited to a Christmas party given by one of the Society's trustees. The family occupied a splendid double-decker apartment, two full floors in one of those classic Park Avenue apartment buildings. The place was full of the trappings of life to be enjoyed: good art, acres of comfortable furniture, soft carpets, tons of books, rooms full of games, teenage detritus, food and drink in delightful abundance. I was chatting up the hostess and some of her grown children while Baz was picking up the shaky looks of my department colleagues. He noticed that message: drive fast and avert your eyes so as to get past the bloody highway accident fast.

Oh no, I told him on our way back home to Brooklyn that night. I put the nervous avoidance down to my outsider status.

Two days before the New Year holiday I was summoned into Elsbeth's office. My job is eliminated for the coming year, she told me. I was to sign a "no-sue" agreement and receive my full salary with all benefits for a whole year. End of story.

I found out later that Elsbeth was bailing out: within a year she would leave New York for a safer, smaller ultra-respectable position in New England. The top doc was stepping down, and Elsbeth who prided herself on her timing was cleaning her house before the departure. As Jack the lawyer had predicted, there was nothing I could do.

Ending the *Drizzle* was the least of my worries. (Note: The Rare Books collection at SUNY Buffalo has the complete *Drizzle* archive. I have donated correspondence, mockups, and all my files in addition to the complete set of the issues. The collection has a list of all 132 contributors, both living and not, to whom, once again, I extend my thanks.)

The truth was stark: I was 54, without academic degrees, with a checkered work history, without public accomplishments, armed only with a crazy personal purpose. Only a few years earlier Baz had endured an art world betrayal so gruesome he'd thought of calling a halt to his life in the toxic water of Gowanus Canal. The negative stories thus set in motion would, he recognized, polish off prospects for showing his art in the New York art scene for years if not forever. Baz had come through the despair somehow. He'd begun to write. He was now writing substantially, making a new path, spending half his day at his desk at one end of his huge studio on 39th Street and the other half at the other end, painting on the big rolling walls he'd built. There was much to support and to be supported and now no clear way to do it.

Ah, the all-too-boring resolution aka the same-old solution arrived in time. A bit more than two years later I found another office job. This time I was to head up publications at the National Multiple Sclerosis Society. And we went on going on.

A Vicente Interlude

In Bridgehampton, in the cool of his grape arbor, Esteban Vicente told Baz that his paintings were magnificent. It was July in the late 1980s. He turned to me and said how much it meant to him that Baz had learned such discipline and acquired the means to do his work. He told me I wouldn't believe the wayward, desperate kid who'd been his student at Black Mountain. How hard everything had been for him. How unruly he was. I didn't tell him that I did. I knew that desperate wayward boy had become a man who was still struggling and might need do so all his life. That wasn't what Esteban wanted to tell.

Earlier that year he had visited Basil's big studio on 39th Street and looked Baz's work for the first time in maybe thirty years. "I thought he was going to cry," Baz told me afterwards. Then, as Baz drove him up the West Side Highway back to his city digs at Hotel Des Artistes, he suddenly punched Baz on his arm so hard he nearly lost control of the car.

"You're being ignored," Esteban shouted repeatedly pounding Basil's arm. "It's shameful!" There was white foam in the corners of his mouth, and no way for Baz to pull the car off the road because the West Side Highway was still in a half-demolished state, hemmed in by Jersey barriers. Baz showed me the bruise. At least Vicente hadn't made the car crash.

In Bridgehampton, while we ate lunch, Esteban grew morose, and told long rambling stories about how he had never lacked a dealer or a place to show. Had the world changed or had he simply had some of those inexplicable strokes of luck that turn lives? He'd come to America a foreigner, painting European infused cubist abstraction. Always elegant and nimble, he'd briefly had some sort of job with Voice of America, and met people, and had entrée. Now he was well respected, regularly exhibited, and holding down teaching gigs at Princeton and the like. The summerhouse he and Harriet had was glorious: a plain old farmhouse set well back from main road, with a modest barn they'd converted into a studio. They had added a modern guesthouse, acres of tended garden, and a wild-flower meadow. We ate under a large trellis covered by grape vine. Harriet kept calling Baz "Esteban's oldest student" and none of this, I realized, my stomach churning over Harriet's exquisite food, was going to be of the slightest help in getting Basil's work seen. Had the world changed? Oh yes.

But the visit wasn't to end like that. Suddenly that afternoon Esteban asked if we'd like to see Stefan. He meant Stefan Wolpe, the composer. They had been friends in New York for years before and after the summer Esteban spent at Black Mountain. Stefan was a special friend of ours too. Our daughter Mallory gained her name because of an epic dinner party at Stefan's apartment in New York in 1962 when I was in the waddling stage of pregnant. But that's another story. Including the two years of

413

diaper service Stefan and Hilda gave us as a baby present when Mallory was born, despite my refusal that night to name our daughter-to-be Stephanie. ("And on no account Stefan if it turns out to be a boy!") We countered him by selecting the name of one of the cooks at Black Mountain – Mallory Few. Wonderful Mallory, Baz remembered, who loved regaling the students about her former job, cooking in the North Carolina State Hospital for the Insane, and thus, "I have no problem putting up with *you*!"

In Bridgehampton Baz and I exchanged nervous looks. See Stefan? He had died in 1972.

"Oh, suuure," Esteban drawled. "He's just over in Springs. Just a little drive. Harriet can take us. You know when Adolph died (he meant the painter/sculptor Adolph Gottlieb) his family took him away to Queens somewhere and now we'll never see him again."

So Harriet drove us all as asked and there was Stefan's grave, and Frank O'Hara's, and Jackson Pollock's, and my dad's old lover Jean Stafford's as well. Some marked with headstones. Pollock's with a large native boulder. Lots of pine needles. A stone wall fence. Notices. "Grace / to be born and live as variously as possible" on Frank's.

After that we would never doubt Esteban's deep Spanish identification, his surety that death is among us always. But when I asked if *he* wanted to be buried in Springs as well, he got huffy and changed the subject.

As it happens we'll never see *him* again. He died in Bridgehampton in 2001 and Harriet took him back to Spain. He's buried in a plot on the grounds of the Esteban Vicente Museum in Segovia. But I tend to think bodies are dead but art is not. So I say we saw him again in the winter of 2014 in North Carolina, where the Asheville Museum mounted a luxurious exhibition of his collages. And there will be more.

Goodbye, Ma

She's still where we put her in 1989. At the back of our backyard,
just to the left of a large blue hydrangea. The remains of a cat are
close by: Mallory's beloved Zeke, aka Mr. Nibs, the Dignified
Duke. But he's wrapped in a blanket, not, like Esther, turned to
ash and packaged in a tin can. It looked quite like a paint can – one
would use a screwdriver to pry off the lid but we didn't want to.

We didn't want the ashes at all.

When Basil's father died six years earlier, Baz opened the
little strong box his dad had given him. "Everything is taken care
of," Mark said when he gave Baz the key. There were three
documents inside: a will, which was a 10-page form signed and
witnessed but with no specifics filled in; a bill, unpaid, from the
uptown law firm that had supplied it; and information about a
funeral home for cremation. Baz called them to confirm and then
went there to sign documents that would permit a pick up. It was
an Irish establishment. Jews almost never elect cremation. The
funeral director, Baz said, was a dead ringer for W.C. Fields. "What
do we owe?" Baz asked.

"Oh Mr. King, this is a trying time for you. I'm sure all the
arrangements have been made," the director said and left Baz with a
cup of coffee. He was gone a long time. When he showed up again

it was clear he'd had a stiff shot or two. His nose and eyes were red and watery as he agreed with what Baz had tried to tell him: No, they hadn't been paid a penny. But, along with a basic cremation they offered simple disposal. The ashes left the city along with a whole barge-full of municipal detritus to be dumped in the Atlantic. This was pretty much what Mark had asked for: to go back to the ocean, "where we all came from." He didn't want a funeral service. He was, he said, "simply passing away."

By the time Esther died the city had passed an ordinance that forbade free disposal of human remains in the ocean. As if horrified that this could be done without ceremony, we wondered. Or was it simply to levy some extra dough? Dead dogs and refrigerators were and are still are carted away free, but a small can of human ash requires a fee. An extra $150 as Basil remembers. I remember it was more. Whichever, it was money we didn't have much of to pay for something we didn't think should have a special price.

    The funeral home called requesting we retrieve the ashes.

    Now what? What had been a simple part of the process for Mark became as complicated as Basil's life with Esther: A mother who had never kissed him. Not ever. A mother who bragged to her girlfriends in front of him when he was four that she had never wanted a baby and had gone through with it only because her husband had begged her so. Also a mother who saved Basil's future constitution by refusing to follow the medical advice of the time.

She threw into the Thames the expensive and sadistic brace he was supposed to wear to correct his birth injury, his semi-paralyzed right side. Right over the Embankment fence it sailed because young Baz was sobbing from the pain it caused. She blandly told him he wasn't going to be a cripple, took him home, and taught him to pick up marbles with his toes. This is also the same mother who gave away the family candlesticks that her only son had particularly asked for, who alienated his about-to-be in-laws by sending them a letter full of lies about him just before his marriage to me, and who announced in front of our half-grown daughters that he should never have been born. Her body language and her daily acts all said that Basil didn't actually belong to her. That nothing did. Her kindness and spunk and inventiveness emerged only when the stakes were completely indirect.

We certainly weren't going to get an urn and keep her on our mantelpiece. We discussed dropping the container into the harbor from the back of a Staten Island ferry. Sounded okay, but I was terrified we'd be observed. In fact we couldn't suss out a place in the city where we could safely scatter ashes. We finally talked about dropping the unopened can into a city litter basket. Then it would go out to sea, we reasoned.

The funeral home called again. They were peeved.

"I'll meet you there," I said. The funeral home was on the East Side about thirty blocks south of Sloan-Kettering where I was working. I walked.

Then we walked downtown together carrying the can. We passed litter basket after litter basket. Basil's face looked like a thundercloud. I simply couldn't do it. It felt too creepy to me. Without the bracing support of rage, I was undone. Was this superstition or civilization? By the time we reached 14th Street the can was getting heavier. Clearly it was pure fright on my part. Did passersby know what I was carrying? What we were carrying? We'd begun passing the shopping bag holding the can back and forth between us. This had to stop. At 14th Street we took a subway home to Brooklyn. The can still with us.

It was Baz who settled it.

When Baz dug the hole in our backyard I had a brief twinge imagining his shovel hitting a cat skeleton. Zeke! But it didn't happen. Now oddly it's fine. Esther's attitude toward the garden apartment we had given her and Mark rent-free was as inconsistent as anything else she ever did. Her stream of intense complaints about that apartment ended when we moved the two of them to a retirement hotel in Long Beach, where Nassau County had more generous senior benefits than the city. Then the complaints did a 180. Both of them, she and Mark, asked us often for a visit "home." "To have tea in the garden," Esther would say. Using the garden was something they had robustly refused to do for the nine long years when the ground-floor apartment, with its back door to the backyard, had been theirs. Now the space belonged not to us but to our tenants. The request rankled us into rigid refusal, even if we could have arranged it with the young couple living there.

But now time has passed again, and the house has been changed again and again. The garden which I had gradually coaxed into flowering grows more abundant every year. Now it's tea every day all day long, down under the blue hydrangea. We've even agreed that we're sorry Mark isn't there as well. There is something salutary about it after all. Tamped down and located, not scattered or dispersed, Esther is exactly where we put her.

Lucia's Memorial
Lucia Berlin (1936-2004)

"Why did Lucia die on her birthday?" Bob Holman was drinking a large Bloody Mary, very spicy, made by the young woman tending his bar.

The Bowery Poetry Club has installed a new bar since we were last in here. A bit high for the old red vinyl bar stools.

"I think she wanted it that way," Baz said. "Lucia was a witch, you know. A lot of power that woman."

The bar girl was unattractive, seemingly. A bit pasty, a bit overweight, loud, clumsy. The bar had just opened and she was still setting up. It took her a while. But she wasn't actually unattractive. She was animated, jerkily, with a random energy. A lopsided smile broke past her untidy short brown hair. She exuded well-meaning as she came puffing past us carrying a very large plastic bag of ice. Bob jumped up from his stool to take it from her. There was some problem with an ice machine. Was ice all over the cellar floor? No, but something was malfunctioning. They both took in whatever it was phlegmatically. Snafu, the old saying. Bet Lucia would remember that means "situation normal all fucked up."

The bar was empty, as you can tell from this. Bob flipped off the work lights, leaving the stage area dark, and the more cheerful lights over the bar dominated. Baz and I had come about ten minutes before two, the advertised time for the event: "Come celebrate Lucia Berlin's life and work. Bring a favorite piece of hers to read."

All the way over from the 2nd Avenue subway stop, Baz had been prepping me not to expect many people. Cold? Too close to Christmas season? Grey? Not exactly, he said.

There weren't even any people up front, where Poetry Club sells coffee and snacks and there are newspapers, magazines, a few tables, some beat up easy chairs. You'd think on an early December Saturday afternoon there might be a few people eating muffins, reading, waiting for someone.

"She was a very private person," Baz said. "She used her life for her fiction and you think you know her from reading it, but you don't. It's all been transformed. You think you see it, but you don't. Which she wanted."

"She really was a witch," I said to Bob. He was wearing his dark leather vest and that leather hat of his that's half yarmulke, half Chinese sage's cap. "She nearly killed our relationship before it began." I told him that Paul Metcalf had given me a copy of her short story "My Jockey" and told me the tale, now legend in San Francisco, about how Lucia had sent it in to a writing contest, typed single spaced, on crumpled coffee-stained paper. The typescript had her name on it too. Thereby breaking every single one of the contest rules, though her name hardly mattered because no one knew her name. But length was an issue; the story was way short. Just a page. Maybe 200-250 words. A tiny story in which every word works like the knots on a jockey's silks. Brightly colored string. Springs back into a knot when pulled and released. The jury gave her the prize, to their credit. Who were the jurors? Jack Foley? Ron Loewinsohn? Barry Gifford? It's a very large jury by now, the way legend grows such things. They had no choice but to break the rules, the story is that good.

Paul Metcalf gave me her address and said I should get in touch with her. I did. I was publishing *Giants Play Well in the Drizzle* then, and I asked her to send me work for it.

She wrote back that she didn't have anything ready – so I asked if I could reprint "The Pony Bar, Oakland" just out in a collection from Tombouctou Books. That was 1984. Did she send me the book, to thank me for contacting her? I don't remember how I got it. "The Pony Bar, Oakland" is unforgettable. Starts with attention to two sounds: "A perfect pool break." "Perfect crack of a cricket bat." Then moves seamlessly from the gray flannels of prep school boys at a country club in Chile to a biker on a bar stool in Oakland, with hinges tattooed on his wrists and elbows.

I put it in *Drizzle* number 6. She and I wrote back and forth after that. She resisted my mention of Basil, which I couldn't figure quite: Was this feminism? Don't talk about yourself in terms of a man? It was more than a whiff; it was total dismissal. And then came a letter in which she referred to him directly. She called him Brian.

Basil flipped. "She's a witch! Where'd she get that name? I'm sorry – she knows *exactly* what she's saying!"

"Brian" was the engraved name. "Brian" had been carved into a wooden banister at the boarding school where Baz was sent the year he was seven. At the Bowery I told Bob the story: "A female Captain Queeg ran that school. When she found the carving she made all the boys sign their names. Baz wrote his the biggest, and that was all she needed. He was the culprit. When he wouldn't confess, he was locked in a closet."

"The whole story is in *mirage*," I said. Bob was listening to me, mouth agape. He's read Baz's book *mirage* and talked to Baz about it, but it was as if he'd never heard the story before. Baz was locked in on a Wednesday afternoon. He thinks it was Friday morning before he was let out. For certain his father was coming Saturday and the headmistress and her cronies had become frightened at being unable to break him.

Brian, Brian! Baz was adamant that Lucia had picked the name by picking up the vibe.

"I had to ask Metcalf to intervene," I told Bob. "Baz didn't want another letter from her coming into his house!" After some time passed, after Metcalf wrote to Baz, Baz calmed down and I resumed writing to her.

Hettie Jones came into the bar. Bob said something fond and rude about her size, and kissed her. He and Baz helped her up onto the bar stool, where, of course her feet dangled. She's tinted her hair and had it cropped in short tufts. It should be jaunty but she looks tired and worried. She's still recovering from the bike accident she had this fall. A skateboarder blindsided her; she flew off her bike seat and into the air before crashing on the pavement. A forearm broken, bruises along her side showing, she was a bit proud, how fine her falling form had been (ankle, knee, hip, shoulder, like the best trained dancer in town) but there was also nerve damage to her foot and leg. And nerve injuries can be the worst.

She showed off her new boots – Ecco's, very expensive. Hiding perfectly the little ankle brace she's been prescribed. Nerve damage is very slow to heal. She's waiting for MRI results, which won't say anything much, she's convinced. The blow was a blow.

"I remember what a good teacher Lucia was at Naropa," Hettie said. "She had that cannula thing in her nose, and the cart for hauling her oxygen cylinder. She was in a wheelchair most of the time. It was all just normal, as far as she was concerned. She dispensed with it. You didn't even sense her 'getting over'. I can really dig that now," Hettie said. "Not that I didn't then."

I wanted to know how Hettie knew her, since Hettie was so close all her life with Helene, Ed Dorn's first wife. And Ed was Lucia's lifelong love, around and among her four husbands, and irrespective of whatever did or didn't pass between the two them. I was thinking Helene might easily have seen Lucia as a rival or even as an enemy. Helene was possessive. For example it was important

– essential! – for Helene to have her children, even Ed's biological son, firmly on "her side" when their union dissolved. At the end of Ed's life he re-established something with those children. Or so Lucia told me. Lucia said Ed saw all of his by then grown children at the end. She said his bitterness had subsided and he'd used his dying time well. As for Hettie's closeness with Helene tainting a relationship with Lucia, well, Hettie said, Lucia just wasn't that way. Ed and Helene's relationship was just another thing. Everyone, everything could be included in her world. Made her sound saintly, unreal.

Soon all three of us were talking about the little we each really knew about her. Start with her name. The many Lucias. Lu-SEE-ah. Lu-CHEE-ah. LU-sha. LU-chi-ah. Then Berlin, a name by marriage – what other last names had she used?

I told about sitting on a gravestone in the St. Marks churchyard and Ed telling me Lucia had caused him to accept the medical model for alcoholism. One resists this kind of reductionism, especially Ed Dorn would. He knew that the subtleties of addiction include a great deal more than most theories palatable to white-coated doctors. But in her, it clearly was disease, a kind of biochemical revenge. He asked me if I'd ever seen her drunk. My answer was no. He said I was lucky. The Lucia he and I loved could be totally taken over by drink; she could become Mr. Hyde, raging and loathsome, Ed said.

Baz loved the story Lucia told him about her experiences with AA. "Such sweet people," she'd said. "They were so understanding. I'd slip up. They'd forgive me. They'd forgive me. They'd forgive me. Again and again. They were so damn nice, well I just went right on drinking! Shall I tell you, a headshrink got me straight. The meanest s.o.b. in the Bay Area. It took about a year."

Two video people came in and sat at our end of the bar. They were working with each other on something and Bob was doing something with their project. He left us to discuss something with them. When they all returned to the bar, we told them we were together to celebrate Lucia Berlin's life – in a fitting way, in a bar, as alcohol had been her nemesis. Hettie remembered another funny story about Naropa. She told it and we laughed and the two videographers lost interest. Neither Lucia's name nor the names in the stories meant anything to them.

Bob asked the three of us to read the things we'd brought.

Hettie began. She had one of her own poems, a narrative piece, called "Doing Seventy" – set on the road from Maine, with Helene Dorn's memorabilia packed in boxes on the back seat. Helene died the previous summer, the same year Hettie turned 70. Hettie loves being the killer driver. Always in fatally flawed cars. So you know before she tells you that her car will break down. Her poem was like a trip to the attic. Why did someone carefully store that large broken pot? Who are the people in this scrapbook? It was sweet too, with Hettie drooling (discreetly) for the tight young body of the wrecker driver, who towed her car and her all the way back to the Lower East Side from somewhere, Massachusetts.

Jane Augustine dashed in, breathlessly. She had promised to meet me here, she was picking up a copy of my poetry collection, *Imperfect Fit*, which she planned to give to someone for a Christmas present. She said couldn't stay, visibly taken aback at the sight of the three of us, sitting together at the bar. She'd left Michael outside – the two of them were late for somewhere. She had told me when we arranged to meet that she wouldn't be able to stay at the memorial very long. Now she furnished too many reasons about where she and Mike had to go and what they had to do, kissed us all, and ran out.

Bob talked me into switching from my bar whiskey drink (finished now) to a Bloody Mary, joining Baz, who was ready for his second. "She really makes them right," Bob said about his bartender. She did.

I read Lucia's story "Pony Bar."

Baz, Bob, and Hettie applauded.

I read another piece I'd put in the *Drizzle*, by no means as edited, stacked, or shaped as "Pony Bar" but full of Lucia's hilarious observations from her stint as a nurse in the emergency room: a wrinkled old lady being lectured by an aging barroom beauty in a voluptuous beige silk slip, recommending Preparation H for facelifts; then the gun. Someone had a gun. The threat of violence is always there. Always permutated, always normal.

Lucia, who nursed people dear in her life to their ends, among them her sister and then one of her ex-husbands, woke up alone on her birthday in November this year. That was it. It came to me: she woke up dead that day.

"Who is Mrs. Booth? " she had emailed in September, after Baz sent her this poem from his new book, *Learning to Draw*:

J.M.W. Turner: Sunrise with Sea Monster, 1845

> I told
> Mrs. Booth
> all I
> want
> is to
> sit on
> my porch
> and watch
> the sea.
>
> She told me
> I don't sleep
> enough. She told
> me the sea corrupts
> frogs and men with
> out hats. I told
> her I was going
> fishing. She told
> me to wear my old
> boots and not to
> forget
> the imagination
> spawns monsters.
>
> I
> fear

vapors
constant
fog
the monster's
big eyes
its many teeth.

Cross
my heart
Mrs. Booth
I am going
to paint
The Monster
at Sunrise.

Baz had so much fun replying that his letter to her became another
section in *Learning to Draw*. He told her how Caroline Booth ran a
boarding house with her husband in Margate, a seaside town where
Turner used to stop on his way to Petworth, Lord Egremont's
castle in Sussex. Turner had a terrific deal with Lord E. who ran a
never-ending house party in the country, a crazy upper crust
commune. The castle was always filled with guests, doing whatever.
Turner had a permanent studio there where he spent months at a
time, painting the meadows, the fornicating deer, the sunsets, and a
few interiors including one very strange woman's back, charged full
of Petworth intrigue. But Mrs. Booth is another story. Her
husband died, and so too did Lord Egremont. The Petworth idyll
was ended. Egremont's children kicked Turner out.

Soon after, he talked Mrs. Booth into moving up to Chelsea
and buying a house on Cheney Walk. It was a rundown neighbor-

hood then. Retired mariners. Grog shops. She opened another boarding house and Turner was known in the neighborhood as Mr. Booth. Mrs. Booth made him see the dentist, wear a hat, and let him cut a hole in her roof and build a high porch for an unobstructed view over the Thames. He gave her many drawings and watercolors, and told her to ask John Ruskin for help if the day came that she might need money. She was in her early forties. Turner was twenty years older. I think of her with reddish hair, not pretty but with terrific eyes. They had a good thing going, Baz wrote.

Lucia liked her too.

While Baz read, Bob closed his eyes. He's a fine listener, with an interesting range from low to high. He is seriously devoted to erasing snobberies that impede access in either direction. Emotion beats the air into undercurrents whenever Baz reads. And his changes demand concentration.

At some point after that – I was by then working on my second Bloody Mary – I thought it was time for the wrap so I read a poem I wrote for Lucia and the poet Laurie Duggan last year, when both had sent me work to read and I'd left the texts on my desk for months, unanswered. (We all know this guilt.)

"Bless every dirty breath I take," is the opening line – guilt breeding sentiment, but it's not so bad. I'm sure it's not. Just asthma. "Working backward" the poem is called. That Bloody Mary was *extreme*. It was still daytime, and the bar was filling up for the Bowery's four o'clock event. Suddenly, there were many people, adults, children, dogs leashed up outside, dogs inside by the front windows, all eating muffins. Bob was becoming busy: he keeps the Poetry Club whirling, every day, every night. A young woman and her friends have claimed his attention. The young woman is holding one of those large fake leather portfolios, zippered all around, and Bob wants to get out of something he must have promised her by persuading Baz to look at her work. Or he wants to put something together, because introducing this one to that one is one of his business-making pleasures.

Baz is cheerful but says he won't give critique "if you don't pay me." He gets a freebie, another of those amazing Bloody Marys, and goes off with the artist and her clique, Bob ambling behind them. They occupy the edge of the stage, where the young woman can spread her work out.

Hettie and I stay on our bar stools and talk family. Ours has had a terrible loss. Our daughter Hetty miscarried her twins on November 12. The same day Lucia died. A month ago. It was the aftermath a whole string of spontaneous miscarriages she had endured. And then healthy pregnancy of twins, and then an amnio-centesis which somehow introduced infection. The means of it mean so little. The fact of it so large and irreducible. Hetty gave birth to two pound-and-a-half baby boys, deep purple in color and so young one's mouth was still fused. They were genetically perfect it turned out. But not to be.

Hettie's daughter Lisa is pregnant. She's due a few months sooner than our daughter would have been. Lisa is old for pregnancy and Hettie is terrified in a way that is completely unfamiliar to her. She can't rely on her innate energy, the power that has supported her all her life, to keep this right. The bike accident has sapped her. So we talk intensely to each other and don't pay attention to anything else. The life of the Bowery Poetry Club goes on. Lucia Berlin's memorial is over.

"It was what she wanted," Baz said to me out on the street. "Lucia didn't really want anyone to come." We headed to the subway. To follow his logic, she chose just us to be there.

So Long. Home Sick. Safe and Sound. Phantom Pain. Manual for Cleaning Women. Where I Live Now. Lucia Berlin, writer.

HOME

Where is what makes you feel home?

In 1961, when we lived on Avenue D, all the way east on the Lower East Side, we had a home. In our mad rush to vacate Ferry Street and escape fines for living in an industrial loft, we managed rented squalor, a temporary device. A bed. A table. A floor, a room with electric lights. A building permeated by the stinks of poverty cooking, feral cats, dirty clothes, fear. It was home.

Later that year we moved into apartment #81, 57-59 Second Avenue at Fourth Street, on the eighth floor, with sun in the windows, and for it we purchased home things: a gold fish and a gold fish bowl. A globe, a pretty yellow one, so old it showed "Palestine, Brit Mandate." A dark maple-wood rocking chair. A bridge lamp with a yellow shade. We painted the walls white and the floor a lovely maroon. And when we were finished, the roof leaked and water softened the plaster all the way through the ninth floor and down to our wall on the eighth and the big round mirror we'd acquired loosened and crashed into splinters. Why had we wanted it? A heavy, frameless circle of glass we bought in a junk store on Allen Street. Well, it had doubled the size of our living room, portholed it, so there was another smaller day bed covered with India print and bright cushions, a second squat brown coffee table. But after the crash there were zillions of sharp glass shards and seven years bad luck.

Just seven?

It is 2001. Baz and I are just back from ten days in Rome. We've gone on a holiday because we're homeless. We are out of the house in Brooklyn where we have lived since 1969, because it is being renovated. Out of the house we often changed by moving around inside it: first living on the top three floors, then on the bottom two, then on all four. Now we're changing everything again.

We have thrown out old furniture. Many paperbacks had turned into orange dust over the years. We've packed up belongings until we're black and blue with it.

Home. We're lightening up, I hope. I want to throw a whole lot of stuff away. Less stuff is my plan, just as it once was when I left home in Chapel Hill fleeing from stuff. I was 19. I wanted two plates, two cups. I wanted to be free of my mother's obsessions, the objects on which she pinned her identity. I wanted to be far away from my father's imperialism. Baz has the opposite feeling. His fractured wartime childhood – and his parents' move to America – caused the loss of so many possessions that he can hardly bear to part with anything unless it is clearly too broken or desiccated to ever use again.

Despite my craving for domestic minimalism it turns out I kept and kept and kept, not only mine but also my mother's stuff after she died. I even retrieved some of her stuff my siblings had discarded. Tell me about it.

Renovation will get rid of the fake-wood plastic walls in the ground floor kitchen, which we had covered with two decades worth of postcards from friends and family. The wobbling toilet, the rust-eaten shower stall – out! I've scribbled "You're history" in dark brown marking pen on the wall in the dining room that I've hated for twenty years, the wall that created a stupid dark little hallway. The workmen will crowbar out the jerrybuilt closets in that hallway, dumpster the patched doors, rip out the bozo storage shelves we put up in the pantry.

Upstairs, Baz will gain six precious feet of painting space and with a wall gone, light from the hallway skylight will finally spill into his front studio. I will have a bathtub, an actual full-size bathtub, in the new bathroom on the top floor. The trade calls this a gut renovation. We're replacing many worn out guts.

Out go all the old wiring and original plumbing – the improvised and the antique. Down come the patched and re-patched ceilings. Out go closets that are in the wrong places, doors that open on the wrong side. We'll have French doors in the kitchen out into our garden, French doors, a dream of Basil's since his childhood. We'll have a big room for a big party.

In 1969, we had our stash of lobster money, two children, and we needed to move. The equation was pretty stark: we could stay squeezed in on Second Avenue, fix the place up a bit, and pay to send the kids to private schools or we could move to a neighborhood where public grammar schools were possible.

The house we bought was just four blocks from Prospect Park, jewel of Brooklyn, and three blocks from an ordinary public school. It was on a street where kids played hopscotch and jacks on the sidewalk and little girls sat on the stoops to dress their dolls. It was a house riddled with holes, broken walls, and 95-year-old plaster too brittle to repair. The entrance had a tin screen door in front stamped with a cocker spaniel. Ugh. A block down, on 5th Avenue, was a dangerous park, littered with crack vials and broken bottles. But we didn't need to go there. What we had was home.

In 2001 we've selected a minimum of stuff to make do in a three-room apartment on the top floor of Mallory's house in Jersey City. A table with two chairs barely fits into its kitchen. That's where we'll eat. A minimum of pots, pans, and dishes to fit into the two built-in cabinets. Remember two cups, two plates? A windowless middle room holds our two desks, two chairs, two computers. We fit in back to back, each facing a wall, and mustn't both shove away from work at the same moment or we'll collide. Mallory and her husband Sansana are happy to have us but a bit dismayed as we moved our stuff in and they grasped what we were actually doing.

"Are you going to be okay, dad?" Mallory asked, the worry in her hazel eyes shining through her glasses.

In the front room we've crammed Basil's easy chair, our big brass bed, a chest for clothes with our TV on top, a bookcase with space for our CD player at the bottom, and by the window furthest from the radiator, Basil's studio table. Four feet by three feet. Rather smaller than a cell. This space will be his art world, his medium, his only studio space from March to August 2001, and then we can go home.

Is this like house arrest? What is home when it changes? To home is a verb.

After my father died, my mother moved from their modest house in Chapel Hill to what was termed a deluxe apartment in a retirement center. It was an intense compression of her living space although she had a bedroom, a living room with a wide picture window, a kitchenette, bathroom, luxurious walk-in closet and a large storage room.

Once there her apartment had a look and style quite like her old house. The furniture and pictures were familiar. Her old rugs were spread out covering the standard issue beige wall-to-wall. There were glass doors opening onto a common, with a personal patch of concrete just outside the apartment's back door where my mother put some outdoor chairs and flower pots.

Like our Jersey City apartment, it was functional – and trapped. Perhaps it's the truncated pathways. How few steps it takes to go from room to room. How close our faces are over the small kitchen table.

Baz and I have chosen books to support work we hope to do while we are here. We will fight this feeling of being trapped. Our family, our daughter Mallory, her husband Sansana, and their little kid, our two-year-old granddaughter Satrianna, are just down the stairs. How mean to complain of feeling trapped when I can see my daughter and granddaughter quietly blowing bubbles together in their brick paved back yard? When we can we share an evening meal with them. But first, before our exile kicked in seriously, Baz planned for us to go to Rome.

After all the packing and preparation all I wanted to do was sleep. "I'm too done in for a trip," I wailed.

"Trust me," Baz said. "Rome. We'll stay put there for ten days. Won't go anywhere else," he promised. We're going home, I finally agree, to Rome, the center civ of Western civ. He and I don't believe Greek propaganda. Without the Romans, Greek art and ideas would be as dead as dust. Like any power, the Romans changed what they saved. And so we're going to Roman Rome from which all of Europe was shaped.

Home.

In Rome we find a favorite last stop of the day not far from our pension. It's a bar/restaurant with an ample covered terrace on the broad road that circles below the big park where the French Academy is. We've also discovered the free elevator inside the metro stop that hoists you up the Spanish Steps when you'd rather not climb them. On the terrace, and from that road, you see repeats of Peter's dome, in church after church, from one neighborhood to the next. The boxy office towers are banished to the suburbs. They sulk in the haze far to the right of our view, way across the river to the north.

We order Campari and orange juice: we have appetizers of black olives, anchovy, and tiny artichokes. There's a small fountain in a rectangular tiled basin, with four dark green turtles living in it. The sun is setting. We wear dark glasses, looking very Dolce Vita, because the slanting western light is dazzling, and we talk about where we might eat dinner and what art and architecture we want to see the next day. We have shucked time. It's too early to go home and change for dinner. Home is a dark pension with two extremely narrow beds. I messed up big time by asking for a double bed. They reserved a room for us with twin beds. We now know, too late, we should have asked for the *matrimonial*. Old Mother Latin one more time.

Two weeks later we are home again, back in our old brass matrimonial, which has been uneasily transplanted to Jersey City. Where Baz will sit at that table and do a series of graphics employing three different iconographies, and many many pieces of drawing paper. He will do an homage to Rimbaud who has been with him most of his life. Rimbaud who mastered classical forms and never abandoned them; Rimbaud who blew French language apart to make room for the contradictions of modern times.

There will be one set for "Drunken Boat" in ink washes black and white; one set for "Illuminations" in saturated stained glass colors from high-tech colored pencils and turpentine; and one set for "A Season in Hell" in pastels and charcoals, greys and pinks. He'll do almost a hundred of them in all, in between trips back to Brooklyn to review what's happening at our house.

Most of the time he'll take the Path train, cross the huge underground mall at World Trade Center, and hop the R train to Brooklyn. But once in a while, he'll walk down to the bottom of Liberty State Park, about twenty minutes from Mallory's house, and treat himself to the water taxi, a five-minute ride over the river to North Cove, right under the World Trade towers, under the iconic double-dash late-capitalism shrine, huge, shining, minimalist, and blank.

"No wonder they don't like my paintings," Baz said to me on a bright summer day late in August 2001. "This is their ideal. All surface. Impervious. Nothing comes out."

I'm back at my job in Manhattan five days a week, giving my weekdays a familiar pattern. And in early mornings, or in hours on the weekends, I keep working at becoming a prose stylist.

I am not an innovator. I write short narratives. I practice no faith, every day. I find it as hard to imagine going back to our home in Brooklyn where everything is now new as I do staying here, where my daughter and her family are at home, but we, loving them, nevertheless strain with the unreality of waiting to go home.

Where unreality awaits all of us. Our return takes place just two weeks before Tuesday, September 11, 2001.

What Rolls On

When I walked into my office Carolyn said, "A plane just crashed into the World Trade Center."

"That's crazy. It couldn't be a clearer morning."

I was thinking of the small plane that had crashed into the Empire State Building in a fog years before.

"No," she said.

A bit later, after we looked at newsfeed images, weird and tiny, on Sarah's desktop computer, I got it together to phone Baz.

"I'm okay," I said.

"Okay? Why shouldn't you be okay?" Yes, he'd heard some fire trucks down on 4ᵗʰ Avenue earlier. It hadn't seemed unusual at the time. When I hung up my sister Charlotte phoned him from California.

I'd always liked our view of the towers over the treetops in the park at the end of our street because the exact opposite view was available from a corner by Mallory's house in Jersey City. Triangulation. Bouncing a note of hello between us.

Now waves of stinking smoke bearing tiny scraps of burned paper rolled over all our part of Brooklyn, sticking in the grass and flowers. Baz knew that stink from the Blitz. More phone calls poured in: Australia, England, North Carolina. One before I got home was from Andrew in Manhattan. He was yet to become our younger daughter Hetty's husband. He was crying. "I've lost her. Her cell phone doesn't answer." No one's did. Only landlines functioned once the giant WTC mast was down.

The F train from Manhattan ran as usual. The water ran. Electricity and gas were undiminished. The sun kept shining. Traffic lights switched from red to green and back again. We normally take in the faraway sound of jet planes without really hearing it. Planes cross the sky to and from New York's three airports, almost continuously, mostly high enough to hum not roar. Abruptly the sky was completely silent. Mid-afternoon a military plane flew loud and low over 9th Street when Baz was on the corner. It waggled wings at the people on 5th Avenue, who waved and cheered. Downhill, crowds from lower Manhattan still filled the four lanes of Fourth Avenue…stunned and silent, walking toward their homes. Not ghosts. Just white all over with the dust of destruction.

Why did we think the ghost of old lady Campbell was in our Brooklyn house when we first moved here in 1969? She left behind old rags stuffed into the window frames so her ground floor would stay warm when she turned the thermostat way down and to hell with the seven old men upstairs in their single-occupancy rented rooms. She left behind kitchen wallpaper featuring large red tomatoes. Behind it was a massive cockroach nest. There was a square of cement in the sidewalk just in front of our house with a dog's paw print in it. Neighbor children told our kids it was a witch mark.

Of course there was horsehair in the plaster. The house was built in 1886. Old lady Campbell had been as nasty as a fairy-tale witch.

Of course the smell from 9/11 was the one Basil knew all too well.

Of course the driver of our second-hand Volvo wasn't a ghost. But I think she went on smoking and screwing people over for years after it wasn't her car any more. She was still in there. The front seat sagged heavily to the left and the ashtray lid wouldn't stay closed. She was smoking as she drove, shifting her huge hams that no way were comfortable, and making smug remarks about other people when she smashed the car into something on the left-hand side. The car was so cleverly repaired even our smart mechanic didn't spot it when he picked it up for us at an auction. He was so guilty about his mistake that he fixed that car for us over and over charging only a little and a little less. Chug chug it went, like all Volvos of that era, but the whack the frame had taken, or maybe the constant insult of her weight, meant the car was never any good.

In 1942 I went to the Dalton School in Manhattan. But first I went to P.S. 6, the "good public school." I mainly remember the hugely noisy cafeteria and how frightened I was when the sixth graders crashed in. Giants slamming their trays. There are as ever "good public schools" in the city, the one on Greenwich Avenue in the Village and P.S. 321 here in our Brooklyn neighborhood. But today the rich are so rich and the middle class has to copy them so they choose private schools whenever they can. The rich are so rich, and the middle class has to copy, so middle class teenagers don't babysit, work as lifeguards, deliver groceries, or hold any kind of blue-collar job in the summertime. Mundane employment might hurt their college chances I've been told.

Back in the long gone, Basil escaped the draft. Dirty Gertie returned our rent money because I needed a dentist. Muhammad Ali ran past us on Broadway, so large and lovely we gasped like gaga tourists. Back in the long gone, we walked down Broadway after it crossed Canal Street and it was dark all the way to the Battery. In the present, in the future, we're buying art supplies, stretchers and pigment, and new computers and I'm learning how to keep my website fresh and get good photographs with my little digital camera.

In Brooklyn we woke up and the young guy who delivers our morning *New York Times* had built a miniature snowman on our bottom step. Dead oak leaves for arms...and a smile intaglio on the face. Was that the winter with seventeen snowstorms when March meant tossing snow up over our heads to reach the top of the pile?

In Florida, the Miami Beach Bridge and all the big hotels along the ocean are being rebuilt for a third time, even though the beach itself, the sand part, is now so very narrow. Forgetting King Canute, mini-dozers push sand around "rebuilding" it. There are plastic bags and tiny pebbles of Styrofoam everywhere. How bad is it really? Neanderthals were smart enough to adapt to several cycles of dramatic climate change but they had a straightforward incentive: the animals they lived on were leaving for elsewhere so they did too. The weather was colder and the marshes dried, so they made thicker clothing and walked toward Italy. We find it very hard to move. People say the world might collapse, but very few of us really believe this.

When we left San Francisco we didn't leave a forwarding address; we were going back to New York to live and anyone who knew us would find us. Basil's ex-employer, Railway Express, found him! We were no longer staying with old friend Lynn on Patchin Place. We had moved to that almost deserted office building on White-hall Street, where no one lived and who would know, but the letter was addressed to 33 Whitehall Street, and offered him a job in New Jersey. New Jersey! Baz must have left a ghost behind. Baz had been fined by the Railway Express union for working too hard; then the big boss had called him into his office upstairs to tell him the story of *his* life, how he too had started "on the floor."

The personnel lady in charge of Sloan-Kettering's human resources glared at me. Doesn't "human resources" make people sound like rolls of copper wire or bales of cat food? She was married to a guy who served Huntington, Long Island as head of its volunteer fire department. He'd received awards and honors; he was a model for volunteer firefighters nationwide. She could not believe anyone would not work hard to acquire credentials, badges of rightness, or have unqualified respect for institutional requirements. She faced me over her desk because it had become clear to her that my resume was loaded with unproveable assertions. Seven years before I'd passed through a similar sieve at Mercy College thanks to my credentials from Caligula University. (Oh Caligula! Priceless jewel. Created by old friend Charles, artist manqué.) I'd gone on to teach at Mercy quite successfully. But Sloan-Kettering had a tougher gatekeeper. The personnel lady's eyes were hard as marbles. After my interview, the V.P. who had hired me must have put on one glorious show. He wouldn't tell me what he said. Clever s.o.b. But I kept the job. I daresay I became another crazy long-winded story for him to recount to his bar buddies. He's the one who decamped with a fat payoff, leaving the whole department to the tender mercies of Miss Elsbeth.

Our children never saw a gunfight in the city, never their whole New York City lives. But in Grand Haven, Michigan, population

30,000, when they were eight and ten, they witnessed a man with a buckshot-loaded shotgun going after the man who was schtupping his wife. In the middle of the afternoon he fired through the open front door of the small counter restaurant where she was a waitress and got the man right in the backside while the lady in question was screaming. So were a lot of the people watching. The girls didn't actually see the victim, his pants in tatters and blood streaming down, because he ran out the back of the restaurant and down the street on the other side. They saw and heard the gunman clearly enough and many people concocted excited versions of the story right on the spot. I didn't know the girls knew about marital infidelity but they assured me and Baz that none of the witnesses blamed the man with the gun. This happened three blocks from our Grand Haven house.

On our block in Brooklyn Irish Tom wanted a green lawn in the tiny front square by his brownstone's stoop. He'd rake and seed. Up it would come, fragile May-green threads. And Tom would rake. Poor grass. And every day his little brown dog would use the square to relieve himself. Tom would watch. His dog knew better than to scratch. The grass pulled by the rake and burned by the piss dried in neat little rows. Tom would lean his large arms on the fence that separated his front yard from the sidewalk and shake his heavy head. "I dunno. It never seems to catch." By and by, he'd be replanting. He did it three or four times every summer, patiently, and without a shred of hope. You don't have to wonder where Beckett got it from.

The counselor. Was she the camp girl in a dark green T-shirt or the psychologist behind a white desk, in a suit with a circle pin on her lapel? Space cadet, a real one in a NASA stretch suit. Or a guy in a rabbit suit, on hourly wages from a fried chicken joint?

Birdman, Snakeman, Flyman, Buzzard! A story better materialize!

Found in my files: "American television is full of smiles and more and more perfect-looking teeth. Do these people want us to trust them? No. Do they want us to think they're good people, that they'd never hurt a fly? No again. The truth is they don't want anything from us. They just want to show us their teeth, their smiles, and admiration is all they ask for in return. They want us to look at them, that's all. Their perfect teeth, their perfect bodies, their perfect manners, as if they were constantly breaking away from the sun and they were little pieces of fire, little pieces of blazing hell, here on this planet simply to be worshipped."

I wish I knew who wrote this because I do know why I saved it.

Birdman, Snakeman, Flyman, Buzzard! Does this story need updating? Where do we plan to have our bodies go? It won't be so many years. What has happened to the Bowery Poetry Club since Lucia's memorial? Exhibitions of Basil's art on walls in North Carolina and New York. Exhibitions to come? His published books, almost always subtitled as part of his master document *Learning to Draw.* Our grandchildren, four of them, two biological, two adopted – a beautiful bouquet of America's promise with only Australia and Antarctica missing among the continents that supplied their DNA. Published essays on Basil's poetics. Loss after loss of old friends. Yet *another* renovation here on 4th Street to ensure we can "age in place." Little pieces blazing.

We are not Buddhists. Nevertheless, Baz wrote this in *mirage: a poem in 22 sections:*

> "Eight miles outside of Northampton, my Buddha
> sits. Cross-legged and straight-backed, it sits
> surrounded by light, the essential condition of
> vision, the opposite of darkness."

That poem is a long ghost story and this is another, but it's shorter.

After Baz wrote that poem I wanted to buy a Buddha for our backyard. He agreed. We went looking in and out of shops along Greenwich Avenue one early winter evening. It had been snowing and thawing, so it was nasty and slushy and we were late for a Pauline Oliveros concert. There, in a corner window was an exquisite very young Buddha, carved in very old stone. Someone had put a necklace of bright green and red beads around its neck. It had no Buddha smile. The shopkeeper in a white knitted skullcap was Afghan. He told us the piece was at least 2,000 years old and could be purchased for $6,000. Whether it was authentic or a forgery wasn't the point. The authenticity of it was implicit. It radiated spirit. We went home and actually figured out how long it would take us to pay it off at say $20 a month. Craziness.

Two months later that year and it's full spring. I'm on 7th Avenue in Brooklyn walking past our neighborhood grammar school where there's a flea market every weekend. On the wall nearest the 2nd Street corner, a vendor sells garden ornaments, awful stuff – Praying Hands, gazing balls, bathtub Madonnas. But on this day there was a Buddha, not the strange young Buddha we saw on Greenwich Avenue, but a reproduction of a classical South Asian version, seated in lotus position, with slightly stretched ear lobes, hair dressed in a triangular pile of curls, eyes down, soft Mona Lisa lips. It was that lovely it stopped me in my tracks. I hadn't seen the vendor before. A long-hair, somewhere in his thirties. A bit grubby looking.

"How much?" I asked.

"Twenty bucks."

I started to pick the piece up, thinking for this price it must be hollow plaster but I couldn't lift it.

"Wait," said the vendor. "You'll need help."

But I wanted to wait. I know how Baz hates a compensation for a disappointment, and he might feel the piece was a poor substitute so I told the guy my husband would have to have a look before we bought it and I went home.

Baz was unconvinced that this thing was even worth a six-block walk to see. Cement? Twenty dollars? But he did go. I made him promise not to buy it unless it felt right to him. By and by he came walking back down the street with the long-haired vendor trailing behind him. The vendor had put on a wide leather back brace and was calmly carrying the thing. It's solid cement and about 24 inches high. He marched through our house out into the garden and told us that he wanted to put it down where green vegetation would grow up behind it. Which he did, choosing a flagstone in front of a patch of daylilies.

Baz had to push the $20 bill into his hand. He didn't want to take it. And I haven't seen him since that day. Sorry this sounds so X Files but I did say this was a ghost story. There's still a garden vendor by the wall on 2nd Street. This week the top of the wall is full of miniature Davids and truncated Greek columns topped by more of those blue and green gazing balls. In our neighborhood, bathtub Madonnas are out now. Victoriana is in. No Buddha anywhere.

Baz is doing our bills this afternoon but it's time to get him away from all those slips and scraps so dear to auditors and accountants. It's getting dark. It's daily life. In the summer our Buddha grows green algae in his drapery folds and in the crevasses around his curls and, in the summer, he stares down into a pool of blue ajuga, jump-ups, and the violent ever-invading never-shy violets. In the winter, stoic and industrial, with dead daylily stalks on the ground behind him, Buddha is still a question. Absorbing the essential condition of vision. Being daily life. Being art, Basil King's and Martha King's.

Sometimes I fear our persistence, Basil's and mine, to be looked at, seen, and read. But I know there is much more to it. It has to do with a need to give.

END

Glossary or Dramatis Personae

Who are these people?

...in order of their appearance

Basil King (1935–) Painter and poet, attended Black Mountain College off and on from 1951 to 1956. Married Martha King in 1958. See www.basilking.net for information about his art, publications, exhibitions, and art for small press publications.

Franz Kline (1910-1962) Leading member of the American Abstract Expressionists, best known for large black and white paintings. Lived in New York City from the early 1940s until his death; was a teacher at Black Mountain College in 1952 and an occasional visitor later. Works in major collections worldwide.

Robert Creeley (1926-2005) Poet, essayist, author of more than 60 books. Began a connection to Black Mountain College through extensive correspondence with Charles Olson starting in 1948. Edited *The Black Mountain Review*. Taught at Black Mountain in 1955-56. Major awards including the Bollingen Prize for poetry.

Charlotte Furth (1934–) Professor Emerita of Chinese History, University of Sothern California. Author, among other titles, of *A Flourishing Yin: Gender in China's Medical History 960-1665.* The author's sister.

Lambert Davis (1908-1993) Editor and publisher. From 1948 to 1970, director of the University of North Carolina Press. Also noted as the editor of Robert Penn Warren's masterpiece, *All the King's Men*. With his wife, Isabella Symmers Davis, the author's parents.

Charles Olson (1910-1970) Poet, essayist, literary theorist, polymath. Served as Rector of Black Mountain College from 1951-1956, having first taught there briefly in 1948. Best known for *The Maximus Poems*

(1953-1970), *Call Me Ishmael* (1947), a study of Melville and the writing of *Moby Dick,* and the influential *Projective Verse,* first published in 1950 in *Poetry New York.*

Constance Wilcock (aka Connie Olson) Olson's partner and mother of their daughter Kate. Their relationship ended in 1956.

Dan Rice (1927-2003) Painter of delicate abstracts, sometimes landscape based. An early talent for music was destroyed by hearing damage in the Pacific in WW2. Student at Black Mountain College intermittently 1946–1955. Works in the collections of Yale, Princeton, Wadsworth Atheneum, and the Black Mountain College Museum & Arts Center, which showed his work in a solo exhibition, "Painter Among the Poets" in 2014.

Jorge Fick (1932-2004) Abstract painter who studied at Black Mountain 1952-1955, lived in New York 1955-58, and then moved to the Southwest where his work was greatly influenced by Pueblo culture. Works in the collections of Smith College, the Whitney, Asheville Art Museum, New Mexico Museum of Art, and others.

Gerry van de Wiele (1932–) (Gerald) Painter, studied at Black Mountain College 1954-56, Later a founding member of The Wells Street Gallery in Chicago. Work shown at Leo Castelli, Peridot, and Washburn galleries in New York,1963-73.Work in the Asheville Art Museum, and in major Black Mountain exhibitions, one curated by Vincent Katz in 2002, another by Helen Molesworth in 2015-16.

Stefan Wolpe (1902-1972) German-born, DaDa influenced, atonal composer. Taught at Black Mountain College, 1951-1956, and tutored major American jazz players including Gil Evans, as well as avant guardists Ralph Shapey, Morton Feldman and David Tutor. His work is now widely recognized, performed and recorded in Germany, which he fled in 1933.

Hilda Morley Wolpe (1916-1998) Poet, born Hilda Auerbach, often wrote ekphrastic poetry influenced by friendships with New York abstract painters before her marriage to Stefan Wolpe. Taught at Black Mountain College 1951-1956. Was not published until 1976. Died in London, after many years in New York City and Sag Harbor.

Tony Landreau (1930-2009) (Anthony) Painter, weaver, textile historian, who was a student and then a teacher at Black Mountain College, 1953-1955. Later director of the Textile Museum in Washington. At 65, after an eventful life in California, Peru, Iran, Maine, and Pennsylvania, he earned a PhD in anthropology and taught at Yakima Valley Community College, Washington, to be near one of his three sons.

Joe Dunn (1934-1996) Poet and publisher. Student at Black Mountain 1955-1956. Founded White Rabbit Press in San Francisco in 1957 at the urging of poet Jack Spicer producing chapbooks by Spicer, Robert Duncan, George Stanley, Helen Adam, and others including Denise Levertov, Charles Olson, and Joe's own poetry, *The Better Dream House* (1968). Left California to live in his home state, Massachusetts. Information on Joe now greatly amplified by Carolyn Dunn's memoir *Eyewitness: From Black Mountain to White Rabbit* (Granary Books, 2015).

Tom Field (1930-1995). (Ralph Thomas) Abstract and abstract-figurative painter. At Black Mountain 1953–1956. Lived and worked in the San Francisco area thereafter, supporting himself as a merchant seaman. Works in the collections of the San Francisco Museum, SUNY Buffalo, the Asheville Art Museum, and others.

Michael Rumaker (1932–)Writer and memoirist, perhaps best known for *Black Mountain Days*. Other semi-autobiographical prose often focuses on life as a gay man: *A Day and a Night at the Baths*, *My First Satyrnalia* and *Pagan Days*. A rare graduate of Black Mountain College in 1955; his outside examiner was William Carlos Williams.

John Chamberlain (1927-2011) Sculptor, who first gained prominence with large abstract pieces using colored metals from cars and other manufactured items. At Black Mountain 1955-56. Works in major museums worldwide including the Whitney, Centre Pompidou, Tate Modern, and the Hirshhorn.

Elaine Chamberlain (dates unknown) John Chamberlain's wife until her early death; studied sculpture at the Art Institute of Chicago, where she met him. At Black Mountain 1955-56.

Ed Dorn (1929-1999) Poet. Most well known for the marvelous, satiric multi-part poem *Gunslinger*, 1968-1974. Studied at Black Mountain

1950-55. Author of some 30 additional books of poetry and essays. Edited the magazine *Rolling Stock* at the University of Colorado, Boulder, with his second wife, Jennifer.

Helene Dorn (1927-2004) Sculptor and collagist. Ed Dorn's first wife. At Black Mountain in 1955. A collection of the 40-year correspondence between Helene and Hettie Jones, *Love H*, was published by Duke University Press in 2016.

Wes Huss (1918- 2018) (Wesley J.) Theater teacher and treasurer at Black Mountain 1950-1956. Was a Quaker relief worker and C.O. during WW2 and served in Civilian Public Service work camps for the duration. After Black Mountain closed he returned to the American Friends and for years oversaw fieldwork in Oakland with urban, rural, and Native American people. After retiring, lived with his wife Sonia in California.

Joe Fiore (1925-2008) (Joseph) Artist and teacher at Black Mountain College 1949-1956. Exclusively abstract work during his BMC days, Fiore later incorporated landscape. Taught at institutions including Parsons, Philadelphia College of Art, and Artists for the Environment in the Delaware Water Gap. Works in the collections of Maine Farmland Trust, Asheville Art Museum, the Corcoran, and the Whitney.

Mary Fitton Fiore (1924-2017) Student at Black Mountain from 1949-56. Married Joe Fiore while both were students. Ceased writing after leaving the school.

Jonathan Williams (1929-2008) Poet, publisher, photographer, essayist, founded the Jargon Society to publish "Black Mountain" poets. However the house list mirrors Williams' capacious taste for inventive writing: Mina Loy, Lorine Niedecker, Paul Metcalf, Ronald Johnson, and many others. Author of some 10 books of poetry and photography including *An Ear in Bartram's Tree* published by the University of North Carolina Press while the author's father was director and editor-in-chief.

Fielding Dawson (1930-2002) (Fee)Writer and artist, at Black Mountain intermittently 1949 to 1953. Among his more than 18 books —novels, memoir, and brilliant short stories — is *An Emotional Memoir of Franz Kline* which covers some of the same period as this memoir.

Paul Metcalf (1917-1999) Writer of monumental multi-voiced works between poetry and prose exploring American histories, the best known of which may be *Genoa: A Telling of Wonders.* Nancy Blackford Metcalf was his wife. Lived for a number of years near Asheville before returning to his native New England.

Robert Duncan (1919-1988) Poet and devotee of the Western esoteric tradition. Early and eloquent voice for gay rights. Taught briefly at Black Mountain in 1956, but lived most of his life in California. Eschewed publication for long periods but was nominated for a National Book Award for *Groundwork: Before the War-Part I* in 1984. Works are now widely available from New Directions and other publishers.

John Wieners (1934-2002) Boston-born lyric poet, variously identified as San Francisco Renaissance, gay rights, Beat, or Black Mountain school, and currently having a re-evaluation, with new collections of his poetry, journal entries, and letters published by City Lights and Wave Books. More publications are in progress.

Jack Spicer (1925-1965) Poet and leading member of the San Francisco Renaissance. Fired from the University of California Berkeley's linguistics department in 1950 for refusing to sign a loyalty oath. American Book Award for the posthumous *My Vocabulary Did This to Me*, 2009, a major collection of his poetry.

John Allen Ryan (1928-1994) Poet and bartender. Unofficial mayor of North Beach in the late 1950s. Along with Jack Spicer, painter Wally Hendrick and three others, founded The Six Gallery in San Francisco, today remembered as site of the first public reading of "Howl" by Allen Ginsberg.

Ron Loewinsohn (1937-2014) Poet, novelist, and literature professor. His early poems were included in Don Allen's seminal *The New American Poetry* in 1960. He left bohemian life to obtain a BA from Berkeley and a PhD from Harvard. Joined the English department at Berkeley in 1970 from which he retired in 2005.

Dora FitzGerald (1934–) Widow of the artist Russell FitzGerald. Marriage Commissioner of Galiano Island, BC, where she has lived since the 1990s.

Avery Russell (1937–) Editor, researcher. Grew up in Chapel Hill. Previously a project director at the Carnegie Foundation in New York. Currently married to Alfred J. McLaren, US Navy, Retired, a noted polar explorer.

George Butterick (1942-1988) Poet and editor of Charles Olson's works. Curator of Literary Archives at the University of Connecticut at the time of his early death. Received American Book Award for his *Collected Poems of Charles Olson*, 1987. His own *Collected Poems* published by State University of New York Press in 1988.

Frank O'Hara (1926-1966) Poet, art critic, curator at the Museum of Modern Art, and leading light of the New York School poets, his *Collected Poems* shared the 1972 National Book Award for Poetry with Howard Moss. Shared to the annoyance of his many supporters who see O'Hara as a major influence on U.S. letters.

Allen Ginsberg (1926-1997) Poet and activist. His 1956 poem "Howl" ushered in Beat poetry and changed censorship laws when a charge of obscenity was overruled. A lifelong nonviolent protestor against wars, nuclear arms, and the U.S. "war on drugs" and a popularizer of Buddhism in the U.S. Posthumous publications continue to appear.

Gene Swenson (1934-1969) (G. R.) Art critic and curator. Amazingly, G.R.'s publications, *The Other Tradition* and *Art in the Mirror* (both 1966), have survived as contributions to analyses of mid-20th century American art. His art collection, including a painting by Basil King, can be found at the Spencer Museum, University of Kansas.

Bob Thompson (1937-1966) Known for figurative, expressionist, and symbolic painterly art, Thompson's work is in the collections of the Smithsonian, the Newark Museum, the Whitney and others and he is increasingly being seen as an important 20th century African-American artist.

Virginia Parker (1897-19??) Southern artist, friend of the author's grandmother and mother, studied at the Pennsylvania Academy of Fine Arts, and is said to have exhibited work at the Brooklyn Museum.

Jim Rosenquist (1933-2017) (James) Pop artist, shown and exhibited internationally. Works in major museums. G.R. Swenson was an early promoter of his work. Jim and his wife at that time, Mary Lou, separated many years ago.

LeRoi Jones/Amiri Baraka (1934-2014) Adopted the name Amiri Baraka in 1965 after the murder of Malcolm X. Poet, playwright, critic, activist. His first collection of poetry, *Preface to a Twenty-Volume Suicide Note,* has a cover by Basil King, as do several issues of the magazine *Yugen,* which he and his then wife Hettie Cohen Jones co-edited.

Hubert Selby, Jr. (1928-2004) (Cubby) Fiction writer, best known for *Last Exit to Brooklyn* and *Requiem for a Dream,* both of which have been made into movies. One of his earliest short stories, "Tra La La" was published in *The Black Mountain Review.*

Gilbert Sorrentino (1929-2006) (Gil) Fiction writer, poet, critic, teacher and editor, often tagged "experimental." Taught at Stanford for many years. Of his 25 books, the best known may be *Mulligan Stew,* which owes much to his enthusiasm for the Irish writer Flan O'Brien.

Diane DiPrima (1934–) Poet, author of more than 15 books, publisher with LeRoi Jones of the influential "zine" *The Floating Bear,* teacher at Naropa University, the Poetry Center at San Francisco State, and other poetry venues. Known for her antiwar and pro-feminist activism and her involvement in American Buddhism.

Joyce Johnson (1935–) Writer of fiction, memoir, essays, and investigative journalism. Her *Minor Characters* won a 1983 National Book Critics Circle Award. Author of a recent and important critical biography of Jack Kerouac.

Lynn St. John (1934 –) Photographer, one-time studio assistant to Irving Penn, met Basil King at Cass Technical High School in Detroit when both were students there.

Joel Oppenheimer (1930-1988). Poet and a columnist for *The Village Voice.* Studied at Black Mountain and has ever been identified as a "Black Mountain poet." Two large collections of his work are available, notably *Names & Local Habitations* from The Jargon Society.

Bob Rauschenberg (1925-2008) (Robert) Painter especially known for his "combines" which incorporate objects and non-traditional materials, as well as for performances, printmaking, and collaborations with dancers. Works in major museums around the world.

Bob Beauchamp (1923-1995) (Robert) Painter, student of Hans Hofmann, known for expressionist figures and brilliant colors. Works in the Museum of Modern Art, the Hirshhorn, the Denver Art Museum, and elsewhere.

Jackie Ferrara (1929–) Sculptor and draftswoman. Her minimal sculptures are in the Museum of Modern Art, the L.A. County Museum of Art, the Phillips Collection. She's made large-scale public installations at the University of Rochester, the L.A. County Museum of Art, the University of Houston, and elsewhere.

Jay Milder (1934–) Painter, influenced by Hebrew mysticism and mythology. Student of Hans Hofmann. Currently better known in Latin America than in the U.S., Milder has had retrospectives at the National Museum in Brasilia and the Museum of Modern Art, Rio de Janeiro.

Jean Cartier (dates unknown) Painter. Childhood in Paris during WW2. His studies in art at Oxford, England, were interrupted by a nervous breakdown. Lived in New York for several years in the early 1960s, and subsequently returned to France. Once informed Basil and Martha that he was an illegitimate grandson of Jules Verne.

George Stanley (1934–) Poet, member of the San Francisco Renaissance group. The death of Jack Spicer precipitated a move to Canada where he has lived since. He taught at several Canadian colleges and universities until he retired. Received the Shelley Memorial Award from the Poetry Society of America in 2006.

Danny Lyon (1942–) Documentary photographer, famed especially for covering the civil rights movement. Most recently exhibited at the Whitney in 2016, which may ultimately offer him a much-needed full retrospective.

Lita Hornick (1927-2000) Philanthropist, art collector with her husband Morton Hornick, and publisher—first of the little magazine *Kulchur* which after 20 issues became Kulchur Press focusing on New York School poetry. She ultimately created Kulchur Foundation, which produced poetry readings and theatrical productions.

Henry Geldzahler (1935-1994) Art administrator and curator at the Metropolitan Museum of Art. He later served the National Endowment for the Arts and was New York Commissioner of Cultural Affairs under Mayor Koch. Published several books of essays and interviews with artists. Spent his last years as an independent curator mainly at P.S.1 in Queens and the Dia Art Foundation.

Ivan Karp (1926-2012) Art dealer and gallery owner, instrumental in the launch of pop art in the 1960s. He worked in the Leo Castelli Gallery on 57th Street for ten years before opening his own establishment, the OK Harris Gallery (with his cigar store on the ground floor below) in SoHo.

Leo Castelli (1907-1999) Leading New York art dealer and gallery owner, instrumental in promoting Abstract Expressionism, and later movements including Pop, Neo-Dada, Conceptual, Minimal, and others.

Paul Blackburn (1926-1971) (three wives, Winifred, Sara, Joan) One of America's important lyric poets and a translator especially of Piere Vidal and other Troubadour poets, as well as Octavio Paz, Julio Cortazar, and Federico Garcia Lorca. Known as a Black Mountain poet though he was never at the school. He served as a contributing editor and New York distributor of *The Black Mountain Review* for several early issues. Published some 15 books of poetry during his lifetime, while many others including major collections appeared only after his early death.

Hettie Jones (1934–) Poet and teacher, especially known for her memoir *How I Became Hettie Jones* recounting her life with LeRoi Jones (later Amiri Baraka). Taught writing at colleges and universities in New York and elsewhere, including the Graduate Writing Program at The New School, the 92nd Street Y, and the Lower Eastside Girls Club.

Frank Lima (1939-2013) Poet with roots in New York's Spanish Harlem. He was a student of Kenneth Koch and importantly of Sherman Drexler whom he met while he was an inmate on Riker's Island. Later, he worked as a photographer's assistant and, as a trained chef, in top restaurants in New York. Publications include *Inventory: New and Selected Poems.*

Gavin Douglas (dates unknown) Except for information about Gavin's possible progenitor, the Scottish Bishop Gavin Douglas (1475?-1522) poet and translator of the Aeneid into English, little information about 20th century Gavin or his mother Jean Douglas is easily obtained other than in the author's account, "Another Summer of Poverty" in this book.

Larry Rivers (1923-2002) Painter, sculptor, occasional filmmaker and jazz musician, and mercurial man-about-town. He merged figurative and narrative art with abstraction and produced enormously entertaining works now found in major museums and collections of American art.

Joe LeSueur (1924-2001) New York School poet, Frank O'Hara's roommate and sometime lover for ten years, Joe took part in the social whirl that O'Hara helped create. His best-known book is *Digressions on Some Poems by Frank O'Hara*.

Ivan Micho (dates unknown) Sculptor and craftsman. Worked as studio assistant to sculptor Sylvia Stone when she worked in plexiglass in the 1970s.

Philip Wofford (1935–) Painter of "lyric abstraction" – taught at Bennington College from 1969 to 1995. At one point, represented in New York by the Andre Emmerich Gallery. Work in the collection of University of New Mexico Museum. Married to Carol Haerer.

Carol Haerer (1933-2002) Abstract painter. Her wonderful White Paintings were exhibited at the Sheldon Museum of the University of Nebraska with an essay on this work by Charles Eldredge, art historian and museum director. Her works are in the collections of the University of Kansas, Nebraska, the Whitney, and the Guggenheim Museum.

Edwin Denby (1903-1983) Poet, translator, and notable critic of modern dance. Devoted partner to photographer and filmmaker Rudy Burkhardt. Several collections of his dance reviews were published between 1968 and 1986, and his translation of the Tao Te Ching was published as *Edwin's Tao* in 1993.

Adolph Gottlieb (1903-1974) Abstract painter (but employing many elements of surrealism). Works in major collections of American art, including the Museum of Modern Art, the Guggenheim, the National Gallery of Art in Washington, and elsewhere.

Mark Rothko (1903-1970) Abstract painter, though earlier works employed myth not only in titles but also in imagery. Works in major collections worldwide, including the Guggenheim, the Museum of Modern Art, the Metropolitan, and many others.

Harry Lewis (1942–) Poet, translator mostly of Mayakovsky, and a clinical social worker based on the work of Wilhelm Reich and his follower Victor Sobey. Teacher of psychology at the New School. Poet and publisher with Basil King and David Glotzer of *Mulch* magazine and Mulch Press books and on his own of Little Rootie Tootie Books and the little magazine # (or number).

David Glotzer (1949–) Currently a financial advisor to DeYoe Wealth Management in the San Francisco Bay Area, but in his youth a book designer, poet, and publisher with Basil King and Harry Lewis of *Mulch* magazine and Mulch Press books.

Michael Goldberg (1924-2007) Noted "Second Generation" abstract painter, closely associated with the New York School poets. Works in the Albright-Knox, Baltimore Museum of Art, Walker Art Center, Museum of Modern Art, the Whitney, and elsewhere.

Helen Ives (1909-1994) (Mrs. Burl Ives) Married to the folk singer Burl Ives for 25 years, with whom she adopted a son Alexander (1946-1995).

Thelma Burdick (possibly 1895-1973) For over half a century, she was a voice for sanity in housing, childcare, education, and community on the Lower East Side where she was Director of Activities for the Church of All Nations, 9 Second Avenue.

Dan Gerber (1940–) Poet and formerly publisher, with Jim Harrison, of *Sumac* magazine and Sumac Press which issued 34 books between 1951 and 2007.

Robert vas Dias (1936–) Anglo-American poet and editor, born in London, raised in New York and returned to England permanently in 1974. Marriage to first wife Susan ended shortly thereafter. Organizer of

National Poetry Festivals in Western Michigan in 1971 and '72, and editor of the anthology, *Inside Outer Space*, 1970.

Kenneth Rexroth (1905-1982) Prolific poet, translator and essayist. The Grand Old Man of the San Francisco Renaissance, who fostered American interest in Asian art and philosophy and, usually working with a scholar, translated many books of Japanese and Chinese poetry.

George Oppen (1908-1984) Poet and with his wife Mary an anti-capitalist and antiwar activist, although he served and was wounded in WW2. The Oppens' political activity led the couple to flee to Mexico. They were allowed to return in 1958 and his collection *Of Being Numerous* won a Pulitzer in 1969.

Susan Sherman (1935–) Poet, playwright, short story writer and founding editor of the seminal feminist poetry magazine IKON. Her memoir *America's Child: A Woman's Journey Through the Radical Sixties* was published in 2007.

Ted Enslin (1925-2011) Poet, with a huge body of work, a good deal of it not (yet) published, although some 70 books from small press publishers appeared in his lifetime. Influenced by Louis Zukofsky and an associate of Cid Corman, Enslin worked and lived outside the mainstream in rural Maine for 50 years.

Carl Rakosi (1903-2004) Poet and psychotherapist. Born in Berlin of Jewish parents, raised in Wisconsin from the age of 7, Rakosi was a member of a group of non-mainstream modernists influenced by Pound and dubbed The Objectivists. He abandoned poetry for social work with disturbed children for over 30 years, but prodded by the young Andrew Crozier, resumed writing poetry in 1967.

Ronnie Bladen (1918-1988) (Ronald) Painter and sculptor especially known for large-scale steel works, hard edged and geometrical. Sol LeWitt often referred to him as a "father of Minimal Art." Public works in Storm King, Buffalo, Dusseldorf, Des Moines, Baltimore, and many other sites.

Tod Thilleman (1962–) Poet, novelist, and editor/publisher of Spuyten Duyvil Press, an energetic independent publisher. www.spuytenduyvil.net

Bernadine Loden (dates unknown) No information available after she left Kirkland, New York; her last name may be different if indeed she and "Tubby" did divorce. He was William H. Lohden, former reporter for the *Utica Observer Dispatch*. His investigative work helped win a Pulitzer for that newspaper in 1959.

Dave Gearey (1942–) Filmmaker and teacher of film at the College of Staten Island, a senior college in the CUNY system. Best known for films that were integral parts of multimedia works by Meredith Monk: *Quarry, Tail of the Dragon*, and others.

Bob Hershon (1937–) Poet and publisher. Former head of the nonprofit Print Center devoted to printing small press/self-published books, and an indefatigable editor of *Hanging Loose* magazine for more than 50 years.

David Rattray (1936-1993) Poet, translator, senior editor at *Reader's Digest*, and self-taught pianist, which he pursued to better understand the *In Nomine* music of John Bull. Noted as a very young man for his interviews of Antonin Artaud, Ezra Pound, and H.D. and later for masterful translations of Rene Crevel, Artaud, and Roger Gilbert-Lecompte. His last poetry book, *Opening the Eyelid*, features a portrait drawing by Basil King.

Anselm Hollo (1934-2013) Poet, translator, teacher, born in Finland but lived in the U.S. from 1967. His more than 40 books of poetry were all written in English, starting with poetry created in London before 1967. Noted translator of Finnish, German, and Swedish poetry and for translating Allen Ginsberg into German.

Esteban Vicente (1903-2001) Painter, printmaker, teacher, born in Spain and exiled by the Spanish Civil War. In the U.S. since 1936, he taught at Black Mountain the summer of 1953. Founding member of the New York Studio School. Never exhibited in Franco's Spain but the Esteban Vicente Museum now flourishes in Segovia. So does New York Public School #170 in the Bronx – the Esteban Vicente School, with art programs for the K-2 classes, thanks to a bequest from his foundation.

David Meltzer (1937-2016) Poet, jazz guitarist and singer, influenced by the Beats, Black Mountain, and the San Francisco Renaissance. He wrote more than 50 books and performed lyrical political poetry in venues across the country. Recent publications include *No Eyes*, poems on Lester Young, and *Beat Thing*, an epic.

Lucia Berlin (1936-2004) Fiction writer. Very lately celebrated and posthumously published by the mainstream including *The New Yorker* and Farrar Straus & Giroux. Her rich and checkered career ended on her birthday, when she died at age 64. During her life she published over 70 stories in the small press only. Ed Dorn was a life-long friend and mentor.

Bob Holman (1948–) Poet and poetry activist, especially devoted the oral tradition. Co-founder of the Nuyorican Poets Café, where "Slam Poetry" got its start, and later proprietor of the Bowery Poetry Club. The Club hangs on today with events only two days a week. Bob is currently concentrating on preservation activities for endangered languages, some of which is shown in the 2015 documentary, *Language Matters.*

Jane Augustine (1930–) poet and founder of the poetry publishing collective, Marsh Hawk Press. Books include *A Woman's Guide to Mountain Climbing* and many others; editor of *The Gift by H.D. :The Complete Text.*

Mary Emma Harris (1943–) Independent scholar and director of the Black Mountain College Project. She has been devoted to the history of Black Mountain College for over 30 years and maintains an extensive archive of BMC-related materials. Author of *The Arts at Black Mountain College,* MIT Press, 1987 (2nd printing, 2002).

Martin Duberman (1930–) Historian, playwright, gay rights activist. Author of *Black Mountain: An Exploration in Community*, 1972, among many books of contemporary history. Professor Emeritus at Herbert Lehman College and winner of a number of distinguished awards including a Bancroft prize and three Lambda Awards.

Andrew Crozier (1943–2008) British poet and activist, associated with the British Revival. Editor of *The English Intelligencer* and of the independent Ferry Press. On a Fulbright in 1964 which took him to SUNY Buffalo, he became interested in Charles Olson and the Black Mountain poets and was instrumental in Carl Rakosi's return to writing poetry. *All Where Each Is* collects his wide-ranging and rigorous poetry.

Vincent Katz (1960–) Poet, editor, translator, critic, and curator. Leading member of The Friends of Basil King and co-curator of "Basil King: Between Painting and Writing" at the Black Mountain College Museum and Arts Center in 2016. Among many other publications are his translations of Sextus Propertius, which won the 2005 National Translation Award and *Black Mountain College: Experiment in Art*, MIT Press, 2002; second printing, 2013, the catalog for the multimedia exhibition he curated in 2002.

Nicole Peyrafitte (1960–) Multimedia artist, filmmaker, and singer, and partner of Pierre Joris, poet and translator, most recently of the prize-winning *Breathturn into Timestead: The Collected Later Poetry of Paul Celan*. Nicole's film promoting this work led The Friends of Basil King to select her to make a film on Basil King.

Miles Joris-Peyrafitte (1993–) Filmmaker, actor and director. While still a student at Bard College, worked with his mother Nicole on *Basil King: MIRAGE*, a 23-minute documentary portrait completed in 2012. His first feature film, *As You Are*, received the special jury prize for outstanding direction at the 2016 Sundance Film Festival.

Kimberly Ann Lyons (1958–) Poet, essayist, publisher of Lunar Chandelier books, and founding member of The Friends of Basil King. A recent book, *Rouge*, from Instance Press, has a cover by Basil King. Other recent books include *Approximately Near* and *Calcinatio*. Recent essays include those on Bernadette Mayer, George Quasha, and on Basil King. Now living in Chicago, she was for many years a psychiatric social worker in various NYC hospitals and shelters for women.

Mitch Highfill (1958–) Poet, publisher of the former little magazine *Red Weather* and of Prospect Books. Coordinator of various reading series in New York including Leonard Street and the Poetry Project at St. Mark's. Works appear in many small press publications. Member of The Friends of Basil King.

Burt Kimmelman (1947–) Poet, editor, scholar of medieval literature and of contemporary modernists, including William Bronk and Michael Heller. Has published nine collections of poetry. Professor in the Department of Humanities, New Jersey Institute of Technology. Former senior editor of *Poetry New York*. Member of The Friends of Basil King.

Note: This book uses a few pseudonyms when the actual name is not particularly pertinent: e.g., Tanner and Susan in "Moving Money," Athena in "Another Summer of Poverty," Elsbeth, Amanda, and Gerri in the Public Affairs Office at Memorial Sloan Kettering Cancer Center and all the members of The Society of MSKCC mentioned in "It Starts to Drizzle."

Not included in this glossary is the complete list of poets whom Baz drew – e.g., Paul Auster, Joan Silber, Rochelle Ratner, Bill Berkson, Armand Schwerner, and many others. Some but not all of these sketch portraits are published in *The Poet,* with text by Basil King, New York: Spuyten Duyvil. www.spuytenduyvil.net/the-poet.html. Others are "collection of the artist. "

A Postscript

I opened this book with a note about my belief in the value of the art of Basil King. Never discussed is *why* I think so.

I'm *seriously* wary of the hoary trope of troubled artist with his ever-loyal wife. That's way off the mark. So is the notion that I want to secure for him the recognition I alone think his work deserves.

I am not alone. And I haven't been, for any of the years I've lived with him. In fact, I've sometimes been led to recognition of his accomplishments by other people who saw more than I did.

While recognition of his boundary-breaking work in visual art and in poetry is still a bit "outside" the "inside," cracks are forming as indicated, for example, by 13 recent essays on Basil King's work in issue #48 of *Talisman* magazine (to be issued in print as a Talisman Book in 2019). Moreover, the generation of which both he and I are part is now almost gone. Aesthetic history is full of examples of important contributors who were locked out by their contemporaries to be embraced by others who came later in time and were not embarrassed by or frankly hostile to unexpected accomplishments.

Whatever else this book is, it is not and cannot be a full consideration of Basil King's contributions! Clearly that's for later. That's for others. I invited readers to enjoy this ride, here and now, and I hope that's what happened.

Martha King's fascinating memoir bristles with a unique kinetics of purpose, struggle, reluctant parents, loyal friendships, and of a lifelong partnership with brilliant artist Basil King forged in a utopian dream of communality and the powers of alternative art praxis and passionate bohemian life. What a headstrong young woman she was taking off to Black Mountain upon receiving a note from then rector Charles Olson to "Come with all the money you have and what you are used to for cooking." And what a long life that continues unabated! Indeed this book is a way of seeing with others in and out of place in the maelstrom of heady American art and poetry life. I think of Clifford Geertz's terms "consociational": all the bustling intersecting realities and persons and the work itself that makes such a grand fabric and warm salute to an amazing time in our culture's complicated relationship to its geniuses.

I couldn't put OUTSIDE/INSIDE down until way after dawn, captured by King's patience, and the urgent "call" to tell this palpable art-driven love story, an archive of trenchant and luminous particulars. —**Anne Waldman**

I've just finished with this splendid memoir. It has so much life to it, and brio, and so much deeply felt reflection that I'm hooked. I loved hearing about everything! The picture of San Francisco life at a certain moment in the mid-fifties has not been equaled elsewhere...but the Lucia Berlin chapter was to me the emblem of all the rest—a long look, with a hundred cunningly observed details, that builds to an heroic thesis. —**Kevin Killian**

Martha King's writing brims with a forward propulsion that makes her memoir a page-turner, until you deliberately slow down to relish many passages. You end up appreciating a well-lived life, even if you are not familiar with all of its characters. She says early on that she, perhaps unfashionably for today, lived/lives a life (partly) in support of her partner rather than in self-focused exploration. That's not something to criticize when her partner, painter-poet Basil King, manifests an integrity that earns any support for it. Besides, hindsight shows that Martha ends up fulfilling her own potential as a poet and writer. The very last word of the memoir sums up Martha's life — it is a word worth discovering in a book worth reading for her definition. —Eileen R. Tabios

Here it is, kids, the Martha King chronicles. An insider's account of the real late Black Mountain College, starting with Charles Olson's enigmatic but clearly motivated postcard: "Come with what money you have in hand and what you are used to for cooking." The trip stretches wide and far but comes home to a real sense of living. And living for art. Eventually, and then always, with partner in crime and much else, painter and poet Basil King. She gives us what we really want and need — textures: "rotting mattresses, worn-out boots..." She tells what radical women's lives were like, they "...improvised their clothing, cooked exotic peasant food, tied nursing babies to their waists with Mexican scarves." She cuts to the essential: "Black Mountain is important because it grew a language – in collision – that is still available for use." She gives us close-up accounts of goings on inside the Cedar Street Tavern. Denizens, avatars, pass through and by: John Wieners, Frank O'Hara, Hettie Jones, Bob Thompson, Paul Blackburn. And then she goes beyond that, all the way to the present. King clarifies, edifies, entertains. She gives the reader all that freely, and the reader is duly gratified. —Vincent Katz

Martha King's lively, always insightful memoir provides an intimate account of not only the artists and writers constellated around Black Mountain College in the 1950s but the evolution of many of its figures—famous ones like Charles Olson and John Wieners as well as those less so—while the scenery changes from San Francisco to the East Village, from the ragged clapboards at Black Mountain to the Park Avenue apartments of art dealers. Against the backdrop of her proper Southern upbringing King charts her sentimental education, one done in the company of her husband Basil King, with both eye and ear attuned to the urgent disputes and minor key joys that animate the ordinary days of poets and painters. By turns a family remembrance, a gossipy tale, a love story, and a bildungsroman, *Outside/Inside* gives vivid account of lives lived in pursuit of *making*. —Al Mobilio

The book is an incredible picture of life in the art/writing scene over that period. A great picture too of New York. I'd been reading part of Edmund Wilson's diaries which gives a detailed account of the city some thirty years [earlier]. Martha King's account is just as sharp and dense with detail....it's the period just before the money people completely took over. I like the take on the sixties counter-culture, its naivety in being part of the advance of capitalism without knowing it. And I think that what is says about women in that period (or now for that matter) is absolutely on the money. —Laurie Duggan

Martha King was there, and her book is a testimony to the moment when modernism transitioned into contemporary poetry and painting. From Black Mountain to Frank O'Hara and James Rosenquist, she and her husband, the much accomplished and respected painter and writer Basil King, were there, and the result is a personal and detailed guide to a critical moment in the history of the American arts. This is an essential book. Don't miss it. —Edward Foster

Photo by Sanjay Agnihotri

Martha King was born Martha Winston Davis in Charlottesville, Virginia, in 1937. She attended Black Mountain College for three months as a teenager, and married the painter Basil King in 1958. They have two daughters and four grandchildren. Before retiring from day jobs in 2011, Martha worked as an editor and science writer. She also edited 2+2 chapbooks with Susan Sherman in the late 1970s and published 31 issues of *Giants Play Well in the Drizzle*, 1983-1992. Currently she co-curates a long-running prose reading series with Elinor Nauen at the SideWalk Café on the Lower East Side. For more information, see basilking.net.

Made in the USA
Middletown, DE
19 October 2018